Growing up
on
The Times

Growing up
on
THE TIMES

Louis Heren

HAMISH HAMILTON · London

First published in Great Britain 1978
by Hamish Hamilton Limited
90 Great Russell Street London WC1B 3PT

Copyright © 1978 by Louis Heren

British Library Cataloguing in Publication Data

Heren, Louis
    Growing up on *The Times*.
    1. Heren, Louis   2. Journalists—Great
    Britain—Biography
    I. Title
    070'.92'4   PN5123.H/

    ISBN 0-241-89 886-2

Printed in Great Britain by
Western Printing Services, Bristol

*To Pat, whose unfailing affection and understanding
over the years proved that a foreign correspondent
is only as good as his wife*

...

Contents

Introduction

This book is about my years as a foreign correspondent of *The Times*. It is not a history of events which shaped and occasionally shook the world between 1947 and 1970, but a very personal account of the fun, adventures and the growing up of one fortunate correspondent who travelled the world with his family on an expense account. Similarly, the conversations recalled are not verbatim reports. They are faithful accounts of what was said and recorded at the time, but they have not been transcribed from detailed shorthand notes.

I am grateful to the editors of *The Times*, especially Donald Tyreman who helped me make what would now be the impossible jump from messenger to junior reporter, foreign correspondent, foreign editor and now deputy editor of the paper. *The Times* must be one of the best papers to work for, because few other journalists have been allowed the freedom of expression I and my colleagues have enjoyed. In a very real way it is our paper, it belongs to us and not the proprietor, and when it has been less than great the fault has been ours. We cannot blame the machinations of the proprietor or the advertisers, although in recent years industrial disputes on the production side have impaired the service we tried to provide to readers.

My one gripe was that before Lord Thomson bought the paper the management took advantage of the enthusiasm and dedication of writers, most of whom did their best for the paper, and risked their necks, on salaries less than the pay of union men in the production departments. I can still remember a couple of acts of unforgivable meanness, but the choice was mine. I was offered better-paying jobs, but I stayed with *The Times*. This book will explain why.

1 What Really Happened?

I am a lucky man. I survived the second world war in one piece although I was in the army for nearly seven years, and soon afterwards became a foreign correspondent of *The Times*. I lived and worked abroad for nearly a quarter of a century and saw the world on an expense account. I was married in 1948, and my wife Pat also enjoyed the gypsy life we lived in the early years. We camped out in hotel rooms and furnished flats from Tel Aviv to Singapore. We were a couple of international tramps following the news and instructions cryptically telegraphed from Printing House Square. Proceed Damascus soonest. Times, was typical although under the terms for minimum rate telegrams more words could have been sent without extra charge. Once in India, when we had just checked into a hotel in Simla, the following telegram arrived. Hillary lost Makalu. Proceed find him soonest. Times. Hillary was the conqueror of Everest, which he had climbed two years before, and Makalu was a lesser but more dangerous mountain. I left the next morning to mount what must have been the only one-man expedition into the higher Himalayas, and was away for weeks.

We nearly always travelled together before the children came, Pat with two suitcases and me with a grip and the typewriter. Always the typewriter, a little Swiss-built Hermes which survived tens of thousands of miles of travel, hundreds of thousands of words bashed out with a heavy impatient hand, wars and other misuses until one day in 1968, when I was hurrying between planes at La Guardia airport in New York, it dropped out of its metal case and was damaged beyond repair. Apart from overnight bags, this luggage contained all our worldly goods for some years. We were young, romantic and no doubt silly, and I can remember collecting the bags at some airport and Pat saying, 'With my worldly goods I thee endow'.

On another occasion, when we were flying to Eritrea, the bags were mislaid at Cairo airport and then returned to Cyprus from whence we had flown. We checked into the Semiramis Hotel just with the two overnight bags and typewriter, as if we were spending an illicit weekend together. I can still remember the raised eyebrow of the Greek reception clerk and the disdain of the *sephragi* as he carried the two small bags up to the palatial room overlooking the Nile. Pat's was rather smart, but mine was an American army musette bag, stained from long use and lumpy because of the camera and inevitable whisky bottle. We waited three days for the other bags, but for the first time in living memory Cyprus had a heavy snowfall and all planes were grounded. I could wait no longer, and we took off before dawn for the Horn of Africa in an unheated Dakota with two overnight bags, the typewriter, and our love to keep us warm.

Even in those childless days I occasionally had to go off alone. One morning in 1949 I took off in a UN plane from Tel Aviv for Gaza with the American photographer Bob Capa, a British international civil servant and 2,000 gallons of industrial alcohol in four-gallon, non-returnable cans. The plane had to fly by way of Ramallah, a town outside Jerusalem with a short airfield at the foot of a rock-strewn hill. The young American pilot, wearing a red jockey cap and a cigar, had previously flown freight to Berlin during the blockade, and apparently thought he was landing at Tempelhof. Capa and I instinctively knew that he could not stop in time—we had both been in earlier air crashes—and as the plane ploughed up the rocky hill, losing its under-carriage and propellers, we opened the door and did forward rolls to safety; Capa with his cameras clutched to his belly and me with my typewriter. Miraculously the plane and its load of industrial alcohol did not catch fire, and rather shame-facedly we sauntered back. The first to emerge from the wreckage was the pilot with the cigar still clenched between his teeth, and then the civil servant. He brushed industrial alcohol from his moustache, muttered, 'Bloody bad show', and stalked off in the direction of the Mount of Olives.

The crash was reported on Israel radio, and when I got back to the Almond hotel in Tel Aviv Pat was sitting on the verandah wet-eyed, and reading the *Palestine Post* upside down. A maid, an Israeli of German origin, was cleaning the room and rather inhibited our fond reunion after my return from the dead. Never at a loss, Pat asked the maid to fetch me a dry martini and the girl, with whom I normally conversed in German because she knew no English and I no Hebrew, hurried away and brought back three martinis. It was a suitable celebration.

Flying was very much part of our lives in those early gypsy days. They were before the introduction of economy fares and packaged tours, and the airlines tended to treat passengers as pampered persons of wealth. By today's standards, the planes were primitive. The workhorse all over the world was the Dakota, or DC3, which carried about 22 passengers except when it was also carrying freight. I once flew on a Dakota with a drugged bull lashed to the floor. On inter-continental flights, the Americans used the Constellation, which was probably the most graceful-looking aircraft ever built. The British first had the York, a converted bomber, and then the Argonaut, a pressurized DC4. The stewards and stewardesses were always attentive, and the captain would come back to chat with the passengers and discuss the progress of the flight with the aid of charts which were circulated among the passengers at regular intervals. If the progress was comparatively royal, it was also slow. These old propeller jobs—we afterwards remembered them as steam planes—could at best do about 350 miles an hour. On the long flights to the Far East they would stop at night, and the passengers would sleep in hotels or resthouses. The next and last generation of steam planes, the Stratocruiser and DC6, had bunks, and I can remember sleeping across the Atlantic between sheets after the steward had offered me a selection of sleeping pills. I awakened as the plane was flying down the New England coast, and stepped ashore in New York refreshed and ready to work.

If flying meant occasional separations, we accepted them because they were the price we had to pay for a wonderful life. I always thought that the absences made our hearts grow fonder, but there were awkward moments. I nearly missed my own wedding because I had delayed leaving India and the plane lost an engine somewhere over Iran. Pat was alone when our first baby was born dead, and soon afterwards I had to fly off to cover the Korean war when Ian Morrison, *The Times* war correspondent

there, was killed in battle. Pat was a very serene person with an
inner stillness beneath her rather fey humour. She was only
punctual in delivering babies. For that reason I nearly missed the
births of two of our four surviving children. The first was in
Singapore. I flew back that night from Sarawak and was met at the
airport by my Malay driver, who told me that Pat had already
gone to the hospital. She was in labour when I arrived, and
delivered Patrick in the corridor because in effect, she had
jumped the queue and all the labour rooms were occupied. The
hospital was appropriately called Kerdang Kerbau, Malay for
rampant bull, because about 70 children were born there every
day. I had no difficulty in recognizing our boy among the other
babies wrapped in swaddling clothes and laid on shelves. There
were more than 30, an average night's production, but he was
the only white, or pinko-gray. The others were yellow, brown
or black.

Kate was born in Delhi, and we were living in Bonn when
Sarah came. Germany was the first assignment where I had to
wear a collar and tie every day, and where I had an office, an
assistant correspondent and a secretary. It was not exactly a nine-
to-five job, but I was beginning to feel settled when about a month
before Sarah was due I was asked to do some stories in Africa. I
remonstrated, but the foreign news editor said that I should be
back in Bonn for the birth. The trip included visits to Aden,
Hargeisa, Mogadishu and Addis Ababa as well as a week in the
Haud, then a disputed territory between Ethiopia and the old
British Somalia. It was a tight schedule, but everything went like
clockwork. The planes actually arrived and departed at the
announced ETAs and ETDs, even from the small town with the
improbable name of Jigjiga. Finally I climbed aboard a London-
bound plane at Addis for Frankfurt where I had left my car. It was
the winter of 1956, and when we landed at Cairo to refuel I
bumped into a senior Egyptian special branch man whom I had
known during my Middle East days. He did not seem pleased to
see me, but accepted my offer to buy him a drink.

He asked what I was doing in Cairo, and I told him about the
baby due to be born on the morrow. He congratulated me, and
then said that Britain was about to invade Egypt. I swore. That
meant I would have to get off the plane and cover the fighting.
'You don't seem to understand,' he said. 'Our two countries will

be at war, and you will be interned'. I bought another round of drinks, and hardly noticed that there was not enough ice. 'But what about my wife? I can't miss another birth'. He stood at the bar smoking a little cheroot. Nothing was said, and then with an almost imperceptible nod of the head, the gesture common to Arabs and Indians, he indicated that it was time to leave. I followed, not knowing where we were going and fearing the worst but he took me to the departure gate, waved a minion aside, and although it was not time to depart we walked out to the plane. We climbed aboard, and he turned to me and shook hands. 'It can't last long,' he said, 'And when it is over we can be friends again'. With that he clattered quickly down the steps, leaving me immensely relieved and with one more reason for liking Egyptians.

The plane took off for Rome where a fresh crew took over. I recognized the new captain; he had flown for Cyprus Airways when I was bumming around the eastern Mediterranean, and he later invited me up to the flight deck. There was an easy camaraderie between the likes of us in those far-off days, and I sat in the co-pilot's seat while we chatted about old times. I told him about Pat, whom he remembered, and he said not to worry. The weather was deteriorating, but he would deliver me to Frankfurt on time. Then ground control reported bad weather over the Alps. It suggested that the plane should turn left and fly direct to London, but the decision remained with the captain. I went back to my own seat, and the two pilots, strapped in, struggled with the bucking aircraft. I was convinced that we were heading for London, and that Pat would be let down once again. Then lightning drew my attention to the window, and there were the Alps with jagged peaks rearing through snow clouds to just under the wing. Or so it seemed. It was a fantastic sight, both terrifying and reassuring. The storm passed, we began to lose altitude, and the captain came back to say that he had called the tower at Frankfurt to have my car ready. We would be landing in about thirty minutes. His tired eyes smiled. An international regulation had been broken, but that was what the old camaraderie was all about.

We landed in thick snow, and as the plane came to a halt at the terminal building I saw my Mercedes being driven towards us. Whatever had passed between the plane and the tower, my

arrival was being treated as an emergency. I thanked the captain,
and went down the steps carrying my typewriter and musette
bag. My grip had been taken from the luggage hold, and was
being put into the back of the Merc. The customs and immigration officers ignored the usual formalities, and wished me a
boy in German and English as I headed for the *Autobahn*. Snow was
still falling, but there was no traffic at that early hour and I
skidded happily towards Bonn. Dawn was breaking as I crossed
the Rhine, and there was a smell of coffee as I opened the door of
our house in E.T.A. Hoffmannstrasse. I just had time to give
presents to Patrick and Kate when Pat, looking enormous and
beautiful, said it was time to go to the hospital. Young Sarah
arrived a couple of hours later at the Johanniterkrankenhaus. A
nice hospital staffed by nuns. Pat long remembered it because
she was given *Malzbier*, or stout, twice a day.

There were fewer comings and goings when we were transferred
to Washington in 1960. We stayed for ten years, long enough to
put down roots, buy a house on a mortgage, make friends, and
learn to love the United States. The sixties were wonderfully
newsworthy, and one of the most decisive decades in the history
of the Republic. There were fundamental changes which at one
time seemed to threaten its very foundations. I believe that I
sensed their dimensions and directions before most Americans.
That was not particularly clever of me. A sympathetic and
reasonably well-informed foreigner can often sense change before
the most prescient natives, but it obviously helped my reporting.
I also had more confidence in the future because I sould see the
great strengths of the American system when others were near to
despair. This perhaps explains why I was invited to contribute to
the final report of the National Commission on the Causes and
Prevention of Violence. The report, honest down to the last
comma, was written at the request of President Johnson after
the murders of Dr. Martin Luther King, Jr. and Robert F.
Kennedy. It made bleak reading, and I was asked to write a
chapter on the strengths of America. I can think of no other
country inviting a foreign correspondent to make a contribution
to a report of the equivalent of a Royal Commission investigating
the weaknesses of its own society. It was a great honour.

We especially enjoyed those years because for the first time we
had a home of our own. For me, it was the first time I lived a

settled life since marching off to the wars on September 3, 1939. I cannot say that I enjoyed every aspect of domestic life. American crabgrass is too tough an enemy for the reluctant gardener. I never really got accustomed to commuting, although we lived in the District of Columbia and I did not have to travel far, but it was worthwhile. We did not live in Georgetown, the fashionable colonial section of Washington where most of the people we knew lived. As we explained at the time, we could live in a picturesque slum anywhere in Britain. I live in one now, the Vale of Health in Hampstead. Instead, we lived in a real American house, with central air-conditioning and a swimming pool in the backyard.

It was the first time we lived in quiet affluence. I was miserably paid until Lord Thomson—God bless his memory—acquired *The Times*. I was paid £700 a year when I first went abroad. I was still earning under £1,000 a year as a war correspondent in Korea. I was paid less than a junior reporter on the *Washington Post* when I was appointed chief Washington correspondent of *The Times*. £2,000 a year to be precise. I had a cost-of-living allowance and a modest expense account, but in the early years we would have had a hard time of it without the occasional lecture fee. These were generous, and in effect I subsidized *The Times*. Not that the management was grateful. One year when we returned to London for our biennial leave, Francis Mathew, the then manager, stopped my CoL although we still had to pay taxes and the mortgage in Washington and of course our accommodation in Britain.

My modest income had not bothered us unduly. We enjoyed life and the world too much to complain, although very early I had spent my war gratuity and savings—another subsidy for *The Times*—and only had a few quid in the bank. That was one reason why the middle-class comforts of America were so pleasant. There were others. The comforts were intrinsically pleasant, but most of all we could live as a normal family. The children had an uninterrupted education, and made friendships which still survive time and distance. I did not have to throw away books because the excess baggage charge to move them from one country to another was too excessive. Pat proved that she was a splendid cook after serving a prolonged apprenticeship on a single hotplate in innumerable hotel bedrooms. We could go to the movies with English sound tracks. Enjoyable as it was, the change of life style and rhythm took getting used to. After being in Washington for about two years, Pat became aware one afternoon that the children were suspiciously quiet. She went upstairs, and found Kate and Sarah packing. Their little built-in time clocks, accustomed to another rhythm, had warned them that it was time to move on.

Washington was a wonderful place for a reporter. It was in effect the capital of much of the western world as well as of a vast country. More hard information and good stories were to be had in the White House, the State Department and the Pentagon than in any other continent, and they were to be had without flying thousands of miles. I just had to cultivate people, walk a few blocks or telephone, and the stories flowed more or less unendingly.

Actually, it was not that easy. I was in competition with literally hundreds of journalists, but I had clout because I was the chief Washington correspondent, and later the first American Editor, of *The Times*. The dimmest congressman had heard of the *London Times*, and the name opened doors that were rarely ajar even in that most accessible of cities. My American colleagues were cooperative. My experience was most helpful. For me, Berlin, Saigon, Aqaba and other places which made the headlines, and kept the President up late, were not just exotic names. I knew most of them well, and the reasons why they suddenly demanded the urgent attention of the new imperial city on the Potomac. I knew many of the foreign service officers in the State Department and the diplomats in the embassies because we had served together in those faraway places. All the fun of those early years became a kind of treasure trove of information and contacts not readily available to most of my rivals, at least not when we were writing against the clock.

Time, not distance or official secrecy, was the enemy in Washington. In the Middle East I had had two hours in my favour, five in India and eight in Singapore. I could file a story at the telegraph office in New Delhi at, say, 7 p.m. local time and go home safe in the knowledge that it would arrive in London about teatime. In Korea and Japan, I had had nine hours in my favour, which was too much of a good thing. For instance, I was expected to cover the briefings at MacArthur's headquarters

during my so-called rest periods in Tokyo, and after the discomfort
and danger of Korea the problem was to stay sober for the
midnight briefing. But apart from that occasional occupational
hazard, time had been a friend east of Suez, and even east of the
Iron Curtain. The extra hour or two made my visits to eastern
European capitals less unpleasant.

Eastern standard time in the United States is five hours behind
Greenwich mean time, and this simple chronological fact
dominated my life for ten years. It became even more demanding
when I moved westwards. Midnight in London was 6 p.m. in
Chicago and only 3 p.m. in Los Angeles. I had to move words,
hundreds of words, while my American colleagues were having a
ruminative drink before sitting down at the typewriter. It said
something for the British press that we were the only European
journalists who tried to get the day's American news into that
night's newspapers. The deadline for my German friends of *Die
Welt* and the *Suddeutscher Zeitung* was lunchtime. The correspondent
of *le Monde* never even tried, which helped to explain that
newspaper's timeless prose which so many Britons pretend to
admire. It was left to British journalists, representatives of the
world's most inefficient industrial democracy, to beat the clock,
and most of us succeeded with impressive regularity.

The discipline was harsh, but on the whole beneficial. Most
British journalists in Washington were masters of their craft.
Washington was the plum foreign job, as Paris had been before
the second world war, and they were posted there because they
were good. Malcolm Muggeridge, Bill Hardcastle and David
English were but a few of the men who worked there, and most
of us became even better at our jobs because of the demands of
the clock. It sharpened our news sense, that indefinable sixth
sense which is the difference between an adequate and really
good journalist. We had to be well informed, and in a constant
state of rehearsal, if we were to respond correctly to late-
breaking news.

Fortunately, the communications were superb. *The Times*
Washington office was connected to the communications centre
in Printing House Square by a private teleprinter line open day
and night, and we had a Telex machine as backup in case the line
failed. Working outside Washington the overseas telephone
operators at White Plains, New York, would connect me to

London in seconds. They never failed, but excellent communications tended to increase rather than relax the discipline of the clock. We were encouraged to write or phone late news right up to edition time in London. I would run back to my office in the National Press Building after a late presidential press conference, and write straight on to the teleprinter.

This was instant communication. The words would appear on the teleprinter in London as I typed them in Washington. I would write in short takes—or short sections of two or three paragraphs—so that the London operator could tear off the paper and rush it to the sub-editors. I would pound out hundreds of words, often until London told me to stop because the last edition was about to run. Johnson gave an unannounced press conference one night when we had people to dinner. Being Washingtonians, they wanted to see the President on television. I watched with them, called London just before the end, dictated 750 crisp words, and then had another martini before sitting down to a dinner of clams, poached Canadian salmon and an eight-way critique of Johnson's performance.

The New York office covered most of the news outside Washington, but my assistants and I were not always confined to the capital. We covered the space programme, the civil rights demonstrations in the South, and the presidential and mid-term election campaigns. We also occasionally accompanied the President when he went out of town. *The Trip of the President* as the White House baggage labels said, and the most cynical reporters were reluctant to remove them from their typewriters and grips. The trips were always worth covering because from the moment we stepped aboard the air force bus at the south-west gate of the White House for Andrews air base until our return we were members of the President's entourage. The atmosphere was relaxed. We did not have to worry about baggage, hotel rooms, transport or phones. Everything was taken care of by the White House travel staff. The cabin service aboard the special press plane was superb, and the liquor flowed from the moment you stepped aboard, when a stewardess always stood at the door with a tray of Bloody Marys no matter the time of day, until the besotted handlers of television equipment staggered off at the end of the trip.

The self-protective guard between the White House staff and

the press was also partially lowered. Men with access to the Oval Office and Air Force One tended to talk a little more. This was not wholly unintentional. A presidential trip invariably had political or diplomatic significance, and they wanted to make certain that it was understood—or that the White House line was fully explained. To that extent the trips were but an extension of the briefings and private chats in the White House, but in the relaxed atmosphere of the plane, or a hotel room at the end of the day, they tended to unburden themselves. I could never be certain, even when the night caps followed each other in rapid succession, whether or not I was listening to an engineered leak. Not at the time, at least, but vanity can be an uncontrollable force. Information is power, and in unguarded moments most men who possess information are compelled to reveal it to prove that they are powerful.

The civil rights demonstrations and riots in the South were entirely different. There was no comforting White House cocoon. Indeed, we were regarded by the whites as the enemy, and with good reason. I did not share the liberal certainties and superiority of some of my American colleagues. The situation was too complex and tragic. The whites as well as the blacks were caught up in a violent liberation from the dark southern past. The process was essentially more painful for the whites, even when they were clobbering the blacks. I was impressed, even inspired by black courage. I learned a great deal from Dr. Martin Luther King Jr. and other black leaders. They also reinforced my professional instinct to report and understand and to shy away from instant judgement or condemnation. The average southern white was not to know that of course. Any stranger with a type-writer or a camera was the enemy because we were breaking down the self-imposed silence which had protected the South since the end of Reconstruction.

The silence had been shared by the North, including most of its liberals. Despite the Civil War Amendments, ratified between 1865 and 1869, the *1896 Plessy v. Ferguson* decision of the Supreme Court established the doctrine of separate but equal, the euphem-ism for American apartheid. Franklin D. Roosevelt, the folk hero of American liberals, was party to the silence in return for southern Democratic support in Congress. The so-called solid South was his reward. Northern connivance survived until

Hubert Humphrey inserted the civil rights plank in the Democratic platform in 1948 and Chief Justice Earl Warren handed
down the *Brown v. Board of Education* decision, which desegregated
schools, in 1954. Even then little was done until Dr. Martin
Luther King Jr. led the bus boycott in Montgomery, Alabama, a
few years later.

Northern liberals, and the press, had nothing to be proud of,
which helped both to explain their belated moral indignation
and southern fury. I was shielded from the fury to some extent
by my English accent. Many southerners were proud or fond of
their English blood. Governor George Wallace of Alabama once
boasted to me that there were no ethnic mongrels in the South.
He made my toes curl. Were we really blood brothers? There
was certainly a trace of nasal Cockney in his southern drawl. I
felt vaguely ashamed, but not for long. Too many southerners
were protective, and eager to explain that some of their best
friends were Nigras. I discovered afterwards that their claims
were not always spurious. The two races shared a great deal, and
not only the inexplicable love of grits or catfish and hush puppies.
That was proved years later when the vast majority of blacks
voted Governor Jimmy Carter of Georgia into the White House.

My English accent did not always have its blessed effect. I was
refused hire cars at Hertz garages in more than one southern
town, and the police were often nasty. Driving between Meridian
and Vicksburg in Mississippi, a car full of youngsters repeatedly
tried to force me off the road. The hair-raising ordeal ended
when I tagged behind an unsuspecting Highway Patrol car—
unsuspecting I am certain because he would have joined in the
hunt had he known that he had a reporter on his tail.

The accent was of little help in crowds and mobs. I had seen
black, brown and yellow mobs all over the world, but none was
as frightening as a southern white mob. I suspect there was a
surviving trace of racial chauvinism in my reaction. I had never
dreamed that whites, many of them of the college-educated
middle class, could be capable of such abandoned violence, or
that the local law enforcement agencies would allow them to run
riot. In places such as Calcutta and Singapore I had watched mob
violence with some detachment if only because I knew that at
least some police detachments would do their duty and reimpose
law and order with *lathis* or gunfire. That rarely happened in the

American South until the federal government intervened, although its earlier efforts were occasionally ineffectual. I can remember when the federal marshals were sent to Alabama. After a movie diet of Wyatt Earp and other frontier marshals I expected some fast action, but alas they were post office employees, many of them middle-aged and bespectacled, unarmed and apparently untrained in riot control. I began to giggle until they were rushed by the mob, and I was swept with many other frightened people against a wall. We seemed to be out of danger, and I began to worry about getting my story away. I saw a phone on the wall, a pay station as Americans call them. I edged my way to it, put in a dime, dialled the overseas operator and placed the reverse-charge call. Within a minute I was through to the communications centre at *The Times*, and began to compose and dictate my story. Harold Hiley, the shorthand writer, complained of the noise in the background, but where else in the world but America could I have worked so efficiently? And I got back my dime.

*

Norman Mailer once wrote that writing for newspapers is like running a revolutionary war. You go into battle not when you are ready but when the action presents itself. A romantic view perhaps, but basically a many-sided truth. For a start, a great deal of news is unpredictable. Much of my wild scrambling about the world was a desperate effort to catch up with the news. The best newspapers and the most alert journalists can be caught unawares by events, and I am not only thinking of earthquakes and what are generally described as acts of God. Whether or not God should be held responsible only for disasters, they can rarely be anticipated. Mailer of course had more in mind than the unpredictability of news. He saw himself as another Castro, whom he greatly admired. In his *Presidential Papers*, he portrayed himself as a guerrilla, an involved writer fighting for existentialism against what he saw as the totalitarianism of modern society. More disciplined or less imaginative reporters might have dismissed this as unbuttoned self-indulgence, but he posed anew the very fundamental question of the function of the reporter.

Reporters are supposed to be concerned with the truth, but what is the truth? Keats said that it was beauty, and that was all you needed to know, but his advice could not have helped the reporters who had to report the effects of the atomic bomb dropped on Hiroshima. Scott of the old *Manchester Guardian* said that comment was free but facts were sacred. As with much other high-minded dicta, this was mealy-mouthed cant. Comment is indeed free, which was probably one reason why Scott wrote so much of it, but what are facts? The proponents of the New Journalism claimed that there was no such thing as pure fact, and that it could not be separated from comment. This is of course nonsense. There are events which can and must be objectively reported. The Vietnam war and the assassination of President Kennedy, to mention but two major events in recent years, did not wait in some mysterious limbo until comment made them real. Instant analysis and comment can also be dangerously misleading, but the reporter knows that facts, let alone truth, can be very elusive.

Many years ago, *The Times* ran a promotional campaign with the slogan 'What really happened?'. It was hardly a winner, the circulation remained modest, but it suggested the true function of a newspaper, and I did my best as a young reporter to tell the readers what really happened. I soon discovered that it was not easy. I was not often able to witness the event I was supposed to report, and eye-witnesses were more often than not unreliable. Official spokesmen had axes to grind, and parties to a dispute had interests to defend. Wars were easier to report than politics. I just had to walk or ride towards the sound of gunfire, but what I could report was often only one tiny segment of what was happening. Unless there was a major advance or retreat, I still had to depend upon official versions of what had happened.

Many political events I covered, such as international conferences, took place behind closed doors, and again I had to depend upon official spokesmen or participants anxious to publicize their version of what happened. Official communiques were frequently drafted before negotiations were completed, and had little to say.

I gradually learned that the best I could hope for was to write an honest report which did not mislead, and leave the rest to further investigation or history. It was the true beginning of learning my curious craft, of humility if not wisdom. It remains the indispensible discipline of journalism, along with deadlines, space restrictions, and the laws of libel and contempt.

Time and the nature of the medium—newspapers, radio or television—are constraints that can rarely be overcome. Great stories cannot be neatly packaged. They do not necessarily have a beginning, a middle and an end, at least not in the time scale of journalism. The real story can dawn in a reporter's mind long after his version has been written, printed, perhaps read, and wrapped round fish and chips. Carl Bernstein and Bob Woodward, the young *Washington Post* reporters who revealed the Watergate crimes, must have realized these limitations after they had been honoured for their triumphs. They tried to rise above them by writing a book which some critics dismissed as a fictionalized version of what really happened. Successful or not, and I think it was a very good try, the urge to tell the whole story must have been overwhelming.

All good journalists have this almost physical urge to report. You can recognize them when working on a story—lone wolves with hungry eyes and the adrenalin in full spate. Americans rationalize this insatiable appetite for news with the claim that the public has the right to know. It does indeed, but the principle is nothing without the good reporter's urge to know what really happened. They are the guerrillas of journalism, and I was a willing recruit when I enrolled in Mailer's revolutionary war.

I was intensely curious. If I had not taken to journalism, I would have been arrested for peeping through keyholes. I have always wanted to know how things work, what people think, why they do one thing and not another, and, above all, what really happened. I derive intense satisfaction from reporting. The writing of a lead story is comparable to a good shit. When the last word is on the wire I feel emptied, and at peace with myself and the world. The story—the reporting, the realization of what has really happened, and the writing—is for me more important than the event. Today's scoop is tomorrow's cold type, as the old newspaper saying goes, but no matter. There will be more scoops, and meanwhile the herogram, or message of best thanks from the editor, is sufficient reward. I feel edgy and frustrated when the next good story is slow in coming. Death will be the final frustration. I can see the beginning of the first take: 'DATELINE LIMBO TUESDAY FIRST BEGINS. . . .' Alas, it will never be written.

If death is to be the last enemy, for all reporters the enemy on earth is authority. He comes in many guises, benign, authoritarian, democratic, elitist, populist, ideological, stupid or just plain nasty. He can stand at the dispatch box in the House of Commons or above Lenin's tomb in Red Square. He can sit in the Oval Office of the White House in Washington or in the TUC headquarters in London. He is the enemy because he holds, and can seek to deny or falsify, information the reporter wants. What is more, what he says often has to be reported, including the half-truths and prevarications. To that extent he holds the high ground and dominates the terrain. In these circumstances, the reporter has two defensive weapons, scepticism and experience.

I learned to be sceptical, or rather my natural scepticism was sharpened, very early in my career when, just out of the army, I helped to cover the 1946–7 fuel crisis. One of the main sources of information was the old Ministry of Labour, and the officials were defensive and unhelpful. I was also resented because I was a general reporter hurriedly assigned to the job and not a member of the professional group of industrial writers. I was even refused handouts, which are the official version of the truth, and was dependent for a sight of them upon a nice man who was the industrial correspondent of the old *Daily Worker*. In other words, the readers of *The Times* read the official version only because a communist was a helpful colleague. A strange situation indeed, and it should once and for all dispose of the old lie that *The Times* was the official mouthpiece of the government. The *Worker* man was also a mentor of sorts. One day, when I asked him for some advice before interviewing the permanent secretary, he said, 'Always ask yourself why these lying bastards are lying to you'. I still ask myself that question today.

I must admit another reason for regarding authority as the enemy in Mailer's revolutionary war. I was born that way, as I believe most good reporters are. I was born that way because I grew up poor in the East End of London in the thirties. They were bad times, but they did not have to be that bad. The distress of the unemployed, the stunting of their children, and the entrapment of their wives did not have to be ignored by elected and self-appointed authority. I was, I suppose, an angry young man, although I do not look back in anger. My mother was a widow without a pension, but we did not go hungry because she ran a 'caff'. The schools were good and I enjoyed myself immensely, as I have described elsewhere. I was not embittered. I was too much of a Cockney for that, but I was angered by uncaring authority.

My idea of right was well to the left, and I nearly joined the Communist party. Looking back, it seems that the major attraction was the girls, who were wonderfully intense, but there must have been more to it than that. I am still suspicious of British Tories, American Republicans and European Christian Democrats. Not that my battle kit in Mailer's war was ever partisan or ideological. I quickly learned to distrust all ideologies, of the left as well as the right, because of the great harm they have done to human beings. I remained intensely interested in politics, but my scepticism and experience, growing up poor in London and working as a foreign correspondent in many countries made me apolitical.

My attitude to authority suited *The Times*, although successive editors were occasionally embarrassed by complaints from the high and mighty. Dr. Adenauer, the chancellor of West Germany, called me a *Drahtzieher*, or wire-puller. Others called me a communist, nigger-lover and anti-Semite. *The Times* always defended me, for which I am grateful. Together with the freedom of expression it allowed me and the complete absence of political direction and censorship, it made up for the miserable pay. One editor devised an impregnable defence. I had Basque blood, he used to say, and it was well known that Basques are against the government, any government.

He could have used another defence except, I suppose, he felt that he could not quote from the columns of his own newspaper. After being rebuked by Lord Derby in 1852, for in effect waging a guerrilla war against authority, *The Times* defined the functions of a free press in two magisterial leading articles. 'The first duty of the press is to obtain the earliest and most correct intelligence of the events of the time, and instantly, by disclosing them, to make them the common property of the nation. The statesman collects his information secretly and by secret means, he keeps back even the current intelligence of the day with ludicrous precautions until diplomacy is beaten in the race with publicity. The press lives by disclosures: whatever passes into its keeping becomes a part of the knowledge and history of our times; it is daily and for ever appealing to the enlightened force of public opinion—anticipating, if possible, the march of events—standing upon the breach between the present and the future, and extending its survey to the horizon of the world. . . .'

As to the journalist, *The Times* said, 'The duty of the journalist is the same as that of the historian—to seek out the truth, above all things, and to present to his readers not such things as statecraft would wish them to know but the truth as near as he can attain it.'

Inspired by those words I set off in 1947 'to the horizon of the world' to do battle—and enjoy it immensely.

2 The Captains and Kipling Depart

I told myself on the plane going out that it was the greatest story since the birth of Jesus Christ. A slight exaggeration, but the withdrawal of the British from India was a great historic event, and it was my first foreign assignment. For Britain, to quote the leader writers, it was the end of a chapter of imperial history, and for India the most momentous event since the battle of Plassey in 1757. More than that, it meant the end of the British Empire and European colonialism. The British army would have to fight rearguard actions in Palestine, Malaya, Kenya, Cyprus and Aden. The French would have to be kicked out of Algeria and Indo-China. The Portuguese would hang on to their African provinces for nearly thirty years, but once the last British troopship left Bombay bound for old Blighty's shore the world would never be the same again.

The end came very suddenly. Negotiations had gone on for years, and failure threatened once again in January 1947 when the Muslim League rejected the Cabinet Mission's independence plan, but the Labour government in London was determined to quit India. Clement Attlee, the sheep in sheep's clothing according to Churchill's sneer, announced in the Commons that power would be transferred into Indian hands not later than June 1948. Lord Louis Mountbatten was sent out to be the last Viceroy, and soon announced that independence would be granted on August 15, 1947, ten months before Attlee's deadline.

It should have been a great and splendid occasion, but the price exacted was the partition of the sub-continent which Britain had united, and the creation of Pakistan as a Muslim state. This meant the division of the Punjab and Bengal, but millions of Hindus, Muslims and Sikhs were left on the wrong side of the lines. Many fled and died in a wave of violence which must have been unprecedented. Estimates of the number of refugees ranged from 10 million to 12 million, and one estimate put the number of dead at 1 million. The worst violence was expected in Bengal, where in the previous year 6,000 people were killed in the Calcutta riots, but the presence and sheer force of Gandhi's will and perhaps memories of the earlier slaughter maintained the peace. Instead, the palls of smoke which had been rising for weeks from riot-torn villages in the Punjab ignited and burst into an uncontrollable conflagration. I headed towards it soon after landing at New Delhi, and on and off for the next few weeks spent most of my time watching the collapse of the Indian Empire and, worse, the collapse of everything which is supposed to separate men and women from animals.

I was utterly unprepared for what I was about to witness although I had seen the smoke rising from the Punjab plain as the plane came into land, and knew about communal hatred, but the first terrible impression was the heat. I had served in India as a soldier before going on to Burma and Southeast Asia, but the temperatures in the Punjab in 1947 were said to be the worst in living memory. The thermometer soared above 115 degrees during the day, and rarely dropped below 95 degrees at night. It was bad enough in New Delhi, where I could take refuge in my darkened hotel bedroom with the desert cooler roaring away. In the Punjab it was intolerable, although I was young and physically fit and still had the mental discipline instilled in me after nearly seven years in the army. I also had a large American Ford V8 car fitted with a sun visor projecting over the windscreen and two petrol pumps to prevent the petrol from vaporizing in the fuel line. I had to wear gloves because the steering wheel was too hot to hold otherwise, but in the back was my bedroll, rations, thermos flasks, water cans and a case each of whisky and gin. I was better equipped for campaigning than I had ever been in the army, but I doubt that I would have continued for long if it had not been for that urge to know what was happening.

I quickly discovered what was happening as I drove westward on the Grand Trunk road, along which Kipling's Kim had walked with his holy man. At first it was very much as I had remembered it, a strip of black hardtop with wide soft shoulders and sparse and repeatedly interrupted lines of trees. The road had been the backbone of British India, for without it the old *Raj* could not have controlled a sub-continent and hundreds of millions of people with so few troops. Before the arrival of trains and the internal combustion engine, troops had made forced marches along it to restore unruly situations or 'to support the civil power', as the euphemism had it. The lifeblood of India had also flown along it, strange to my young western eyes in the war years but colourful and friendly. I had loved it, perhaps because of Kipling but mainly because of the panorama of Indian life endlessly unfolding.

It was different in the summer of 1947. For as far as I could see the road and surrounding countryside was empty and dead, and not only because of the great heat which had burned up most of the vegetation. I had the impression that it had been visited by vast swarms of locusts, and then in the distance I saw a cloud of dust approaching. The cloud grew until it seemed to fill the western sky, and I pulled off the road and stopped near a Persian well. It was stuffed with Muslim dead, and in the arms of a woman was a baby, its belly bloated and covered with flies. I was mesmerized—I had never before seen anything so horrible—until the cloud was upon me.

I could see little at first, I must have been weeping, then I saw the head of a bullock with soulful eyes plodding at the edge of the advancing cloud. The cart behind was overloaded with bundles, cooking pots, *charpoys* (Indian beds) and a huddle of women and children. It was the first of more than a hundred bullock carts, moving nose to tail, and on the soft shoulders of each side walked hundreds of men and boys, each with a headcloth over his face against the dust. They looked like apparitions moving through one of those London fogs in Hollywood movies, except that the fog was searing, dry dust. The feeling of ghostliness was enhanced because they plodded past unseeing, and silently except for the squeaking cart axles. It was as if I did not exist, despite the large car. Occasionally one of the men stopped at the well, obviously looking for water, and seeing what was there moved on without gesture or exclamation. One little boy, barefoot with a pair of old sandals slung round his neck, beseechingly raised a brass pot. Unthinking, I emptied a pocketful of annas into it, and he resumed the march without salutation.

The caravan took more than an hour to pass, and then suddenly it was gone except for a few men picking up bullock droppings for fuel. I could see them better because the dust was subsiding, and they looked like scarecrows, caricatures of human beings with bones protruding through tight skins. I was accustomed to Indian misery, but these were not the jetsom of Indian society whose only homes were the pavements of Calcutta and other large cities. They were Punjabi peasants, men who had once owned land and had grown big and husky—huskier than the average Englishman—on a plentiful diet. Judging from the length of the caravan, more than one village was on the move. Only afterwards did I realize how lucky they were. They had abandoned their homes and irrigated fields in West Punjab and knew not what was in store for them, but they had survived.

In Pakistan a few days later I met another caravan, but it was still in great danger. I was driving from Lahore, the old majestic capital of the undivided Punjab, to Multan, when soon after dawn I saw a group of Muslims by a railway embankment. They were armed, and while they let me pass unhindered, they were obviously looking for trouble. A few miles on I met the caravan, smaller than the one outside Delhi, led by a mounted Sikh elder. He was an old *subahdar*, and he sat on his horse straight-backed as if he was leading a troop of cavalry in a Viceroy's review. He wore a pistol belt, and a *kirpan* protruded from his saddle bags. He raised his right hand in the cavalry signal to halt the caravan, and waited for me to get out of the car. The men walking alongside the bullock carts rested on their *kirpans*, shotguns or farming tools. One of them had a modern American pump gun, which suggested that he was a man of substance. In the surrounding fields, outriders mounted on ponies maintained a vigilant watch. It was like a military operation. Clearly there was more than one old soldier in the caravan.

I exchanged greetings with the old *subahdar*, and warned him of the ambush down the road. He looked at me with level eyes, and then rhetorically but quietly asked what could be done. They could not go back. There was nowhere to go except forward, across the new frontier to the safety of East Punjab. His stoicism was impressive, but appalling. He was prepared to die, although he would fight to the end. My Englishness could not accept such a fate, and I told him to wait while I fetched help. He looked at me quizzically, and I guessed what he was thinking. I was English and drove a fine car. I was a *sahib*, but not a *pukka sahib*. My half-forgotten Urdu was not nearly good enough for a regular officer or an ICS man, I was also too casually dressed and wore an old American army fatigue cap which must have accentuated my longish hair. I could almost see the calculations clicking through his mind, then finally he agreed to wait, but only for two hours. They had to get across the boundary before nightfall.

I raced back, passed the Muslim mob, to Lahore, and drove to the office of the assistant police commissioner, whom I had met the previous day. He listened patiently, although he was a Muslim, dead tired and harassed by a mob of supplicants outside. He said that there was trouble in the Old City, and he had few men available. They were also tired, and the communal mass-acres had eroded their discipline. Many of them came from villages in what was now East Punjab, and some had lost their families. He offered me a cup of tea, and I suggested a whisky from my mobile cellar parked outside. Perhaps the whisky un-wound him, but he was a good man. He gulped down the whisky, and said, 'Let's go'.

He climbed into my car, and followed by two police trucks we drove back to the scene of the ambush. Some of the police dis-mounted to disperse the mob at the railway embankment just as the caravan appeared down the road. One truckload of police were detailed off to accompany the caravan, and I returned to Lahore with the assistant commissioner. Later he called me at Faletti's hotel. and said that the caravan would be crossing the boundary that evening. Would I like to see it cross? He would pick me up in about half an hour.

It was half dark when they hove in sight led by the *subahdar*. His *kirpan* and pistol belt were now hidden, and the bullock carts were moving faster, their axles shrilly protesting. Illogically I was reminded of an old cowboy movie with covered wagons seeking safety from the Indians. But they are Indians, I told myself. Real Indians. The old man was still straight-backed and somehow en-larged by a great dignity. He raised his hand in a half military salute, but did not pause or speak. The outriders and the other young men moved by impassively. The man with the pump gun, which was now wrapped in a mat, alone acknowledged me. Some of the old men in the carts looked petrified, and the children were wide-eyed with incomprehension. Only the women showed any emotion. Most were big and buxom. Some were handsome in their shifts and trousers. Heaven knows what they looked like at journey's end, wherever that was, but that evening they were full of spirit and anger glowed in their large dark eyes. More than the men perhaps, they seemed to know the great injustice done them. I decided that I would not like to meet them alone in the dark, but then, being young and spirited myself, decided just for a fleeting moment that it would be an interesting experience.

The policeman, whose family was safe in the Murree hills, accepted my invitation to dine. I had curry and he ate pomfret and steak and chips. We drank a lot of beer, and afterwards sat in the hotel garden drinking whisky. I was determined to get tight in order to sleep soundly that night, and the policeman was similarly determined, but for another reason. He wanted to unburden himself, and for an hour or more told tales of horror which I knew from my own experience were not exaggerated. He was loyal to his newly-created country, and before the first drink gave the toast *Pakistan Zindabad*, but he was not a religious fanatic. He did not seem to hate the Indian Union. I was sure that he would have shot Muslims attacking Hindus or Sikhs. What angered him was the weakness of the military force which was supposed to have maintained law and order during the transition period. Look at what you managed to achieve today, he said. You saved a village. A few British battalions could have saved the Punjab.

My pinko-gray face got me into the assistant police commissioner's office, but he saved the Sikhs. Nevertheless, the security arrangements for the population migrations were criminally inadequate, and in those early days many Indians and Pakistanis still associated Britons with authority. Some were still in authority in Pakistan, especially in the armed forces, and the governors of West Punjab and the Northwest Frontier Province were Britons. This might have explained why so many desperate people appealed to me for help, but I think it was the association of my skin with the imperial past. The appeals were painful and embarrassing. Some supplicants were so desperate for help that they knelt and tried to kiss my shoes. There was little or nothing I could do. I did help to rescue one abducted girl, and another refused to be rescued and seemed to regard me as a kidnapper or rapist.

I have no idea how many girls were abducted during that period, probably fewer than was claimed in the local press, but obviously violence and sex fed on each other. The number of raped women proved that. The first abducted girl I met was in a village outside Jullundur. I had stopped to speak to an Indian army lieutenant when she ran out of a house and flung herself at my feet. I tried to lift her up, but she clung to my ankles screaming. I could not understand what she said, and the lieutenant, embarrassed for a very different reason, explained that she was a Muslim girl claiming to have been abducted. In education and experience he belonged to my world and not hers, and clearly did not want an ugly incident reported. She was just a simple village girl, he said, probably only separated from her family. He would take her to the refugee camp which he was guarding.

The girl refused to go with him, and I had to take her to the camp where there was a centre for abducted girls. There were about thirty of them in the care of a determined but kindly-looking woman whose English suggested that she had been to Cheltenham or Roedean. She wore a sari, but would have looked equally at ease in a twin set and tweed skirt. I could see her running the Women's Institute in an English village, with suggested equality but undeniable authority. She was instrumental in my meeting the second abducted girl some weeks later.

The two provincial governments were by that time cooperating in the search for abducted girls, in part because wild reports of their fate in the vernacular press led to retaliation and further violence. Search parties crossed the frontier, which was why I met the Cheltenham *memsahib* again in Montgomery district in West Punjab. She told me that she had come to rescue a Sikh girl, and did not object when I followed her into a house identified by her police escort. It was brick built, the best in the village, and the suspected abductor was a handsome, well-dressed man in his early twenties. The girl, who was perhaps seventeen, was cringing in a corner of the living room. She was afraid, not of the man but of us. Whatever had happened, the two were in love and the girl did not want to leave. The *memsahib* spoke to her firmly but the girl could not be persuaded, and screamed when a policeman was signalled to take her away. The policeman was nonplussed, and I suggested that we should not interfere. I said that the man was obviously a decent chap, and the girl would be happier here than in a refugee camp. It was unlikely that she could be reunited with her family, and in any case her future was grim. An Indian girl could never hope to marry after living with a man, willingly or otherwise.

The *mem* would have nothing of it. The girl was carried screaming from the house, bundled into a car and driven off in the direction of Lahore. The alleged abductor was distraught. He told me in quite good English that the girl came from a neigh-bouring village, and that they had known and liked each other for some years. His father, a grain merchant, had done business with her family, but there had never been any question of intimacy because of their different religions. Then the girl's mother and father were killed in the early days of the riots, and she had sought shelter with his family. She had been in the house for more than a month, and they had hoped eventually to marry. He asked me if I would explain this to the authorities and bring her back. When I went to the centre the next day the girl had already been sent on to India although a few of the girls I saw during my first visit were still there. Whatever motivated the *memsahib*, a stern sense of duty or religious bigotry, she had tried to ensure that the two would never see each other again.

I remember these incidents clearly because I was personally involved, but they were only small part of the greater tragedy. The migrations and the slaughter continued for weeks, and still largely out of control. The military was more or less powerless. About 200,000 refugees, mostly Sikhs, were safely moved in a single column from the Lyallpur district of West Punjab to India under the protection of Gurkha troops. By any standards, it was an impressive operation, and it proved the point of the assistant police commissioner in Lahore. The Gurkhas belonged to the British and not the Indian army. They served under British officers, and while Hindus were neutral because their families were safe in distant Nepal. They also had a great contempt for the Hindus of the plains. The millions of refugees could have been convoyed safely across the Punjab, if there had been sufficient time and neutral troops. The first was denied for political reasons, and for me this was the ultimate barbarism.

The fate of most of the victims was sealed when the date for independence was moved forward from June 1948 to August 15, 1947. That decision, announced by Mountbatten on June 4, allowed only nine weeks for the transfer of power to two new governments. Violence was then simmering in the Punjab, but the Punjab Boundary Force, which was to maintain law and order during the transitional period, was not formed until August 1. Partition had long been anticipated, but millions of Hindus, Muslims and Sikhs delayed their departure in the hope that their towns and villages would not finish up on the other side of the line. They waited and waited, but the new frontiers drawn by Sir Cyril Radcliffe were not announced until two days after independence.

The dam burst when Mountbatten, Nehru and other politicians were still celebrating independence, and the Punjab Boundary Force proved to be utterly inadequate. Its commander, General Rees, could not be blamed. He was an experienced soldier with a good war record as a field commander. Among his lieutenants were proven soldiers, Brigadier K. S. Thimayya who afterwards became the commander-in-chief of the Indian army, and Brigadier Ayub Khan who lived to become President of Pakistan. They had 50,000 men under their command, among them the 4th Indian division, one of the best fighting units of the second world war. Most of them were disciplined war veterans, but they were also Hindus, Muslims and Sikhs, and in the end most of them refused to fire on their own communities.

I still find it impossible to agree with the complacent assertion that Britain withdrew with honour and dignity from India because in 1947 I was overwhelmed by the horror of it. I saw a few heroes on both sides of the line, and men such as the assistant police commissioner in Pakistan who rose above hatred and killing. Some were army officers who did their best in an impossible situation, and others were volunteers of all religions working in the camps. I met Tarlok Singh, a Sikh who afterwards worked in the Indian Planning Commission, who even then, in Ludhiana I think, was planning for the future and the resettlement of refugees. But the most impressive by far were the engine drivers who belonged to the despised Anglo-Indian community.

Rejected by the British expatriates who had fathered them, and disdainful of the Hindus, Muslims and Sikhs who had given birth to them, the Anglo-Indians had lived as a separate community for

decades. The few who accepted that home was India and not
Britain often did well if only because they had been educated
at good mission schools. One of them became a general in the
Indian army after independence. Frank Moraes, who came from
mixed Goanese stock, was a great editor. The majority performed
essential jobs considered too demeaning for expatriate Britons.
They manned the telegraphs as well as the railways which gave
them a craft clannishness not unlike that of British coal miners.
They were also Christians, but they enhanced their separateness
by looking down on Indians and apeing Europeans. They lived a
life of pretence which could be comic but was ultimately sad.

I first met them during the war when I was one of the many
subalterns briefly stationed at the cavalry depot at Poona while
waiting for a posting to an armoured regiment. Most of us were
young and randy, and we spent our weekend leaves in Bombay
where some educated Indian girls were more liberated than their
sisters at home. When we were short of money or time we went
to the Saturday night dances in the Anglo-Indian club of a nearby
railway colony. We had less success with the girls although we
tried hard, but the club was friendly and hospitable. The food was
always English, roast beef or mutton, and the tipple beer or gin.
The girls danced decorously, and returned to their mother's side
when the music stopped. Some of them were very pretty, but
their dark skins condemned them to this sad nether world. I saw
them occasionally on Sunday after mass. We would gossip for a
minute or two, and then go our ways. I could not take them to the
Poona Club for a pre-lunch drink, and they knew it.

Their time of glory—largely unrecognized and certainly un-
rewarded—came when the land of their fathers quit Mother
India. They were not repatriated, and there was no thought of
emigration to Britain in those days. Instead they kept the railways
running, and because most of the refugees escaped by train they
saved millions of lives.

Trains have never had any fascination for me. I do not respond
nostalgicly as Americans of my generation do to memories of the
lonesome whistle of the night freight crossing the prairie, but I
was drawn to those refugee trains crossing the Punjab. Refugees
sat on the roofs, clung to the sides and even crouched on the cow
catchers. From a distance the first one I saw looked festive, as if
the rules had been relaxed for a jolly excursion and everybody

wanted to enjoy the breeze. White dhotis and saris of all colours streamed in the wind but then an old man, presumably too tired to hold on any longer, fell off and bounced down the embankment. He was dead from a broken neck when I reached him. At night the trains looked awesome with the red glow from the firebox and the silhouettes of contorted humanity on the roofs.

I travelled to Lahore by train one night from Delhi. My bearer escorted me to a first-class sleeping compartment, unrolled my bedroll and checked that there was sufficient ice. In normal times he would have travelled in a servants' compartment, but he was a Hindu from the hills beyond Simla and was naturally terrified of leaving Delhi. He salaamed and quickly disappeared into the mob of refugees milling about on the platform, and the Anglo-Indian guard locked the door of my compartment while I inspected the train. It was already terribly overloaded, and the railway workers were trying to persuade refugees not to ride on the buffers. Few listened. The others, judging from their eyes, were incapable of listening. They were too terrified to think of anything but escape. The footplate also looked crowded, but the Anglo-Indian driver explained that he often had two or three firemen. Shovelling coal was hard work in that heat.

He was a little man, made smaller by a large pith helmet, and he wore a cotton jacket over his singlet despite the fierce heat. He spoke authoritatively to the firemen, and comported himself with fussy dignity and the self-assurance of a man on top of his job. He was in command, and the mob on the platform and the probability of attack that night did not seem to bother him. He sirred me, but had none of the deference of Anglo-Indians. I faced the night with more confidence. Whatever happened, he would not abandon his footplate. It was then that I sensed the drama of that stinking hot night. From Delhi eastwards to Lucknow were millions of Muslims who wanted to escape from death or mutilation, and the Frontier Mail from Delhi to Lahore was the last lap. One more night and they would be safe, and mainly because the Anglo-Indians railway men did their duty.

No wonder their desperate efforts to board the train, but the driver looked down at them with contempt. 'They will never learn to behave', he said. I asked how many would get on the train, and he thought about four thousand. But God knows how many would arrive alive in Lahore. His last train arrived half empty and dripping with blood. The *Jathas*, small groups of fanatical Sikhs who did much of the killing on the eastern side of the frontier, got them when they stopped to pick up water. He spoke without emotion, and it was difficult to tell whether he did not care what happened to the refugees or was just inured to the blood letting. He looked at his railway watch, and said that it was time to get aboard. I would be safe, he added, but I should lock the door. You do not want to be disturbed he explained as an afterthought.

The guard hurried me through the still swarming crowd, and the train, seemingly with more steam but lesser speed than usual, slowly pulled out of the station. The families with their bundles and tin boxes left behind on the platform looked up despairingly. Red eyes shone through the steam, and many surged towards the moving train but were held back by the *lathis* of the police, and then they were gone. I was wafted into the night, alone in the tatty comfort of a first class compartment, while in front and behind me three or four thousand helpless people sat packed in like so many corpses or hung on to the sides. It was disquieting to say the least, and I mixed myself a large scotch and then another. Eventually I fell asleep on top of the bed dressed but with my shoe laces loosened.

I was awakened just before dawn as the train jolted and then shuddered to a halt. The night was silent except for the hissing brakes. I felt cold and stiff although the temperature must have been about ninety, and was pouring hot tea from a thermos flask when screams of pain and terror enveloped the train. The guard came in to report that the emergency cord had been pulled, and the train was being attacked by many *Jathas*. The guard was frightened, and had obviously come into the compartment to share the protection of my white skin. I gave him a cup of tea, and we waited and the screaming came closer. I was lighting a cigarette to hide my own nervousness when the door was violently opened and three or four Sikhs armed with *kirpans* and *lathis* stood in the door.

They were huge men heaving with excitement and breathlessness. Blood blotched their shirts and dripped from their short swords. The first Sikh was overcome by bloodlust, and in retrospect reminded me of a dog on heat. He had difficulty in focusing his eyes. Finally he looked from me to the guard and then at me again. Nothing was said as he took in my bedroll, my grip and typewriter and the whisky bottle on the table. He looked as if he was longing for a drink, and then with a deprecating wave of his *kirpan* he retreated and was gone. This time I poured some whisky into the guard's cup and was about to charge my glass when the train began to move. When we arrived in Lahore a few hours later blood was still dripping from the train. I was afterwards told that only a few hundred refugees had escaped with their lives although I was assured that many more must have fled from the train into the night.

That was not the last time I was saved by the colour of my skin. Driving through Amritsar soon afterwards I had to stop on a bridge over the railway tracks because of a mob which was surging across. The car soon became insufferably hot, and as I cautiously opened the door to get out I collided with a young armed Sikh. His eyes were dilated with bloodlust, and I thought my last moment had come, but when he saw that I was English he apologized and ran on. I looked over the parapet of the bridge and saw that a refugee train, only a few miles from safety, had been shunted into a siding. Every man, woman and child on board was killed, altogether about 4,000 souls. I was physically sick, but drove to a telegraph office and typed my report at the deserted counter. I found an Anglo-Indian telegraphist, who was badly frightened but nevertheless sent the story to London. It was to be some days before I got back to Delhi, but I decided then and there that I had to get away from the mindless slaughter. In any case, the future of India and Pakistan still seemed to hang in the balance, and I wanted to meet the men who were ultimately responsible for the slaughter.

*

On the surface at least, New Delhi was largely unaffected by the communal violence in the Punjab. The *Purana Khila* fort had become a Muslim refugee camp, and the Mountbattens served simplified but hardly simple meals to their guests in Government House, because of the food shortages. Most of the tailor shops put up shutters when the Muslim tailors fled, and a diminution of other services was a rueful reminder of how religion and casts had stratified Indian society. The Lodi golf course was temporarily closed because refugees were encamped on the fairways. Indian and British wives did voluntary work in the camps. The hotels were full, and I had to share a room with another correspondent, but otherwise it was possible to live in the leafy suburban quiet of New Delhi, unaware of what was happening in the Old City let alone in the Punjab. The Delhi railway station with its refugees and overloaded trains seemed a million miles away.

I stayed in the Imperial Hotel, and the grill room was always filled with diners and revellers, most of them Indian. The orchestra played well into the night, and not because the customers were trying to forget the massacres. There was no question of drink and be merry for tomorrow we die. Most of them were obviously little moved by the headlines in the newspapers except that foreign correspondents, the only journalists to venture regularly into the Punjab, were resented. Pandit Nehru warned us not to abuse the hospitality of India, whatever that meant. I am not suggesting that the Indian prime minister was unaware of, or cared little for the tragedy his country was living through. He was too sensitive a man, and too much a patriot for that, but it seemed that he wanted to play down the consequences of the headlong rush to independence. We were accused of sensationalism and exaggeration, which was nonsense. It was impossible to exaggerate the depth and ramifications of the tragedy. Nor could we be charged with exacerbating the situation. *The Times* and the *Daily Express* had no regular readers among the Punjabi peasantry, and nothing was done to prevent the vernacular press from publishing wild reports which encouraged retaliation.

Yet behind the *khus-khus tatties*, the dampened grass curtains hung in windows against the heat in those days before widespread airconditioning, there was a change. The roving bands of murderers in the Punjab were not alone in being sexually aroused. In New Delhi, I was not the only young man who had to resist rape if not necessarily to defend his honour. The number of women on heat was extraordinary. Presumably there were as many men, but being an old-fashioned heterosexual I was unable to make objective comparisons. The aphrodisiac might have been political independence. Indian society was being turned upside down. Indian politicians were being moved into positions of power and authority. The Planning Commission was being planned. No less intoxicating, India was seen to be emerging as an Asian power with its own diplomatic representation abroad and at the United Nations. In conversations, I heard more about diplomacy and how Indian moral force would put the world to rights than about mass murder in the Punjab. Indians seemed sublimely unaware of the contradiction. What kind of moral force committed one million murders? There was a possible answer, and it dawned on me later when I went regularly to the grounds of Birla House to attend Gandhi's prayer meetings.

The mahatma had developed *satyagraha*, or non-violence as it was generally known, against the British for two reasons. The conventional wisdom of the time, once non-violence was proved effective, was that it was the best weapon for a subject people to use against an imperial power supported by a disciplined army and police force. Certainly it helped to persuade the British to quit India, but it was not the only weapon available. There was terrorism as practised in Ireland, and some Indians wanted to bomb and gun their way to freedom. Even Gandhi was attracted for a time by violence. During the second world war he had gone along with the campaign to sabotage the war effort, but he soon changed his mind because, I realized afterwards, he knew that Indians were capable of terrible violence. Hence the return to *satyagraha*. I respected him for it. He really was a remarkable man, but I could not stomach the general Indian assumption that they were more virtuous than the material West.

There was something else in the air of New Delhi that summer and autumn; the belief that Hinduism, one of the most ancient of cultures, was in the process of rebirth. Apart from the more rabid nationalists, I doubted that educated Indians could wholly believe in Hindu mythology. They could not defend caste and its attendant evils, but the frustrations and shame of being a subject people had suddenly disappeared. The centuries of Moghul and British invasions and suzerainty were now history. They were reborn, and they could envisage with varying degrees of confidence a new India all the more noble because of the ancient wisdom of Hinduism shorn of caste and cow worship.

I was impressed, but it was in part sheer romanticism as I was to realize on my return to India some years later. India was indeed an ancient land, and Hinduism an ancient culture. What I did not realize in 1947 was that they meant exhaustion and acceptance.

Nehru spoke about creating a new democratic and secular state, which to my mind made him more noble than Mr. Jinnah, whose intention was to make Pakistan an Islamic state, but he could not defeat the weight of the past. Take Untouchability, surely the greatest injustice in the history of mankind. It was declared unconstitutional, and a national commission laboured with all sincerity to irradicate it, but thirty years later it still exists.

I did not anticipate that back in 1947. I believed in the benign power of representational democracy in general and the good intentions of Nehru and Gandhi in particular. Almost unthinkingly, perhaps because I was young and certainly because I wanted it to be so, I went along with the idea of national and cultural rebirth, as did most Indian intellectuals. This could have been the aphrodisiac, although I suspect that it was an admixture of the assumption of power, violence and an unknown future. I was to meet it again and again over the years which made the life of a foreign correspondent momentarily exciting but ultimately exhausting.

Not everybody in New Delhi was carried away by the romanticism of independence and national rebirth. The Indian Civil Service was again proving that it was the iron frame which held India together. This elite corps of 1,000-odd administrators had ruled India since power passed from the old John Company to the Crown, and it survived because it had been largely Indianized. The Indian ICS men in turn had been anglicized, some had English wives, but they emerged as patriots in both India and Pakistan. They were the essential link between the past and future, and without them the future would have been black.

The most hard-working and effective civil servant in New Delhi was not an ICS man. V. P. Menon, the permanent secretary of the new states ministry, had quit school to support his family after his father died. He had a number of back-alley jobs until a British ICS man took him under his wing and Menon eventually became the reforms commissioner and constitutional adviser to three Viceroys. He was a fierce little Malabari, and we got on well together perhaps because we had both grown up poor. His job in 1947 was to integrate the princely states, and few of the princes and rulers were willing. Under international law they could claim that the states were independent after the withdrawal of British paramountcy, and this could not be permitted. The combined population of the 601 states then totalled more than 80 million, or nearly a quarter of the sub-continent's population. Princely independence would have meant Balkanization and worse. Mountbatten rightly decided that they must accede to the dominion whose frontiers were contiguous with their own. It was also decided that the people and not the ruler must decide the future of states sharing frontiers with both dominions. The obvious example was Kashmir whose Muslim population was ruled—or rather misruled—by a Hindu Maharajah.

Menon set to with persuasion, cunning, an indispensable knowledge of the history of the states, and the determination to use force whenever necessary. Apart from Kashmir and Hyde- rabad which were regarded as special cases and were to be given time to decide, most of the states fell into line, but a few re- sisted. Junagadh opted for Pakistan, although it was surrounded by Indian territory and the population was overwhelmingly Hindu, and Indian forces were sent in. Bharatpur proved stubborn, and Menon went down to persuade the ruler. I went along, as did two companies of Jat infantry. Menon ordered them to stay aboard their troop train and not show themselves until required, and disappeared alone into the palace

It was within an old moated fort, the walls of which were painted with enormous Hindu images and elephants. I was enjoying their bold line and colour when I was beckoned into the palace. Menon winked at me like a Cockney urchin, and an- nounced that he had completed his business. He did not explain how, but the ruler of Bharatpur had signed the instrument of accession. The two of us celebrated with a couple of pink gins and lunch in an apartment which could have been specially created for the occasion. The proportions were generous, even noble, but the gold leaf was peeling and the appointments un- kempt. The splendour that was princely India was crumbling into oblivion.

Not all of them went quietly. The Nizam of Hydrabad held out for quasi-independence, and in Kashmir Muslims rose against their Hindu oppressors and were supported by invading tribesmen. The Maharajah sought the protection of India and New Delhi accepted his instrument of accession. This proved to be a monumental act of folly, and I was soon on my way to my third small war since the last great war to end wars, (I had served in Indo-China and the Netherlands East Indies after the surrender of Japan). The Kashmir war did not stay small, and exacerbated relations between the two countries which are hardly likely to improve in the foreseeable future. But for me it was the end of Kipling's India.

The invaders came from the tribal territories of the Northwest Frontier which Pakistan inherited from Britain. The territories had been a kind of no-man's land between India and what Britain once regarded as the threat of the Russian bear from the north. Strong British garrisons were then established deep inside the territories, but the tribes were largely left alone to manage their own affairs. British agents, in the true Kiplingesque tradition, kept a sharp but benevolent eye on them. The best known was the Khyber agent who was responsible for keeping open the road through the Khyber Pass to Afghanistan. Subventions were paid to the tribes to keep them quiet, the argument being that they were tempted to raid their neighbours because their land was too poor to support them. This was only partially true because the tribes loved to raise Cain. Levies of armed tribesmen were also raised to police the territories, which was rather like hiring a burglar to protect property.

It was expensive, but good fun. It maintained a precarious *status quo*, and appealed to British romanticism and cinema audiences round the world, but Mr. Jinnah, the first President of Pakistan, saw his inheritance in a very different light. He could hardly afford to take up this white man's burden, and in any case the tribes were Muslim and he saw them as citizens of his Muslim state. He was determined to integrate them as the princely states were being integrated. He had little bother with Chitral, Gilgit and Swat, once tributary states to Kashmir, which were situated in the high Karakorams. All of the tributary chiefs opted for Pakistan.

Gilgit in fact had its own October revolution before accession, in which Major Billy Brown of the Gilgit Scouts, the local tribal levy, played the part of umpire. Brown, a mountain of a man, provided shelter and safety for the small Hindu community before allowing the revolution to commence. I flew in later to have a look and it was one of my more hair-raising flights. I took off from Peshawar in a Harvard trainer of the Royal Pakistan Air Force, and headed for the roof of the world. That cliché does not exaggerate. We flew up the Indus gorge in a half-twilight because the mountains on each side were well over 20,000 feet high and blocked out the bright winter sun. We then made a sharpish turn into a valley, quickly losing height, and there was the unmade runway set at another angle and at the foot of yet another mountain. The pilot had to land at the first attempt because there was no room to have another go. Gilgit, one can safely assume, is forever safe from packaged tours.

Most of the people of Gilgit were skilled agriculturalists, and therefore peaceful. Not so the tribes. When word reached them of the troubles in Kashmir, *lashkars*, or war parties, set on a *jehad*, or holy war, and Pakistan was confronted by a real crisis. The tribes were pouring out of the territories as they had rarely done during British times, and apart from the policy of integrating them into Pakistan the Pakistan army was in no condition to stop them. Units of the old Indian army of British India were still being posted to the two new armies. Moreover, the Pakistan government, already beset by the Punjab troubles, was ill-equipped to deal with such a crisis. Unlike the Indian government, it did not inherit the machinery and buildings of government which were all in New Delhi. Earlier, in a quick trip to Karachi, the then Pakistani capital, I met Mr. Laiquat Ali Kahn, the prime minister, wandering aimlessly through the Sind secretariat building. He was looking for an office in which to work.

Outside the offices of the governor general and the commander-in-chief, nobody at the time knew what really happened, but I had a fairly good idea. With the *lashkars* pouring through the passes into the settled districts of the Northwest Frontier Province, Pakistan was confronted with the prospect of a tribal war it was ill-equipped and unwilling to fight. The danger was real enough. The tribesmen, knowing that the British army had been withdrawn, must have been thirsting for loot and adventure. They were a formidable force with enough lorries to travel far and wide because some of their sharper comrades had earlier cornered the transport business through the Khyber Pass. Many of their weapons were handmade, copies of the old British Lee-Enfield rifle, but they were crack shots. They were also reckless and of frightening demeanour. Those I saw later wore cartridge belts over their fur *poshtins*, and most of them carried long daggers or pistols. Some were pale-skinned with red hair and blue eyes, and all of them had the arrogance of born fighters. The only alternative to tribal war was to allow them unimpeded access to Kashmir, and the decision, I understood at the time, was carried out by the Khyber agent in Peshawar.

The capital of the Northwest Frontier Province stands at the end of the Khyber Pass. To the north lies Afghanistan, the Pamirs and Tartary. Caravans from Buhkara and Samarkand once came through the pass with horses, silks, carpets and precious stones, and traders still bring furs and sheepskins. In 1947 Peshawar had the air not so much of a Hollywood frontier town despite the many men who went armed, but of a city poised on the rim of civilization and time. There was an undercurrent of excitement, of living on the edge of a precipice, of not knowing what would happen next. It could be felt everywhere, even in Government House. When I lunched there with the governor of the province, the *tandoori* and lamb *pilau* were served to the accompaniment of a thud against the back of my chair. It was a .45 pistol in a holster slung from the bearer's shoulder. Only then did I realize that everybody in Government House was armed.

Peshawar was a forward fort as well as a city. Even in normal times traffic moved through the Khyber only at certain hours of the day, and men of the Khyber Rifles stood guard on the high ground to ensure safe convoy. The pass was closed at night, as was the bridge across the Indus river to the south. Beyond the river were the fat irrigated acres of the Punjab and, to the southeast, the road to Kashmir. The Khyber agent, as I recall, lived in a house which looked very English, with chintz at the windows and flowers in the garden. His comfortable living room was half office with two or three field telephones among the flower bowls and portraits standing in silver frames. The night came when Peshawar was filled with impatient tribesmen and law and order were gravely threatened. Something had to be done, and the agent finally made up his mind. He ordered the Indus Bridge to be opened. It was like opening a safety valve. The *lashkar* lorries poured over the bridge towards Rawalpindi and then up the Jhelum valley to Kashmir.

The Kashmiris were terrified, and the state troops broke and scattered. The invaders could have seized Srinagar, the capital, within hours. There would have been no war with India had they captured the airfield because the Indian army could not have mounted a major operation over the Banihal Pass. Instead, the tribesmen stopped in the town of Baramula to loot and rape, giving the Indians just enough time to fly in a few battalions of troops. They came in commercial airliners still fitted with comfortable seats. They had little equipment apart from infantry weapons, but they turned the tribal flow and held the airfield until a sizeable force was flown in.

Bill Sidney Smith of the *Daily Express*, who was vacationing in Kashmir at the time, got himself captured by the tribesmen and scored an enviable scoop. It took a lot of nerve, unless you were a Muslim or a Jew and I think Bill was a Catholic. But his scoop did not rankle for long. The early weeks of the war provided wonderful copy for all of us, but, to return to my Kiplingesque theme, none so delightful as a certain night in Nedou's hotel in Srinagar. With the summer gone, it would normally have been deserted after the return of holidaymakers to the plains, but it was filled with elderly British couples seeking refuge. They included former Indian army officers, ICS men, police officers and a few *boxwallahs* as businessmen were known during the days of imperial glory, who had retired to the Vale of Kashmir instead of going home to live in Bournemouth or Cheltenham. They were a disciplined lot, and when word reached them of the Muslim uprising in Poonch and the subsequent tribal invasion they retreated from their bungalows and houseboats to Srinagar. They were met by a diplomat sent up by the British High Commission to arrange their evacuation.

The meeting took place in what I suppose was the palm court of the hotel. Presumably long accustomed to alarums there was no visible apprehension although the tribesmen were only a few miles down the road. A few of the men wore black ties, and some had glowing pink faces after a lifetime of satisfying work and a sufficiency of pink gin and claret. The women were grayer, but looked comfortable and at ease in their embroidered Kashmir shawls. They could have been any well-behaved crowd gathered together after dinner to listen to a lecture on, say, With Rod and Gun in Kashmir.

The diplomat explained that a flight of RAF transport planes would be used for the evacuation. There would be no charge. Each passenger could take a hundredweight of luggage, but no livestock. There was a murmur, and one old gentleman got to his feet and asked if that meant he could not take his dog. The diplomat said that it did. He was sorry, but those were his instructions. The old gentleman said that in that case he would not leave. He could not desert his Fifi, a little terrier to whom I was elaborately introduced afterwards. About thirty odd couples refused to go for the same reason. I met some of them on a return visit years later, and they had worn well.

The war was occasionally ridiculous and sad in those first weeks, especially after Pakistani troops were committed in strength. The two armies knew each other well. Only weeks earlier regiments and battalions had been brigaded with units on the other side, and many Indian officers spoke fondly of their Pakistani enemies and recalled old times. Men were killed, but the impression was that they regarded the war as one of those operations mounted in the tribal territories in the old days; a kind of exercise with ammunition against a sporting adversary. Both armies used the same equipment. Both wore the same uniforms, and both still owed allegiance to the Crown. I was with a battalion on some mountainside the day the then Princess Elizabeth was married and we toasted her with issued Rosa rum in enamel mugs. The colonel then toasted the King, and we all stood to attention.

I treasure that memory, not because I am an ardent royalist but as a reminder of what might have been. Partition is always savage, especially when a country is divided along religious lines. Nehru and Jinnah also despised each other, but India should never have accepted the accession of Kashmir. The subsequent charges and counter-charges, the double-talk and double-think, could not disguise the natural justice of Pakistan's claim to Kashmir proper if not to Jammu, the southern part of the state. The overwhelming Muslim majority wanted to join Pakistan. There was no possible doubt about that, but Nehru's family were Kashmiri Brahmins and he was determined that the land of his fathers would become part of India even if it meant, as it did eventually, the imprisonment of Sheikh Abdullah, the Kashmiri political leader and his old friend. Even without the Kashmir problem relations between the two countries would have been difficult, but there was enough good will between senior government officials and service officers to have ensured correct relations. The passage of time might have brought about a general reconciliation but for this unnecessary war.

The immediate effect of the war was to divert attention, both in New Delhi and Karachi, from urgent problems. The refugees still had to be resettled, and new government organizations established. The India constituent assembly was eager to proceed with the drafting of the constitution. In Pakistan, the tribes were still threatening. Not all of the fighting men had gone to Kashmir. Some went marauding, and reached as far as Lahore. They took what they wanted from the bazaars in the Old City, and swaggered down the Mall, passed Kim's Gun and the offices of the *Civil and Military Gazette* where Kipling had once worked, to the civil lines and cantonments. One day a group of them reconnoitred the Punjab Imperial Gymkhana Club, known as the Pig, where I was having a drink in the bar. It was an incongruous situation. The walls of the bar were lined with Spy cartoons, giving the impression of a London club, and in the doorway stood this wild bunch cluttered with weapons and smelling of sweaty sheepskins. We stared back. Eventually they sauntered away, and we had another round of drinks.

Clashes were reported in the Old City, and one night I stayed at Government House where Sir Francis Mudie reigned as governor. Flames from the Old City reddened the sky, but inside was a timelessness suggesting that Victoria, whose statue stood in the Mall, was still the Queen Empress. It was misleading, however. I was awakened by a bearer with early morning tea and a copy of the *C & M Gazette*. On the silver tray was a gold-edged card giving the day's events. It read, there will be no racing today. Grim reality had penetrated Government House, even if some people in the bazaars still apparently believed that Queen Victoria was still alive. Her statue was freshly garlanded every day.

Despite the tribal incursion and the refugees, Lahore was full of ebullient Punjabis. They were big, hearty men, the kind who would play rugger in Britain, and they were convinced that a new Moghul empire had been born. I was not persuaded, but I warmed to them. Hindu nationalists had always claimed that the British preferred the Muslims, and this was partly true. They also liked the Sikhs, and for much the same reason. Unlike most Hindus, the three races were relatively uncomplicated, and liked muscular pursuits. This is of course a very broad generalization. I had

many good Hindu friends, and for much the same reasons, but
these Punjabi Muslims were an engaging crowd. They were
shrewd enough, but did not lose me in conversation. They ate and
drank with gusto, and took me shooting. We shot quail, and I had
four for breakfast washed down with beer. They liked the
British, who had remained in larger numbers than in India, and
probably got on better with them than with their fellow Pakistanis from Sind, the Northwest Frontier Province and West Bengal.

They were especially resented in the Northwest Frontier
Province where support for the Muslim League had always been
lukewarm. The Pathan inhabitants were not prepared to exchange the *Raj* for Punjabi rule. I could understand the resentment. The Punjabis were confident of their superiority, and
assumed too much. Even then there was talk of a separate Pakh-
toonistan, and with the loyalty of the tribal terrorists still in
question, Jinnah decided to make a grand tour of the frontier. I
went along.

It was like a royal progress. Carpets were laid on the roads
over which we drove. Joy shots were fired constantly, and there
was tribal dancing and feasting. In Kalat, the Khan presided over
a feast I shall never forget. It was a sharp, invigorating day, we had
come far, we ate in the open and I was ravenous. Great platters of
tandoori and *kebabs* vanished within a few minutes. I discovered
later that the *kebabs* were made from the flesh of unborn lamb,
the wool being required for astrakhan. I was not so keen when I
heard that, but they tasted delicious at the time. Uncomfortably
stuffed, I was contemplating some exercise when we were
beckoned into a large tent where the real banquet was to be
eaten. I could only force down some local grapes and oranges,
which were superb.

We went on to Sibi, the winter capital of Baluchistan. It was a
bleak place, standing in an immense and desolate stone desert.
There was more feasting with local khans, again in the open. We
sat on saddles, and were served from large cauldrons. Dundass,
the agent, was the third member of his family to serve in India,
and he was not looking forward to his departure for home. One
reason was that in that awful desert he had carefully cultivated a
garden with a lovely lawn. It was probably the only patch of green
within a day's ride, and he had become deeply attached to it.

On the way to Swat, we flew over what was once a British fort large enough to quarter thousands of troops. They had withdrawn only a few weeks earlier, marching through the Khyber Pass with bands playing and colours flying while the tribesmen watched from their hill crags. That withdrawal was really the end of the Indian Empire, and I wondered then how Kipling would have reported it. I sat next to Jinnah in the plane as we circled over the abandoned fort, and already the tribesmen had removed the roofing, windows and doors. Soon nothing would be left to commemorate the forward policy of imperial India, and all that it had brought about. No wonder Jinnah looked thoughtful.

Swat was a passable *Shangri-la* with clear running water, fruit trees and a ruler with the title of Wali. As we approached I hummed to the tune of the Wizard of Oz, We're off to see the Wali, the wonderful Wali of Swat. He was a young man, thoughtful and intelligent-looking, and with an ambition to do well by his tiny state. We had a long discussion about the possibilities, presumably because he regarded me an expert from the world beyond the mountains. He was eager to grow olives as a cash crop, and stock the streams with trout. His modest hopes seemed eminently sensible after all the grandiose plans for steel plants I had heard and read about down on the plains, and I suggested that he get in touch with the appropriate UN agencies. I hope they did well by him.

We spent part of the weekend in the fort of the Tochi Scouts, another irregular force raised by the British to maintain the peace on the cheap and satisfy their romanticism. The officers' mess was comfortable and looked out to a walled garden, a combination of military and Home Counties life. For the British officers still serving with the Scouts it must have been like returning to the womb when they came back from patrol. We drank beer before tiffin, and they sirred everybody as if nothing had changed after independence. I felt that very strongly after dinner, when the furniture in the ante room was pushed against the walls for a game of British Bulldog. One man stood in the middle of the room, and as the remainder of the company charged from one end to the other he tried to bring down one of the pack with a rugger tackle. Those successfully tackled joined the guard, and at the end of the game the pack had become the guard in the middle of the room and the victor had to barge through alone. The game had been played in British officers' messes round the world. It was always rough, and occasionally savage. I was never amused by it, but I suppose in that woman-less land the British had to work off their aggressions somehow. Jinnah was amused when he heard about it the next day. At least there was a slight ripple across his cadaverous face indicating an indulgence for the odd tricks of the natives.

That week spent in the tribal territories was much more than a nostalgia trip. It gave me an unusual opportunity to watch Jinnah at work, to converse with him, and to compare him with Nehru. Both of them were physically impressive. Jinnah was over six feet and without an ounce of superfluous flesh. He was always beautifully tailored, and in western or Indian clothes presented the silhouette of an Edwardian dandy. He was graceful despite his 70 years, but imperious. He commanded attention and respect, but outside Pakistan he commanded less respect than did Nehru. Age might have had something to do with it. Jinnah was a dying man in his year of triumph, and looked it. Nehru, 13 years younger, was still sexually attractive for women of most ages and races, and from men he commanded more than respect. Young, and only recently out of the army, I felt at the time that I could have followed him into battle. Nehru was even more fastidiuos than Jinnah, although he always wore homespun north Indian dress. He was no less vain and conscious of his good looks and appearance.

Jinnah came from a well-to-do family and had read and practised law in London, but Nehru was a patrician. His years at Harrow and Cambridge had, as it were, made him a double-barrelled patrician. He had the habits and outlook of an English gentleman before the post-war years of doubt and loss of confidence, and the instinctive superiority of the Kashmiri Brahmin. He was doubly arrogant, which probably explains his earlier refusal to take Jinnah seriously. It certainly explains his closeness to the Mountbattens. They were his kind of people. Gossip had it that he was physically attracted to Lady Mountbatten, but I doubted it. She had not worn well. She was beginning to look old, but she had great presence. She carried the majesty of Government House well, as did Mountbatten who looked every inch the Viceroy. Nehru was relaxed and happy with them because they were his peers. The three of them were living proof of a class system nurtured by birth, wealth and privilege.

Nehru was one of the great leaders of history's largest political movement because he was a patrician. He was not a great politician. His miscalculations over Jinnah were proof of that. He would not have got very far without the moral and religious force which Gandhi radiated, or the organizational ability of Sardar Vallabhai Patel. The Sardar was a real pol who ran the congress party as Mayor Richard Daley of Chicago ran Cook county. Nehru's political philosophy was also derivative, absorbed ready-made from the pages of the *New Statesman & Nation*. It was his favourite reading, and his temper was shorter than usual when it arrived late from London. He was a fervent believer in parliamentary democracy because it was part of his English heritage. I doubt that he ever thought it through. If he had, he would surely have accepted a variation of the American political system which was better suited to India. But he was suspicious of Americans, in part because they were beginning to look, at least from New Delhi, like neo-imperialists, but perhaps also because he had inherited the dislike of upper-class Englishmen, if not their envy, of most things American.

He was not an impressive public speaker, perhaps because English and not Hindu was his first language. Yet none of this mattered when he addressed those huge gatherings of Congress supporters. They would sit patiently in the sun in their hundreds of thousands to hear Panditji speak. In regions where Hindi was not spoken, the vast majority could not understand what he said, but it was enough to be in his presence. He appeared to them as a reincarnation of Asoka, the Buddhist emperor, who, according to ancient mythology, ruled India in its golden age. Patel could not hope to be the new Asoka, but Nehru was because he was a patrician as well as a patriot and instantly recognizable as such.

It remained that nobody really knew what the hundreds of millions of poor Indians and Pakistanis, wanted, apart from full bellies, some elementary justice and a better opportunity for their children. This was more than enough for any new government, but the average Congress party leader knew less about the villages than the departed British district commissioners. Not that I blamed them. The ordinary Indian village was a miserable place, understandably but regrettably, shunned by educated Indians such as doctors, teachers and the like, but the gap between the rulers and the ruled weakened the parliamentary democracy to which Nehru aspired. Nehru recognized the gap, and tried to bridge it by sheer force of personality. Eventually it was to exhaust and kill him, but I admired him for it.

Jinnah was entirely different. On that tour of the frontier he behaved like a medieval monarch receiving tribute from feudal barons. Nehru would have been impatient long before the end of the first afternoon, but Jinnah loved the ceremonies and the obsequiousness of those who came to offer tribute. His luminous eyes glowed the more as the khans pledged their fealty. He accepted the gulf between the ruler and the ruled. He was the *Qaid-i-Azam*, or Great Leader. It might have been different if he had not known that he was dying. For those who suspected it, his public appearances were seen as a Roman triumph, the only fruit of victory he would live to enjoy. I did not think that this explained Jinnah. I was convinced that he saw himself as the heir to the British *Raj* and the Moghul emperors. For Jinnah, this was the only way to govern.

He might have been right. I did not entertain the idea at the time. I was too much of a Cockney radical, and I also read the *New Statesman*. Nehru no doubt dismissed his imperial approach as a pretension of the middle class, but it seemed to be successful in the short time left to him. Not that many developments in the early months of independent India and Pakistan could be described as successful. Chaotic was the more appropriate word, and the strain was evident one night when I called on General Ismay, who was Mountbatten's chief of staff.

Pug Ismay could look pugnacious, but although a soldier by training he had many of the qualities of a diplomat. He also had great personal charm, and was very approachable. He was never indiscreet to my knowledge, but was worth knowing. I looked forward to our occasional drinks, although their quantity and strength were a hazard until I learned to leave at least half of them under the chair. He began his career as a subaltern in an Indian cavalry regiment in the far-off days when the men who enlisted brought their own horse, saddle and sword with them. Only the rifle was issued by the army. He had also been Churchill's military assistant during the second world war, when no doubt he learned his diplomacy. Because of his affection for India, partition and the riots had hurt him dreadfully, and he had had an attack of dysentery. This might have explained his mood when I last saw him just before he had decided to return to London. He spoke at length that evening, and was unusually bitter. I cannot remember all that he said, but I did make a note of one remark when I got back to my hotel room. Speaking of Mountbatten, he said, 'Tricky Dicky is going to fall off his tightrope one day, and he is not going to take me with him'.

I was no less depressed, which was one reason why I accepted an invitation from His Exalted Highness the Nizam of Hyderabad to spend Christmas as a house guest at his palace in Hyderabad. The Nizam, with the assistance of the then Sir Walter Monckton, the British lawyer and later Tory minister, was fighting a rearguard action against the increasing demands for accession to India. My visit was a public relations exercise, which misfired. I was wined and dined in extreme luxury, being assured the while that the Nizam, reputedly the wealthiest man in the world, was a benign ruler devoted to civil rights and religious freedom. On Christmas Eve I asked if I could attend midnight mass, and a Rolls wafted me down to a Catholic church in a poor part of the city. Most Hyderabadi Catholics were former Untouchables, and the church was crowded. A man from the palace led me down the aisle, and seeing the front pew crowded with ragged people sharply ordered them to leave. I was appalled. It was Christmas after all, and I was at best a sentimental Catholic while for the cringing people in the pew midnight mass was almost certainly a great religious and social event. I protested, but even as I spoke they sneaked away to the back of the church, and I sat in lonely and sickened isolation.

This was but a minor example of religious contempt, of no importance, but in India and Pakistan the religious zealots were reacting violently to the secular policies more or less pursued by both governments. In Pakistan, Islamization of the state was in fact well advanced but not enough for the Shariat, an orthodox movement strongly influenced by the mullahs. In India, the Hindu Mahasabha and the Rastriya Sawayam Sewak Sangh were restless, and in the new year Gandhi was assassinated by a young zealot of the Mahasabha. The assassin, a young Brahmin journalist, greeted Gandhi as he crossed the lawn from Birla House to the meeting and then fired three shots at point-blank range.

His death, appalling as it was, was not wholly unexpected. A crude bomb had been exploded at his prayer meeting ten days earlier, and Gandhi had only recently broken his fifteenth fast for Hindu-Muslim unity. Thousands had signed a pledge to implement his programme for communal amity, but he infuriated the religious bigots. He was old and terribly frail at the time, but announced that he hoped to live his full span of life in service to humanity. He had added, 'That span according to learned opinion is at least 125 years, some say 133'. That was apparently too much for the zealots.

Whether or not he believed that he would live for 133 years, Gandhi did at times speak and act like the half-naked fakir who aroused the contempt of Winston Churchill. He was beyond my simple understanding. Obscurantist, reactionary and with other qualities that infuriated the more rational, he was nevertheless the soul of the independence movement. He was Hindu India. He was also a shrewd politician and tactician. The admixture had infuriated the *Raj*, and had led some to doubt his integrity, but for hundreds of millions of Hindus he was a holy man. I accepted their verdict when his ashes were scattered at the confluence of the holy Jumna and Ganges river near Allahabad. The occasion also reminded me that India, the so-called real India, was very different from the India of the Constituent Assembly, the Planning Commission and other air-conditioned offices in New Delhi.

The disposal of his ashes was postponed until the astrologers chose a propitous day. Inevitably it was a holy day which brought literally millions of Hindus to the Sangam, or holy confluence. Among them were *sadhus*, celibate devotees to Shiva, the god of life and destruction. They were naked except for daubs of dirt and ashes, but their eyes rather than penises demanded attention. Beneath the fringes of twisted hair they glowed like coals. They seemed not of this world. I had seen their like before moving up and down the roads of India, unencumbered by worldly possessions except for a brass pot and an occasional trident. Then they were just part of colourful India which visitors glimpsed from their cars. In Allahabad that day they were a reminder of an India incomprehensible for most foreigners.

It collided rather than contrasted with the official occasion. A fleet of American-made amphibious vehicles were provided by the army to take the ashes and the official mourners to the holy spot, and a temple-like structure was fitted to the vehicle carrying the ashes. Alas, it got jammed under a bridge and the tires had to be deflated to allow the vehicle to scrape through. Then when the fleet was driven into the river the fast current swept it downstream before the drivers could engage the proper gears. Nehru was in a frenzy of frustration, waving a short stick in anger, like a field marshal surrounded by mutinous troops. Eventually the fleet formed up in some sort of order and chugged back to the Sangam. At that moment light aircraft flew over at a low altitude dropping rose petals. At least that had been the arrangement, but there appeared to be more buds than petals and they rained down like hailstones causing consternation and havoc among the floating mourners who might have thought that they were being strafed.

It was impossible not to giggle. It was hilariously funny, but few of the correspondents present reported the incidents. Rightly or wrongly, each decided that they would detract from the solemnity of the occasion. What I remembered more vividly than this disastrous attempt to mix modern machines and ancient custom were those glowing eyes and the immense crowds. They stood in the chilly waters with hands folded in prayer, frequently immersing themselves with what appeared to be jerky movements, and standing on the bank were even greater crowds awaiting their turn to wash away their sins. This was the India of the villages, Gandhi's India and not the India Nehru dreamed of creating with a succession of five-year plans.

Gandhi's India was probably only two generations behind me in technological development. Those millions could catch up, given the opportunity, but culturally and spiritually we were light years apart. I was willing to be persuaded that they were closer to Nirvana, but the grip of their past was tangible. There was no sense of the national rebirth I had felt in New Delhi. They had not turned a new page in India's history. The enormity of Nehru's burden was never more apparent. I wished him well, but was nevertheless relieved some weeks later to receive one of those telegrams from Printing House Square. This one ordered me to Palestine where the civil war between the Arabs and the Jews was expected to burst into full-scale war when Britain withdrew. Another continent, another war, and another story. I packed my grip, closed my typewriter and was off on the first available plane.

3   It's Tough to be a Goy

I flew to the Middle East by way of London to get married, and only just made it. The Pan-Am plane lost an engine as we approached Karachi, and more mechanical trouble caused further delay along the route. The journey took three days, and I arrived only a few hours before the wedding. All should have been well. I had cabled my measurements and the Moss Bros. suit was ready. The banns had been read three times—I was a bachelor of New Delhi—but Pat's family had forgotten to notify the local registrar. His presence at the wedding was required because the Roman Catholic church did not recognize any civil jurisdiction over its sacraments, and the priest could not therefore register the marriage. He could marry us in the sight of God, but not in the eyes of the law. A civil registrar had to do that, but the Regans, ever contemptuous of anything or anybody outside the true church and Ireland, had not given him a thought. I phoned the local man, who was nice to come at about an hour's notice, and I made a respectable woman of Pat. I also made her a grass widow before the end of the week by flying off to Haifa to cover the birth, or stillbirth of Israel.

I first had lunch with Ralph Deakin, the then foreign news editor of *The Times*. It was the ritual luncheon given at the Reform Club to all foreign correspondents leaving for new assignments. Deakin was a prim and precise man, and the ritual never changed: a sherry in the cavernous rotunda, the club claret with lunch and port with the coffee. We talked about everything except my new assignment, but he did manage to make an oblique reference to it afterwards as we stood on the steps outside waiting for a cab. Fiddling with his umbrella, and carefully avoiding my eye, he said, 'Be decent to those chaps, Heren, be decent'.

It was the only editorial direction I ever received in all my years with *The Times*, and it was, to say the least, obscure. Which chaps? I got no help from Deakin. As we rode back to the office, he stared out of the window as if he had never seen the Victoria Embankment before. As far as he was concerned, the ritual was over. The oracle had spoken, and it was for me to puzzle out what he meant. I finally decided that he meant the Israelis because I was unlikely to meet any Arabs on account of the war. I was relieved. I was wholly in favour of the Jewish state despite the violence done to innocent British soldiers by Jewish terrorists. I was also interested in what I had read about the socialist experiments of the Jewish settlers under the British mandate.

There was a second reason for my relief. Being young and relatively inexperienced, I was perhaps overly sensitive to any suggestion that I should compromise my editorial independence and professional integrity. With other members of *The Times* editorial staff, I remembered how Geoffrey Dawson had misused his editor's authority to bend the news in the cause of appeasement to Hitler. I was doubly determined to report without fear or favour, but I must admit that my attitude was not entirely selfless. The independence traditionally granted to correspondents of *The Times* was a wonderful gift. It gave me freedom to report the world as I saw it, regardless of the views of the editor or proprietor. I was not completely free, of course. If the editor was particularly interested in a story which did not interest me, I was clearly bound to give it due attention. I also had to respond to requests for hard news, but beyond these entirely reasonable qualifications I was one of the most fortunate journalists in the business. The news columns of *The Times* were mine and not the proprietor's, although basically I was still a hired man.

If I was relieved that that freedom was not threatened, however obliquely, I realized later that the Arabs, the Palestinians kicked out of their homeland, played no part of my calculation. In spite of my holier-than-thou concept of press freedom and professional integrity, I was unconsciously prejudiced. Not that I was a racist in the accepted sense of the word. Looking back, I genuinely believe that I was never guilty of racial prejudice. I went to India as a supporter of independence and an admirer of Nehru. I liked India, and accepted it for what it was despite the more distasteful side of Hinduism. I lived happily among Indians, and a

Hindu, Colonel Unni Nayar, was a kind of honorary best man at my wedding. I even chewed *pan*. I was liberated long before the word acquired its new meaning, but the so-called white man's burden had left its mark even on a slum kid such as myself. I lived among the blood-letting in the Punjab without much trepidation because, as Wellington said of the troops he commanded in India, I instinctively felt that I was superior. I accepted Gandhi's claim that Indians had the right to misrule themselves, but secretly doubted that they could rule themselves with justice and efficiency.

Similarly in the Middle East. I was not ridden with the fashionable guilt over the Jewish holocaust. The Germans and not I were solely responsible, and I had done my bit by joining the army to fight them. I had done rather more than the Jews in Palestine. The Jews had first claim to my attention because they belonged to what I unquestioningly regarded as the superior civilization of western Europe. The Arabs came off second best. It was not a matter of colour, theirs is generally more attractive than my pinko-gray, but I just assumed that their civilization was inferior to my own. I still shudder when I recall this hidden and instinctive prejudice which, alas, to some extent influenced my judgement until I was finally liberated after years of foreign reporting.

Such thoughts were not of course on my mind when I flew to Haifa. I did not even think of my newly-married wife alone in London. I was about to cover another war, and witness the birth of a nation, and my jounalist's mind was oblivious to everything else. My arrival was also dramatic. I was the only passenger left on the plane when it took off from Athens, the last port of call, and smoke was rising above the fighting on Mount Carmel as we touched down at the deserted airport. The drama was enhanced by the possibility, however slight, that the Israelis could be pushed into the sea. My fingers were itching to get at a typewriter, a sure sign that I was locked into the story.

Haifa was half deserted and quiet except for the distant firing, and there was little traffic on the road to Tel Aviv. The glimpses of the sea, with the sun touching an occasional wave, were immensely inviting but the low line of hills to the east looked ominous. They were held by Arab forces, and at one point the Iraqi forces were only eleven miles from the sea. A determined commander with good troops could easily cut the country in two. No wonder there was so little traffic. I was in a thoughtful mood as the car drove through the rather tatty outskirts of Tel Aviv and stopped at the Kaete Dan hotel on the seafront. I remained thoughtful when, after checking in and unpacking my grip, I went on to the terrace to get something to eat. The sea looked very inviting, but there was obvious apprehension among the matrons sitting over their coffee and Viennese pastry. The food was central European but the local beer was drinkable, and after gulping it down I went for a walk in the streets.

The atmosphere was electrifyingly different. An overwhelming excitement was being generated in the streets. There was no sense of foreboding or of isolation. Every passer-by exuded excitement which somehow joined and created a collective mood of confidence. I was soon to discover that hotel terraces such as the one at the Kaete Dan were almost alien islands in a sea of revolutionary fervour, refuges for the middle-aged and middle-class, for the most part, respectable Yeckers of German origin, who might well have preferred to live under the British mandate. They could perhaps be excused. They had fled once from their homeland, and had obviously prospered under British rule, and now their future was again threatened. They were few, however. The vast majority behaved as if they had just been liberated, as in a way they had.

The old Zionist aspirations such as the Ingathering of the Exiles had at last been realized. The dream and the propaganda had suddenly become true. After all those hundreds of years in the Diaspora they finally had a home of their own; not the nebulous national home of the Balfour Declaration but a country and a flag instantly recognized by both the United States and the Soviet Union. The realization was clearly too much for many of them. They could hardly believe that the Passover prayer of next year in Jerusalem had been answered. Not next year, or sometime never, but now. Many danced the Horrah spontaneously, and in one cafe a group of soldiers with their girls were singing the Negev song. The dance and the song were of eastern European origin, and were to my mind reminders of the Diaspora rather than a celebration of nationhood. Constant repetition made them tedious, but in the earlier days the dance did express the excitement. I felt that I was witnessing a historic event of unusual significance, and was more than willing to be 'decent' to the participants.

Alas, my good will was not at first reciprocated. I frequently met with disdain, contempt and even sheer hatred because I was English and a citizen of the hated imperial power that had endeavoured to abort the birth of Israel. Government officials tried to behave with cool correctness, and had obvious difficulty in so doing. Golda Meir was the only member of the government who treated me with kindness, and she soon left to open the embassy in Moscow. Moshe Sharett, the foreign minister, lectured me on the perfidy of Ernie Bevin. Some American Zionists, who claimed to represent obscure newspapers which had never spent a cent on foreign news, were the worst. President Truman had signally failed to invite Jewish displaced persons in Europe to emigrate to the United States, but a couple of them tried to provoke me. They succeeded, and I offered to fight both of them on the beach. The provocation ceased, but they continued to sneer behind their typewriters whenever I went into the Press Information Office.

This was one aspect of foreign reporting rarely known by newspaper readers. In time of war or crisis, the diplomats are withdrawn, but we stay behind. We are on our own, without consular protection and exposed to harrassment and worse. I would not have had it otherwise, but I had a thin time of it for the first few days in Tel Aviv. It seemed that I was the only English *goy* in the city until, unbelievably, an Anglican cleric arrived to propagate the Gospels to the Jews. No wonder I wrote that immortal song, *Yoy, yoy, yoy, it's tough to be a goy.*

Not all Israelis treated me as something unpleasant accidentally left behind by the mandatory power. Some volunteers from London's East End were happy to reminisce about home. One of them was homesick for the Jewish pub in the Commercial Road, and the pie shop two or three doors away. The Polish waiters at the Kaete Dan went out of their way to make me feel at home, as did the German barman at the PIO. Oddly enough, Menachem Begin, the leader of the *Irgun*, whose terrorists had blown up the King David hotel and murdered British soldiers, treated me with great courtesy when he emerged from the underground. He looked like an eastern European professor with his soft restless hands, thinning hair and wet lips. His eyes, peering at me through narrow-rimmed spectacles, were triumphant but friendly. It was clear, as far as Britain was concerned, that the battle had been won and he was willing to make up and be friends. I met two members of the Stern Gang, which had specialized in assassination, who were also friendly, but I felt oppressed except when I got away from Tel Aviv.

It was not easy. Correspondents were officially not allowed near the fighting. Even the most favoured, the *New York Times* and *New York Herald Tribune* men, were supposed to be content with briefings given at the PIO by Moshe Perlman, a Cockney Jew who looked like Groucho Marx, and an occasional bus ride to the scene of some successful skirmish. Then it struck me that I could pass for an Israeli soldier. I wore the same khaki shirt and shorts, and at that time they did not wear badges of rank. There were many foreign volunteers who could not speak Hebrew, and despite the old anti-Semitic assumption that all Jews look the same the British volunteers tended to look very British and the American very American. After breakfast one morning, with Michael Davidson of the *Observer*, I called a cab and asked the driver to take us to the Negev. He sized us up with a knowing eye, and I discovered later that he had spent most of his working life driving foreign tourists round the Holy Land. Fifty pounds, he said. Forty, I replied, and off we went.

I first met Moshe Dayan on that trip. He was leading a motorized commando column known as Samson's Foxes. The eye patch was not then famous, and he struck me as an unlikely man to be leading a commando. It might have been the language difficulty, he spoke hesitantly, even with diffidence. There was no charisma, and certainly no boasting. He did not say much about his own exploits, but gave us a clear picture of the Negev campaign. Beersheba had not then fallen, but the Egyptian advance had been stopped. A *kibbutz*, or communal farm, had taken the brunt of their attack and had survived. It was still being shelled sporadically, but with care could be safely approached. Our driver, who had entered into the spirit of our little venture, got directions from one of Dayan's drivers, and off he went in his shiny green Chevrolet.

It was my first *kibbutz*, and I was impressed. Not that there was much to see. The heart of the *kibbutz* was underground, where the children took shelter and the women cooked. This was one reason why the *kibbutzniks* had survived, but the buildings, which in times of peace were home for the inhabitants, were utilitarian and drab. They were surrounded by a belt of barbed wire, coils and coils of it, and in the centre was the watchtower which I had read about in Koestler's *Thieves in the Night*. It was not exactly my idea of a socialist paradise, but of course forward *kibbutzim* such as this were designed to play a military role. Offensive to the extent that they had marked the forward policy of the Jewish Agency, which had been determined to establish as many Jewish strongpoints as possible in an effort to extend its territorial claims; they were defensive in that when the Arab nations invaded they were a kind of Maginot Line all the more effective because they were manned by men and women who were literally defending their homes. They appealed to my Cromwellian soul. This group of about 200 men, women and children were a regiment in a new Model Army held together by an inner discipline and motivated by a belief bordering on fanaticism. They were shaping their own destiny, and the destiny of the infant state of Israel. What they had endured, and would endure, would influence the future of the Middle East for all time. Such people could not be driven into the sea. They would never surrender. They had defeated Britain's Palestine policy, and I suspected that they would long remain an indigestible element in the calculations of Britain's successors in the Middle East, the United States and the Soviet Union.

They were modest, confident and at peace with themselves as all good troops are when their backs are to the wall, but they were farmers not soldiers and nearly half their number were women. I was adjusting myself to this new situation when the *kibbutznik* in charge of the defences returned from an inspection of the barbed-wire perimeter. His moustache and red fleshy face looked very English, and this was confirmed when he said, 'Come and have a drink, old man'. He was also a Gentile and, if I recall correctly, a former major of the Brigade of Guards. Certainly I had seen his like often enough during the second world war. We drank Rishon brandy, and I was introduced to his wife, a handsome Jewess in her middle thirties and already looking motherly. I suspected that she disapproved of his drinking but was too fond of him to think of changing his Gentile habits.

I returned to that *kibbutz* later and under unusual circumstances.

The night before the final withdrawal of the British army three tank crews had driven their tanks across the line and joined the Israelis. They were not volunteers eager to fight for the Jewish cause, but a rather unprepossessing bunch who wanted to sell their Cromwell tanks. Presumably there had been negotiations earlier with somebody from the *Haganah* or Jewish Agency, and they were said to have received £25,000 for each tank and forged passports to get them into Canada or Australia. I had met one of them who had delayed his departure because of a Yemeni girl, and looking at his young unmade face marvelled that he had had the gumption and the shrewdness to enter into such a deal. He claimed that he did it for love, but whatever the reason the Israelis were grateful because the Cromwell was a superb tank, the best of its type at that time. One of its many outstanding features was the turret which, although equipped with a 75mm cannon and a medium machine gun, could be completely rotated in ten seconds. The control was also so sensitive that a well-trained gunner could keep the cannon on target while the tank was moving at high speed. The controls were hydraulic and occasionally went wrong, which was where I came in.

One evening an Israeli army officer came to my room at the Kaete Dan. He was English and looked it in his well-cut battle dress and polished shoes. The badges of rank and medal ribbons had been removed from his blouse, but he was the first Israeli officer I saw wearing a necktie. He looked like a staff officer; only the swagger stick was missing. We chatted on the verandah overlooking the sea until the drinks arrived, and he asked me if it was true that I had served in the Tanks during the war. I had. Did I know the Cromwell? Yes, indeed. He had heard that it was a good tank but that the turret rotating mechanism was inclined to go wrong. They all did from time to time, I said, but generally they were easy to fix. Tank crews were trained to do simple repairs.

He paused, and we watched the last of the sunset. When it had disappeared beneath the horizon, he said that they had had trouble with one of their Cromwells. Would I know how to repair it? I had not anticipated such an extraordinary question, and was nonplussed. A number of questions raced through my mind, but uppermost was whether I, a non-combatant and neutral war correspondent, should assist a foreign army. It sounded a bit pompous put in such terms, and I asked why he should expect me to help. He must have known that because of my nationality I was harldy popular. He nodded, but assumed that I wanted to cover the war. You mean, I began to ask and he nodded again. There was only one condition. I was not to report this conversation or refer in any dispatch to the part I might play. It seemed too good to be true. When do we start? No time like the present, he said with a grin, and we finished our drinks and were off.

We drove south in one of those ubiquitous cabs for about two hours, and stopped at what appeared to be the edge of the Negev. We could have been on the moon. There were no lights to be seen and the vast cloudless sky was almost as black as the desert. I felt the desert chill coming up through the floorboards and wished I had brought a field jacket. Then we heard a vehicle approaching and the driver switched on his sidelights. It was a jeep with two men in front and we were invited to climb into the back. We bumped off, and travelled for about half an hour in a southeasterly direction until we reached a group of vehicles. They were halftracks, and I was beckoned into the back of one where some men were sitting. We sholemed each other, and one of the men, who spoke English with a strong eastern European accent, asked me what the trouble was likely to be. I said that I could not be certain unless I inspected the tank, but probably all that had to be done was to reverse the rubber washers in the master cylinder. That was the first immediate action, and in my experience it always worked. He asked some more questions in a rather peremptory manner, and then I was dismissed. We got back into the jeep and returned to the car.

My Israeli companion laughed, and said that they just did not trust me near the tank. He hoped that my advice was good, but in any case I would see the battle on the morrow. The driver unpacked sandwiches, thermos flasks and some blankets from the boot and I took the whisky from my musette bag. We ate, toasted each other and turned in for what was left of the night. There was not much of it, and just before dawn came up we drove forward until we saw a command group crouched on the reverse slope of a low ridge. I was conducted to a spot about 50 yards from the group, and I said, Let battle commence. Before anything more could be said, the guns began firing and soon I saw three Cromwells advancing in extended echelon. The turrets of all three worked beautifully.

The attack, small by second world war standards, worked no less beautifully and the Egyptians were driven back except for the garrison of a nearby Taggert fort. This was one of the many police forts, named after a former British colonial police commissioner, I think, which the British had built throughout Palestine to maintain control. The surrounded troops were Sudanese, and they were tough, disciplined and aggressive. They were clearly determined not to surrender, and finally the United Nations arranged a truce and they marched out proudly with side arms. Traditionally this was the greatest compliment a victorious army could pay to a defeated enemy, and they deserved it.

*

A war is said to be as big as the bullet that hits you, and in the few weeks of fighting before the first truce about 900 Israeli soldiers and 300 civilians were killed. These were heavy casualties for such a small country, which then had a Jewish population of 650,000, but Israel's War of Independence was not much of a war by 20th-century standards. The early casualties were heavy in part because the *Haganah* did not have a unified command and most of the troops were relatively untrained. Fortunately for them, the fighting was not sustained and exhausting. The truces arranged by the United Nations were regularly broken, but they provided breathing space which the infant republic desperately required. Above all, for all their reckless rhetoric, the Arabs had little stomach for fighting.

The Lebanese were most unenthusiastic, and suffered an Israeli advance across their southern frontier in silence. The Iraqis remained inactive although their forward troops were but eleven miles from the sea. One night they folded their tents and stole away without firing a shot—or for that matter, informing their Arab allies. The Syrians and Egyptians fought, but accepted rebuffs which would not have stopped more determined troops. Only the Arab Legion fought with determination, and it seized the Old City of Jerusalem, cut the Tel Aviv-Jerusalem road at Latrun, and with British troops from the Canal Zone in Egypt occupied the ancient port of Aqaba.

Both sides regrouped and brought in more arms, during the

truces. Israel closed the port area in Haifa to United Nations observers while massive supplies from Czechoslovakia were unloaded. The so-called Burma Road was built to bypass Latrun, where the Arab Legion held the monastery, and the siege of Jerusalem was raised. Rations and arms were trucked in for the civil population and military garrison. Life remained spartan, but only water became a problem when the Legion cut the pipeline.

The hero of this decisive period, when the fate of Israel was truly in the balance, was David Ben Gurion, the prime minister and defence minister. He imposed a unified command over the *Haganah*, and insisted that Jerusalem must be held at all costs. Some of his military advisers wanted him to abandon the city and concentrate the armed forces in the coastal belt and the Negev, but he would not heed faint-hearted advice. The course of history and the future frontiers of Israel would have been very different if he had been equally cautious. For him, however, there could be no Israel without Jerusalem. He was determined to hold on, and, in not forgetting Jerusalem, his right hand did not lose its cunning. Indeed, he elevated himself into the pantheon of great war leaders.

Ben Gurion was a short stocky man with a halo of white hair which made him look like a prophet despite the open-neck shirt and baggy trousers. His eyes could be as changeable as an English sky in Spring. They were always alive except in the company of his wife, when they were inclined to switch off. He was probably hen-pecked, for all his forcefulness. Certainly his wife was one of those much-maligned Jewish mothers, over-protective and demanding. She enjoyed her new status, and could be overbearing and rude, but was nice to Pat and me. Not that we saw much of the prime minister and his wife. He avoided the press, and probably disliked British correspondents although not as much as the American Zionists posing as journalists. Why don't they become Israelis and fight, he asked bitterly one night over dinner at the Zion hotel in Jerusalem.

He had had an extraordinary career, and apart from his love of the classics, which he read in translation every night, reminded me of his arch-enemy, Mr. Ernest Bevin, the British foreign secretary. He had helped organize the *Histadrut*, the General Federation of Labour, and had served as its general secretary, as Bevin had organized and run Britain's largest trades union. In some ways they were both the sergeant majors of the international labour movement, good at infighting and tough enough to keep the rank and file in order. Both had a down-to-earth shrewdness and natural tenacity. They could not be deterred from their objectives, but they both had their weaknesses. Their intransigence was no doubt useful when forcing some contested resolution through the TUC and *Histadrut*, but on a larger political stage it could look like a blinkered mind. Bevin could not understand Zionism, and Ben Gurion did not want to understand the Arabs.

Ben Gurion was the greater man, if only because Bevin was old and sick when he went to the Foreign Office. He was accustomed to fighting on more than one front. Before independence, he had to contend with the Zionist Congresses and the Revisionists, an extreme nationalist party, as well as the Arabs and the British. He was still fighting on three fronts after independence, his enemies apart from the Arabs being the United Nations and the *Irgun Zwai Leumi*. The *Irgun* was the terrorist heir to the Revisionists, and had earlier broken away from the *Haganah*, which under Ben Gurion mostly pursued a policy of restraint. It was first known as *Irgun Bet*, or *Organization B*, and was run like the Mafia. Internal discipline was harsh. Members found guilty of breach of discipline were executed. The *Irgun* was fanatically brave and audacious, and during the last days of the Mandate, correspondents used to sing in their cups to the tune of *Love in Bloom*:

> Was it *Haganah*
> That laid it there
> And made Shell Mex go boom?
> Oh, no, it wasn't *Haganah*
> It was *Irgun Zwai Leum*.

They stopped singing it as the terrorism became more and more horrifying. Nearly 100 people were killed when the King David hotel was blown up, and the entire Arab population of Dier Yassin was massacred.

In 1948, the United Nations observers were easily hoodwinked, and the Arabs were soon found not to be invincible. Once their first onslaughts were repulsed, the *Irgun* briefly became the main enemy. Ben Gurion had earlier been ambiguous about terrorism. Richard Crossman, and old friend of Zionism,

wrote that he wanted it both ways: to remain within the letter of
the law as chairman of the Jewish Agency, and to tolerate terror
as a method of bringing pressure on the British administration.
The *Irgun* could clearly not be tolerated when the administration
was the government of Israel and Ben Gurion was its prime
minister. The confrontation came when American supporters of
the *Irgun* chartered the *Altalena*, an old tank landing ship, to
ferry arms from a French port. Its hold was filled with enough
rifles, machine guns, anti-tank weapons and ammunition to
equip a brigade. It also carried volunteers to expand the seven
Irgun battalions already in the field. They had their own officers
whose first loyalty was to Begin. Ben Gurion saw the arms and
reinforcements as a direct challenge to the authority of the
provisional government, and decided that he could not tolerate a
private army and an alternative government. Barely ten weeks
after the creation of the Jewish state, Jews fought Jews in one of
the most amazing battles of the century.

An attempt to negotiate while the ship was still at sea failed
probably because Begin could not believe that Ben Gurion was
determined to defend his authority by force if necessary. He was
still enjoying public acclaim after years of being underground, and
it might have influenced his judgement. Certainly he must have
been persuaded of public support when the ship arrived one
Sunday evening in June at Kfar Vitkin, a little cove north of Tel
Aviv, and local settlers helped the volunteers aboard with the
unloading throughout the night. But at first light Begin discovered that the cove was surrounded by *Haganah* troops and
armour and two Israeli corvettes were patrolling offshore.

Much of the cargo was still on board when Ben Ami, the
mayor of the nearby town of Nathanya, arrived to negotiate, but
the *Haganah* opened fire on the men on the open beach and the
Altalena, with 50 men and a girl aboard and shadowed by the
corvettes, sailed for Tel Aviv. Begin presumably believed that
the *Haganah* would not open fire again if the ship was unloaded in
full view of the largest city in the country. He also had many
supporters there. Audacious as ever, he had the ship beached the
next night in front of the Kaete Dan, where members of the
United Nations truce mission also lived, and the PIO. Even desk-
bound correspondents had a front seat for the final act. It was the
decision of a ruthless and courageous man toughened by years of

terrorism, and determined to achieve his objective whatever the cost, but his audacity only made Ben Gurion the more ruthless.

The slaughter began soon after dawn when machine guns raked the deck of the ship with concentrated fire. Heavy mortars joined in. The firing continued, and was matched by mounting hysteria ashore. *Irgun* supporters pleaded with the troops to stop firing, and some did. Deputations pleaded with Ben Gurion, but he would not be moved, and the ship caught fire after being hit by a mortar shell. A white flag was hoisted and the survivors jumped overboard, but the firing continued. Many of them were killed or wounded as they swam towards the beach. A triumphant Ben Gurion gave a benediction: Blessed be the gun which set fire to the ship.

Twenty-four of the *Irgun* were killed and many wounded. The country was badly shaken, but not dangerously divided. The Arab enemy was still literally at the gates, and Ben Gurion had a majority of the population on his side. Begin submitted to the inevitable, and allowed the *Irgun* battalions to be mustered into the *Haganah*. He could not have done otherwise without destroying the state for which he had fought for years underground. It was a great if bloody victory for Ben Gurion, and his ruthlessness did more than win a battle. Strange as it seemed at the time, Israel emerged from the burnt-out hulk of the *Altalena* as a unified nation, and no less important was seen to be united. The legitimacy of the provisional government was established.

No attempt was made to remove the hulk. I saw it every time I looked out of my window, and it bothered me more than the Israelis who came to swim from the beach between tours of duty. I was accustomed to violence. I had seen more dead and mutilated bodies than most people, but had never before witnessed such ruthlessness. It was difficult to comprehend, in part because it was alien to my experience of Jews. I had grown up alongside them in the East End of London, and thought that I knew them well enough. Most of the Jewish leaders I knew, or had heard about, in London were liberal-minded and highly civilized. I could not imagine a Henriques or a Simon opening fire on men struggling in the water, or even Ernie Bevin. He was cold-blooded enough to send illegal immigrants from the concentration camps back to Germany, but not to shoot them. Certainly the hated British troops would not have obeyed such an order.

The comparison was unfair, but I was made to realize that the Israelis were a new breed of people. Not only the *sabras*, the Jews born in Palestine who appeared to upset all the theories of heredity in that most of them seemed to be big, blond and short-nosed, but the older immigrants from Europe. They had not come from Golders Green or Whitechapel, but from eastern Europe. They had not been influenced by British liberal traditions, tolerance and compromise. They had come from the ghettos, and many remembered the pogroms. This background and the earlier struggle to survive in Palestine, the holocaust, the silent war against the British, and now the Arab invasion were a collective experience equalled by a few people in one lifetime. Rightly or wrongly, many of them believed that it was them against the world. I could hardly blame them, but they were nevertheless disturbing.

They were so uncompromising. Their attitude to the local Arabs proved that. Whatever one thought of the Palestinian Arabs, they had also been victims of Turkish and British imperialism. Their permission was not sought by Balfour before he made his declaration granting a Jewish national home in their country. It was a romantic gesture typical of that generation of Englishmen brought up on the Bible, but it was at the Arabs' expense. Islam, unlike Christianity, was never guilty of anti-Semitism, but again the Palestinian Arabs were expected to do penance for Christian Europe's sin and assuage the pain of the Jewish survivors. I did not meet one Israeli prepared to admit these historical truths, but many with attitudes remarkably similar to the inherited imperial assumptions I was in the process of discarding. Their attitudes had no imperial source of course, but probably were the products of the exclusiveness of their religion. Whether or not they saw themselves as the chosen people, they tended to act as if they did.

They behaved as a colonizing people refusing to learn from the natives and for the most part perpetuating the life styles of their detested homelands. For instance, Arab domestic architecture had evolved over the centuries and was suitable for a hot climate, but Tel Aviv was typical of central European housing projects of the twenties, cubic concrete, peeling plaster and insufferably hot in summer. The food could have been cooked in Poland or Germany, and the seafront cafes were gaudy imitations of the real things in Vienna. Even the *kibbutzim* refused to come to terms with the climate and terrain. Only the underground bunkers built as shelters for the children against aerial and artillery attack were cool and restful.

This and much more was discussed whenever there was time, usually after a late dinner when I was in Tel Aviv. Looking back, it seems that more time was spent discussing the peculiar nature of Israel than covering the war. This was of course another peculiarity of the country. Never before or since have I met a people given so much to introspection and self-analysis. Many Israelis were as eager to defend themselves in political, historical and dialectical argument as to defend themselves against the Arabs. I was invariably defeated. They were much too clever for me, but I was to some extent inhibited by the fear of being mistaken for an anti-Semite. One or two intellectual zealots assumed that was the only explanation for their failure to convert me, which was why I was grateful for the presence of Arthur Koestler.

Koestler was a Jew who had known Palestine intimately. He had made frequent visits over the years, and his book *Thieves in the Night* established that he was a strong supporter of Zionism. He had returned as a special correspondent of the *Manchester Guardian*, and was the most distinguished correspondent in Israel at the time. He had many friends, who provided him with a flat—and a jeep which was immediately stolen by the *Irgun*—but he frequently dined at the Kaete Dan with a group of correspondents. He was a wine connoisseur, who could place most wines, and during the long evenings we used to order a succession of bottles to test his expertise. He was rarely wrong. The wine list of the *Dan* was not extensive, but I learned a lot from Koestler, about Zionism and Jewry as well as wine. I could not have been more fortunate in my choice of teachers, although I disagreed with some of his conclusions.

The *Atalena* horrified him, more so than most other Jews because he was attracted by the *Irgun*. He argued that ruthlessness was essential for human progress. The end could justify the means at decisive moments in history, and the *Irgun's* terrorism was morally justified with the exception of the mass murders at Deir Yassin and the hanging of the British sergeants. He compared them with the IRA, who had a romantic appeal for me as a boy. (I am of course referring to the versions I heard of the Easter

Rising and not to the present mindless violence in Ulster). Koestler's respect for the *Irgun* was further enhanced by his dislike of Ben Gurion and what he saw as the ghetto heritage of the older generation of Israeli politicians whom he despised. For him, their intolerance and self-righteousness diminished their impressive early achievements as settlers. He had a poor opinion of the Hebrew language, and believed that Jewish religious practices were an invitation to anti-Semitism. He seemed at times to argue that with the creation of Israel its citizens should cease to be Jewish.

I could not accept such sweeping arguments. It was true that Dr. Chaim Weizmann, the Zionist leader and President of Israel, had said that the fundamental cause of anti-Semitism was that the Jew existed. 'We seem to carry anti-Semitism in our knapsacks wherever we go'. But surely not in Israel. The older generation would die eventually, and with them the heritage of the ghetto. The *sabras* were already liberated from the past. They did not look like the stereotype Jew of anti-Semitic cartoons. Most of them were not Jews in the religious sense. I probably went to Mass more often than they went to the synagogue. The orthodox Jews with their beards, side curls and beaver hats would soon be reduced to a colourful minority not unlike the Amish in Pennsylvania.

Koestler nevertheless successfully exploded my received ideas of Israel, and broadened my enquiries. I always wanted to know what made people tick, and suddenly Israel became a collection of paradoxes. Behind the united front presented to the world, and on the battlefield, its population of 650,000 was probably more divided than any other country by ideology and religion. Some of the very religious Jews in Jerusalem did not even recognize the new Jewish state. I saw them empty human excrement on the heads of Israeli soldiers driving through their quarter one Sabbath morning because to travel on that day was unholy. It did not matter that the troops were moving up to defensive positions holding the line against the Arab Legion. The sabbath had to be strictly observed. Some of the zealots refused to use Israeli currency, and ran what looked to suspicious eyes a black market in American dollars. A few misunderstood my interest in them, and expected me—an English *goy*—to act as a propagandist for them. I backed away hastily.

The *kibbutzniks* were the elite, almost a nation within a nation. They were popular heroes because they were true pioneers, trying to change human nature as well as making the desert bloom. Their political influence was disproportionate to their numbers. They amounted to about 3 per cent of the population, but about one third of the provisional government were *kibbutzniks*. They were also prominent in the armed forces and the bureaucracy. The movement was not united. Each *kibbutz* was affiliated to one of the political parties, mostly on the left but including the religious and liberal parties. The basic idea of the movement was not only to farm communally and share the wealth—or deprivation in the early days—but also to sublimate self within the community. This went far beyond Anglo-Saxon ideas of consensus. The radical collectives, mostly those affiliated to the Mapam party, demanded ideological collectivism. No minority views or opinions were tolerated. Complete surrender to the majority view was demanded at the threat of expulsion. This was a new and more exacting exclusiveness which replaced that of religion.

To my young mind, it seemed undemocratic and very Russian. They were not communists—Israeli communists were almost beyond the pale and later sought support among Arabs—but philosophically it was a pure form of communism, and no less tyrannical in the absence of secret police. The paradox was that as the *kibbutzim* prospered they became islands of privilege. The wealth was shared by the community and not by the nation. Some *kibbutzim*, as I discovered during subsequent visits to Israel, developed into luxurious estates and members in good standing, that is ideologically pure, were guaranteed a standard of living and economic security way beyond that of most Israelis. I knew Ein Geb, on the eastern shore of Lake Tiberias, in its heroic days when it fought off repeated attacks of the Syrian Army. When I visited it in the 1970s, it looked like a tourist trap with a fish restaurant which could have been imported, lock, stock and barrel from the Sternbergersee in Bavaria.

The collective selfishness of this privileged few was especially obvious in the austere days immediately after independence when thousands of poor Jews began to arrive. Prominent among among them were the oriental Jews, especially those from the Yemen. They had lived there for centuries cut off from the outside world because the Yemen was then a closed theocracy. Their cultural development had been retarded for hundreds of years, and like all desert people they were physically small and delicate. Apart from their distinctive dress they could have passed for Arabs. The Imam had oppressed them not much more than his Muslim subjects, but they were a withdrawn people very different from the average western Jew. Nevertheless, when the news of the establishment of Israel reached the plateau groups of them began to make their way to Aden, then a British colony, and an airlift was arranged to fly them to Israel.

I flew down to report what was an extraordinary event. Most of them had never before seen an airplane on the ground, and after centuries of medieval life they were suddenly expected to board a DC4 and fly off to a new and unknown life. They took it very well. I was told that they had long believed that a large mythical bird would fly them home to Jerusalem. In my experience, myths are manufactured for such moments, but they had the touching trust of the truly innocent. I am sure that they would have willingly flown in a moon rocket to reach Israel. (Later I was to fly in a helicopter with Malayan aborigines who had never seen a train or a ship, and they loved it). The Yemenis were known at the time as 30-kilo Jews, because they were so small, and I took the place of two of them when I flew back with one group. I was more apprehensive than they because the plane was a battered old charter.

Their arrival in Israel was the most exciting event in their lives, but they were quickly disillusioned because of the attitude of Israelis from Europe. The fact that they were all Jews did not resolve the age-old problem of colour, and their personal habits proved to be another barrier. I suppose much of this was inevitable, if only because European Jews were afraid that the orientals, with their higher birth rate, would change the nature of Israel, but the attitude of the *kibbutzim* was indefensible. They refused to accept Yemenis as guests, let alone as members, and some even employed them as day labourers which was contrary to the basic principle of the movement.

These were not the only paradoxes which concerned sensitive Israelis, but for all the internal divisions and inequalities, the overall unity of the country was beyond dispute. It was evident in the new militant nationalism which quickly replaced the earlier

Zionist dream of a pluralist and polyglot Israel. I regretted the chauvinism, and not only because it is always distasteful. I then shared the prevailing view that the age of the nation state was passing, despite the fact that new states were being created or fought for all over the world. That was a universal paradox, although especially applicable to Jews, the most international and polyglot of peoples. Nevertheless, it was just as well. Herzl's dream of Israel would not have long survived in the welter of the new and aggressive Arab nationalisms, but some of my regrets were revived after I met Chaim Weizmann, the first President of Israel, in circumstances painful for both of us.

The meeting came about after the Israel air force shot down some RAF fighters based on the Canal Zone. It can be argued that they should not have been flying near or along Israel's new frontier in the Negev, but there was no fighting at the time and their intention was clearly not hostile. Nevertheless, the Israeli planes attacked without warning and shot them down. The unnecessary killings troubled me. Tribal loyalty can be strong even when one is trying to be objective, and the killings caused great disquiet within the Israeli government. Some members of the cabinet feared retaliation, and it was suggested by devious means that I should go down to Rehoveth to interview the President. Weizmann, a scientist and greatly respected in Britain, was instrumental in securing the Balfour Declaration from the British government in 1971. As the president of the World Zionist organization, he had been a superb ambassador because he represented all that was best in liberal western Jewry. Even his Arab adversaries had treated him with respect.

He was then very old, and was resting when I arrived at his house that warm afternoon. I was shown to my room, and after changing shirts went down to the living room where I found that a fellow house guest was Richard Crossman, the British labour politician who had served on the Anglo-American Palestine Committee in 1946. He was then known by some of his party colleagues as Double Crossman, and I did not warm to him at our first meeting. He first abused the dead pilots for being stupid clots, and then commended the Israelis for the administration of Arabs within their borders. It did not occur to him that the Israelis were performing a colonial function, and he irritably dismissed my mild suggestion. For me it was yet another paradox of the new country, but he clearly regarded me as pro-Arab or anti-Semite. The atmosphere was not congenial in that pleasant sitting room when Weizmann finally appeared.

He was physically frail, partially blind, and greatly disturbed. It was the unnecessary deaths and not the fear of British retaliation which distressed him. He was nevertheless a perfect host, and ordered drinks and asked about my welfare before we sat down to dinner. Then the emotional floodgates opened. Throughout the meal, during which Crossman showed unusual common sense by remaining silent, Weizman spoke about the incident and the parting of the ways of Britain and Israel. The words overwhelmed me like a torrent, and because of his distress much of what he said was incoherent. He was exhausted when the meal was over, and after repeating his regrets and ensuring that I had all I wanted for the night retired on the arm of a secretary.

I was almost as exhausted by his emotion, and troubled by his incoherence. I did not know what to write after failing to understand much that he said. After Crossman had also withdrawn I discussed the problem with the foreign office official who had come down with me from Tel Aviv, and it was agreed that I should write what I thought the President wanted to say. It was an odd way of reporting a presidential interview in a period of crisis, but there was no alternative. My story led the paper, and might have done some good, but driving back to Tel Aviv next day I pondered the personalities of Ben Gurion and Weizmann. Both were considerable men and indispensable to the cause of Zionism. Ben Gurion would have been hopeless as an international diplomat and Weizmann worse than useless as a pioneer and war leader. Ben Gurion was the younger man and, as prime minister, would have the power. There could be no regret about that, and not only because Weizmann was too old, but I regretted his liberalism and humanism. Israel would have been a better country than it became had Weizmann been able to influence its destiny in the few years left to him.

*

For Jews everywhere, Jerusalem and not Tel Aviv was the capital of Israel although the United Nations had decided it would be an international city. It was also a holy place for Muslims. Hence the fierce fighting for its capture. It was supposed to be a holy place for Christians, but you would not have known that from the Christian indifference to its fate. Much more concern was subsequently expressed over Venice. Nevertheless, I once knew Blake's *Jerusalem* by heart. It had been my Red Flag when I was a young radical in London's East End, and while my political idealism was no longer unblemished the city had an immense attraction for me. When the first truce was broken it was still cut off from the rest of Israel except for the Burma road, but one fine morning I decided to hitch a ride. An old British army 15-cwt truck picked me up on the outskirts of Tel Aviv, and I joined the young soldiers in the back. They were clearly new to war, and were excited by the prospect of battle. They were also as interested in me as I was in them. They were innocently thrilled to know that their war was being reported to the outside world, and not a word was said against Britain. One young soldier, who came from Romania but had a smattering of English, seemed sorry for me because I belonged to the losing side.

The truck dropped me off somewhere before Latrun. We wished each other good luck, but progress became very slow because the Burma Road was not much used during the day. It was evening before I rejoined the main road a few miles from Jerusalem, and I was promptly arrested by one of the detachments of troops guarding the approach to the city. My captors belonged to the *Palmach*, Israel's shock troops. Most of them were *kibbutzniks* and belonged to *Mapam*, the left-wing Labour party. They were not impressed by my Israeli press pass, and I gathered that most of them thought I was a British spy. They were polite enough. They shared their evening meal with me, but there was no doubt that I was their prisoner. One of them reported my capture over a field telephone.

Their caution was perhaps understandable. The forward positions of the Arab Legion could be seen on a ridge beyond the road, and it was led by British officers. I protested my innocence, and, because they were Israelis, the exchange developed into a profound political discussion. Within minutes about half of the detachment, or so it seemed, had gathered about me, and those who could not speak English were given a running translation in Hebrew. The misdoings of Britain were rehashed and disposed of, and we were into left-wing politics, the future of the Middle East including the part the great powers were expected to play, and the need to educate Arab peasants. The *Mapam* was seen by the other political parties to be soft on the Arabs, and certainly some of those soldiers were closer to Herzl, the founder of Zionism, than to Ben Gurion. The discussion continued until the field telephone buzzed, and the leader of the detachment was ordered to release me. He stopped the next truck travelling towards Jerusalem, and told the driver to drop me at the Zion hotel.

The next morning I awoke in another world. The hotel was nearly empty, and although the sun was well up the street outside was also quiet. It could have been Sunday in a small English town. About 80,000 Jews had remained in Jerusalem despite the fighting, but the city seemed to be half-deserted. It was a wonderful change from noisy Tel Aviv, where every morning I had been awakened by *Wunderkinder* practising the violin or piano before going to school, and the city was very beautiful. I have never escaped from its spell. Even the new city was handsome enough because the British administration had insisted that all buildings should be clad with the local stone.

Food and water was scarce, but correspondents frequented a cafe in Zion Square where German beer could be bought for four American dollars a bottle. There was also Hesse's restaurant, which served chicken soup and wiener schnitzels despite the heat and Fink's bar where you could get a good dry martini. We also found an isolated and deserted house at the bottom of Princess Shlomzion Street with a large underground cistern. In the early evening we would drive quickly down the exposed road, generally reaching the shelter of the house before the Arab Legion opened fire, and crawl through an inspection plate to swim in the cistern. The water was refreshingly cool, and we would swim for about half an hour before returning in the dark and without lights for dinner. I also moved into the Salvia hotel where the menu was quite lavish and the bar well stocked because, so it was said, the proprietress, Madame Katz, knew blockade-runners belonging to the Stern Gang. Thus well established, I was ready to report the war.

It was in fact a rather disappointing war. The battle for the Jewish quarter of the old city had been fought and lost, and a secret truce between Israel and Jordan was more or less maintained because of the very secret diplomacy conducted between

the two. There were exchanges of fire along the front line which
ran through the city, and the night sky was often illuminated by
tracer bullets, but diplomacy, of which we knew little or
nothing, prevailed. The Israeli and Arab military governors kept
in touch, and Count Bernadotte, the United Nations mediator,
regularly crossed the line by way of the Mandelbaum gate. Actually it was not a gate, but the ruined site of a house once
owned by a Mr. Mandelbaum which provided access between the
two sides. The city was invariably quiet on the Jewish and
Muslim sabbaths.

As their blockade-running indicated, the Stern Gang was
very much in evidence in Jerusalem. I kept in touch with the
gang, or perhaps it kept in touch with the foreign press. Certainly
one of the gang seemed to be always around. Despite the gang's
ferocious reputation for cold-blooded assassination, he could be
engaging. Goldschmidt had helped to run a Middle East review
during the last years of the mandate, and had been commended
by the British high commissioner for his moderation. His true
identity was not revealed at the time but now his audacity was
expressed by a light-hearted approach to life almost alien in
Israel. The gang was left strictly alone by the government, for
whom Goldschmidt had great contempt. He assumed that the
Sternist philosophy, which was never made clear to me, would
prevail. He awaited the day with confidence, and meanwhile
enjoyed himself immensely.

One Friday he invited a few foreign correspondents to lunch
at Abu Ghosh. This is an Arab village near the wadi which had
been the scene of some of the most bitter fighting. The road
verges were littered with the burnt-out remains of Israeli
armoured vehicles. The village was also known for its crusader
church, and the French Catholic priests who made a sparkling
red wine. We drove down, had a good lunch and probably too
much wine, and then returned to Jerusalem for a siesta. After all,
nothing ever happened on sabbath. Thankfully, I put my feet up,
and dozed off. Then I was awakened by Carter Davidson of the
Associated Press, who shared an apartment next door with his
wife and small daughter. 'They've shot Bernadotte', he said.

We reached the scene of the crime just in time to see the body
being taken away. For all the political implications and possible
repercussions, it was basically a police story and easy to cover.

Who shot whom, when, where, why. The frightened Israeli officials spoke freely, and within the hour we were in the PIO typing our stories in short takes of two or three paragraphs in the expectation of heavy traffic at the telegraph office. We then went off to have a $4 beer, and ponder what had to be done next, and Bob Miller of the United Press suggested that we should go down to the telegraph office and see how the traffic was being moved. It was not. Our messages were neatly stacked on the desk of the censor, who said that he had orders not to pass a single word. We swore, retrieved our messages and went outside.

The street was deserted, and we were getting fidgety as correspondents always do when the deadline approaches. Not one of us had a car, the last one having been stolen a few days earlier, and no official transport was available because the sabbath stars were expected at any moment. We phoned for taxis without success, and eventually, as it was getting dark, found one in Ben Yehuda Street. It was an ancient Ford with the name Stalingrad painted on the sun visor. The driver was a Bulgarian who preferred to be known as Gandhi. We discovered later that he was lame in one leg. We bundled into the cab, shouting, Tel Aviv. Fifty pounds, he said, and we were off.

We chugged past Abu Ghosh and waved to the Palmach unit further down the road, and then turned on to the Burma Road. It was a foolish thing to do, but there was no moon and we travelled without lights. Stalingrad could not get up one hill, and we rolled back and went up in reverse. Then we ran into some barbed wire, and the significance of Gandhi's leg became only too apparent. He was useless for heavy work, and so we jacked up the car, took off the wheel and disentangled the wire. With bloody hands we put the wheel back and chugged on.

Finally we reached the main road, and chugged into Tel Aviv. The city, generally pulsing with energy, was also quiet. We discovered later that the assassination of the UN mediator had frightened most Israelis. The UN had been the indispensable midwife at the birth of their country, and the worst possible consequences were feared. The government was no less apprehensive, and apart from censoring our messages had also ordered that the news must not be broadcast over the radio. The news had quickly spread, however, and the official silence only made the future more menacing.

We pulled up outside the PIO, which was filled with foreign correspondents and the local press. They closed about us demanding to know what had happened, but we told them to buzz off and went to the censor's table. The man on duty was a nice chap, with whom I had frequently played chess. He had always been scrupulously fair with his blue pencil, and that night he looked up at our dusty faces with troubled eyes, and apologized. He had strict instructions not to pass any message on the assassination. We swore once again, fought off the pack in the main office and went outside for a beer. It was now about 11 p.m., and I had lost the first edition. Then somebody said we could try Haifa, and finishing our drinks asked Gandhi to head north. Fifty pounds, he said.

We got to Haifa just after midnight, and went to the local censor's office. The man on duty was a recent arrival from Manchester, and quite clearly the government had forgotten to warn him. He had also not heard of the assassination. He read the first paragraph of Miller's story with horror, and then stamped and initialled all the messages and said that he would have them sent to the telegraph office immediately. We told him not to bother, and delivered them ourselves and waited until the last word had gone to London. We suddenly realized that we were very hungry and went to an all-night café and had *falafel* and more beer. Gandhi had a big bowl of warmed-up goulash and a glass of tea. He looked very chipper, and when he asked if we wanted to go back to Jerusalem we answered in unison, Fifty pounds. He grinned, and off we chugged.

The death of Bernadotte was regretted by the Israel government, but it refused to accept his last report. The assassin was never caught, and whatever his political objective the assassination did not influence the course of events in the Middle East. It did succeed in frightening the United Nations observers, which might well have been the objective. Dr. Ralph Bunche, the senior UN representative in the area, flew in from Rhodes the day after, looking scared. His usually black serene face was gray and drawn, and he would not move far from the airplane. The truce observers became totally ineffective. As I was to discover in Korea, men prepared to give their lives for their country were reluctant to die for the United Nations.

The Stern Gang was rounded up by Israeli security forces,

among them Goldschmidt who had got us out of town on the day
of the assassination, and were sent to the old prison in Jaffa. They
quickly staged an audacious escape, but Goldschmidt chose to
stay. When I reached the prison, he was sitting in the exercise
yard and being waited upon by one of the warders. He was in
complete charge of the situation, and sent the warder out for
more drinks. We sat in the afternoon sun, drinking and chatting
until the yard was filled with cool shadows. He asked a favour of
me as he got up to go. He said that he could not stand the local
cigarettes, and he trod out a half-smoked Nelson as he spoke.
Would I bring him a carton of American cigarettes on the
morrow? I obliged.

The Stern Gang was a savage organization which even Koestler
could not defend despite his theory that ruthlessness was essential
for human progress. The argument that it was an inevitable
product of the holocaust and the desperation of the survivors was
at best a questionable explanation and hardly defensible. Ben
Gurion was obviously relieved to get rid of the last of the
terrorist groups. His authority was now unassailable, at least
within the borders of Israel.

The war went well for Israel, and an armistice agreement was
negotiated in Rhodes under the chairmanship of Dr. Bunche.
Moshe Sharett, the Israeli foreign minister, afterwards reported
that the talks were friendly, even intimate. He did not exaggerate.
After a very slow start, with the Egyptians refusing to sit in the
same room as the Israelis, progress was made. Egypt was seen to
have accepted the consequences of military defeat, and even
flew in goodies from Groppi's in Cairo to celebrate the agreement.
There seemed to be no reason for questioning Sharett's assertion
that the armistice agreement was an opening towards permanent
peace, and that peace negotiations would follow.

*

Pat had joined me before the end of the shooting war, and was
almost killed in Jerusalem. I was showing her the Old City from
the French Hospice, and we were suddenly sprayed with machine
gun bullets. We scrambled for shelter behind a column of the
colonnaded terrace, standing side by side because the column was
only about a foot in diameter, and waited until the gunner got
bored. I think they were the last shots fired in Jerusalem during

that war, and soon afterwards the city became alive again. It was still rather sedate compared with Tel Aviv. The social life was generally confined to coffee and cakes and rather earnest conversation, but it was pleasant enough. The people we met were less anti-British. Moshe Dayan was the military governor, and his English-born wife, Ruth, held At 'Homes and introduced us to local society. I first had the impression that Dayan was bored with his new job. He said often enough that he wanted to be with the troops, and that was certainly true, but he enjoyed the secret negotiations with King Abdullah of Jordan and Colonel Abdullah el-Tel, his opposite number, the Arab military governor of Jerusalem. Not that Dayan told me about it at the time, or anybody else outside the Israel cabinet and foreign office. It was a classic example of secret diplomacy, and I did not hear about it until later.

Dayan regularly crossed the line to negotiate with King Abdullah and el-Tel, and between them they established a *modus vivendi* which could have been the basis for a lasting peace. In later years, long after I had left the Middle East, Dayan emerged as a hawkish general, a national hero until the 1973 war, whose fame and popularity rested almost entirely upon his outstanding generalship. He was rarely given the credit for understanding the Arabs, but he established a very close and personal relationship with el-Tel and won the respect of the king.

The two military commanders were very different men. Dayan was a farmer and looked it even in uniform with his baggy trousers and heavy boots. He was also a born soldier and leader of men, and relatively inarticulate for an Israeli. The love of life gleamed in his solitary eye, but he preferred the mess hall of an army unit or of his *kibbutz* at Daganiah to the fine quarters allotted to him in Jerusalem. He had a proletarian earthiness which appealed to me. El-Tel came from a prosperous Jordanian family, was educated in Cairo and was also trained by the British. This was their one common experience, but whereas Dayan harboured no ill feelings el-Tel hated Britain because it was still the imperial power in Jordan. He resented serving under a British commander. El-Tel was a dashing chap, in looks at least better suited than Omar Sharif to play romantic movie roles. He was a good soldier and administrator, who had attracted the royal attention and had been advanced over the heads of more senior Arab officers in the Legion. He was an Arab patriot, cast in the Nasser mould, but was prepared to come to terms with Israel. He was probably impressed by its efficiency, and like many other Arabs of my own age at the time was impatient to break with the feudal and theocratic past.

King Abdullah was also interested in establishing relations with Israel, but not in order to drag his little desert kingdom into the 20th century. He was offended when Israel sent Golda Meir to begin negotiations because he believed that a woman's place was in the tent and not at a negotiating table. He was immensely proud of his lineage which could be traced back to the Prophet. The British royal family looked like middle-class Germans in comparison. He was a small man, as are most desert dwellers, with an unfinished face saved only by grave, unswerving eyes, and by a dignity which had survived a lifetime of vassaldom under the Turks and the British. He was intelligent enough to recognize that a tribal society such as Jordan could not survive alone in the modern world, and he suspected that British power in the Middle East was receding. New arrangements had to be made, and that meant with Israel.

The two countries had in effect carved up Palestine between them, and Abdullah was determined to hold on to the West Bank and the Old City of Jerusalem. The main prize was Jerusalem because in Abdullah's eyes it made up for his father's loss of Mecca and Medina to the Saudi dynasty in 1925. With British approval, he had already formally annexed the conquered territories and changed the name of his country from Transjordan to the Arab Hashemite Kingdom of Jordan. This was unacceptable to Egypt and other Arab countries. The Grand Mufti of Jerusalem was in Cairo, and there were plans to establish an independent Palestinian state on the West Bank. Neither Israel not Jordan was prepared to come to terms with each other, but given agreement between the two countries the Palestinian problem would disappear, or so it was believed at the time.

Abdullah admitted as much when I first interviewed him in the palace in Amman soon after he had completed the secret negotiations with Israel. Not in so many words. Apart from monarchical discretion, I doubted that he was capable of making a forthright statement. That was not his way. Instead, he assumed that I was aware of his earlier agreement with Britain, under which the

Arab Legion would occupy those parts of eastern Palestine which the United Nations partition resolution had awarded to the Palestinian Arabs. He also recalled the good relations his dead brother Faisal had enjoyed with the Jews, and his acceptance of the Balfour Declaration. He then intimated the relationship he wanted with Israel. Jordanian sovereignty over the Old City of Jerusalem and access to the part of Haifa seemed uppermost in his mind, and as our conversation continued over the required three cups of coffee I gradually realized that he was referring to negotiations that had already been held. I sought confirmation in a way I considered oblique enough not to offend the sensibility of a descendant of the sheriffs of Mecca, and he nodded agreement.

My journey to Amman to interview Abdullah was not the first time I crossed the ceasefire line, and not the last. I visited Jordan many times, and the Lebanon, Syria and Iraq. Eventually my wanderings extended to Egypt, the Sudan and farther afield. It was an unusual arrangement because I always returned to Israel, and with the knowledge of the governments concerned. As far as I knew, I was the only foreign correspondent to cross regularly from the winter of 1948 until I left the Middle East in the summer of 1950. It began in a modest way. I requested permission to visit the Old City, and to my surprise a visit was quickly arranged. Pat and I took a cab down to the front line, and then walked through the rubble of war to the Mandelbaum Gate. We were met by an unfriendly Arab lady, who obviously regarded us with the greatest suspicion and dislike, but produced two new British passports issued by the local consul-general. She stuck in the photographs we were asked to bring, stamped the passports and allowed us to proceed.

The first trip was no more than a day excursion. The consul-general gave us pink gins, and his wife, a motherly soul, overfed us at lunch with delicious desert-raised lamb. An official attached to the consulate showed us the Old City, and gave us tea and Bath Olivers. He asked many questions about Israel, which suggested that he was a spook, or intelligence agent, but I had no secrets to share and my observations on life in Israel were generally favourable. Then a quick visit to a butcher near the Jaffa Gate, and with the carcass of a young lamb slung over my shoulder we went home—that is through the Mandelbaum Gate to the Salvia hotel where we had the lamb grilled over charcoal.

The day excursion broke the ice. Whoever was responsible in Israel and Jordan, they had clearly agreed that it was safe or useful to let me cross. I suspect that I was thought to be useful. There was no other explanation because neither side had to cooperate. On the surface, both sides acted out of character. The Israelis still did not like the British, and the Jordanians were supposed to have no truck with Israel. Working on both sides was occasionally embarrassing. For instance, I went to the Lebanese consulate in Amman to get visas to visit Beirut, and accidentally produced the wrong passports—that is, those with Israeli visas stamped in them. The consul knew that I had come from Israel, but the Hebrew characters of the Israeli visa made him weep. Apparently for him they were the final proof of the existence of Israel. It could also be dangerous. I was almost assassinated in Syria, and escaped only because they shot the wrong man.

We had flown into Damascus from Beirut because of a *coup d'état*, the first of three in fairly rapid succession. The revolutionary government of Husni Bey Zaim welcomed me with open arms, and I filed a long story which led the paper. The next day I remembered that we had a stringer, or local correspondent, in Damascus, and called on him. He was Colonel Stirling, who had fought with Lawrence in the desert and had led an adventurous life, including organizing the gendarmerie for King Zog of Albania. He had retired to a lovely old Arab house just outside the city walls, and I found him on the first floor reading *The Times* at his desk. He was a military-looking man of great presence, and because of all my years in the army I instinctively stood to attention. He gazed at me with some distaste, as so many other colonels had done in the past, and pointed imperiously at my story. We were anonymous in those days, and the byline was from our special correspondent. Was I the author? I nodded, and he said that everybody in Damascus would think that he wrote it. It was most embarrassing, he added.

Later I hired a car and we drove up to Aleppo, which is one of my favourite cities, and not only because of the belly dancers who were then known throughout the Middle East. We came slowly back via Latakia, Hams and Homs, and I made the usual enquiries because I intended to do a whither Syria feature after the change of government. We got back to the hotel in Damascus after being away for nearly a week, and the next day was full of surprises. Hearing a babble of voices outside while I was shaving, I opened the bathroom window and saw that they were hanging men in the square below. They were dressed in white shifts, and placards listing their crimes hung from their necks. Fortunately I was using a safety razor. We went thoughtfully downstairs for breakfast, and glancing through the local French-language papers found a couple of excited accounts of the Syrian visit of Britain's master spy in the Middle East. He was identified as *The Times* correspondent who had been visiting Aleppo and other towns to rig the forthcoming local elections. No wonder the concierge had eyed me with unusual respect when he handed me the papers.

We thought it very funny, but in Damascus Colonel Stirling was known as *The Times* correspondent. That evening, three men went to his house and told the servant that they had messages from the Gezira for the colonel. They were shown upstairs, where one of them pulled out a Lueger and emptied the magazine at almost point range. Stirling was wounded five times, but survived. The assassins escaped into the souks of the city, and no more was heard of them. There was a great fuss. King Zog, who had been toppled from his throne and was living in Portugal, sent his bodyguards to look after Stirling's wife while he was in hospital. The Syrian government of the day apologised to the British minister, but his legation did not want anything to do with me. British diplomats overseas in those days never wanted to meet journalists, especially when they were in trouble, but I had the impression that they believed I really was a spy and resented my presence in their territory. Pat and I withdrew discreetly to Amman and then to Jerusalem. The Salvia hotel gave us the usual warm welcome, and sitting at the bar chatting to the German bartender as we sipped our pre-dinner martinis, we really did feel that we were safely home again.

Our forays into Arabia were invariably newsworthy, and of course provided me with a perspective of the Middle East I could never have acquired if I had stayed in Tel Aviv or Jerusalem, or for that matter in Amman, Beirut, Damascus or Cairo. To that extent, I had the advantage of my rivals. Competition between British papers was intense in those days, much more than in recent years because there was more money to spend, or the proprietors were willing to spend more on foreign news. We were generally utterly ruthless in our pursuit of scoops or exclusives. A new boy was always given a helping hand until he found his feet. Colleagues under great stress were helped. For instance, the Reuter man in Israel was outnumbered by the American news agencies, and one of us would always file a bulletin in his name if he was on another story or trying to catch up on his sleep. These were exceptions. Most of the time we each sought advantage over the others, and my freedom of movement across frontiers was an immense advantage.

I was in Tel Aviv when I heard that the Israelis were planning to seize Aqaba, at the head of the Gulf of Aqaba. It was a military prize of great importance because the gulf could provide direct access to the southern hemisphere denied to Israel by the closing of the Suez Canal to its ships. The information available was hazy, it came to me by way of the mysterious process of osmosis which occasionally precedes newsworthy events, but I knew that foreign correspondents would not be allowed to accompany the expedition. I took a cab to Jerusalem, crossed through the Mandelbaum Gate and cadged a ride to Amman. The Arab Legion headquarters there had received intelligence of Israel's preparations, but did not know if their objective was the port or a stretch of adjacent Palestinian coastline. The frontier between Jordan and the Negev lay just to the west of the port and the assumption, because of the understandings with Israel, was that the expedition would only extend Israel's claim to the entire Negev, including the coastline west of the port, but they could not be certain. The port was important for Jordan and British troops were moving from the Canal Zone to secure it, but Israeli forces, moving along internal lines of communication might arrive first. Legion reinforcements were on the way. I was told that I should be at the railway station by midnight if I wanted to go along.

It sounded very promising, but I had checked into the Philadelphia hotel and was sharing a room—not uncommon in those days—with Colin Reid of the *Daily Telegraph*, who was on a swing from Beirut. He was a friend from the India days, but that did not warrant my sharing with him what promised to be a good story. He was getting on in years, but was still a first-rate reporter with a nose for news. I faced the remainder of the evening with trepidation.

We dined together at the Amman Club, and walked back to the hotel in the cool of the evening. Colin had the look of a correspondent who knew that his days's work was done, and was ready to relax and enjoy himself. He suggested a late movie, and I declined. We went to the hotel bar for a nightcap, and he began to reminisce about India. The clock above the bar ticked on, and I became restive. I refused a third whisky, and Colin admitted that it was getting late, that he was not as young as he once was and that tomorrow was another day. He spent a long time in the bathroom, and I undressed and got into bed. He bade me good night at about eleven, and soon began to snore. I had rarely heard such a beautiful sound. Cautiously I got up and dressed, packed my musette bag and crept out of the room. An Arab Legion officer was waiting impatiently at the station, and without further ado we were soon hurtling south while dear Colin snored on back at the Filthydelphia, as the hotel was known to correspondents before it was rebuilt. I must admit that I still feel no shame or compunction for doing down an old chum.

The troops had gone ahead, and we travelled in a rail car powered by a petrol engine. It was fast, but bitterly cold and I gratefully accepted a red-and-white Legion headdress and wound it about my face. The railway line went only as far as Ras en Naqb on the Naqb Ashtar escarpment where it had been blown up by Lawrence during the revolt in the desert. There we transferred to an army truck loaded with troops, and we continued south without lights. Some miles from Aqaba we spotted on our right the Israeli column, moving with blazing headlights. Its commander presumably thought that he had no opposition, or was in a hurry. The Legion officer anticipated a fight, and ordered the men to blacken their faces. He shared a tin of boot polish with me, and I smeared the stuff on my face wondering what would happen if there was a fight and I was captured by the Israelis.

Fortunately we were moving faster along a well-travelled track, and reached Aqaba as dawn was breaking. It looked peaceful enough despite the hurried preparations for its defence, and we drove to the little fort by the sea and drank hot tea laced with rum. I was starting on my second mug, when a wireless operator came into the room and announced that the British had arrived. We went down to the beach, and they were already coming ashore from tank landing craft. I approached the command

party, and introduced myself to the brigadier as Louis Heren of
The Times. He looked at me suspiciously, and no wonder. I was
wearing the Legion headdress and an old American army field
jacket, and my face was still blackened. I produced my press pass,
but alas it was the wrong one, the Israeli and not the Jordanian
pass. His orderly quickly unslung his rifle and the others closed
in. I seemed forever destined to be mistaken for a spy, but fortunately a Legion officer identified me and all was forgiven. I
filed my story, and finally relaxed after receipt of the final take
was acknowledged by the telegraph office in Amman. I was dirty,
tired and hungry, and spying a British frigate anchored offshore
cadged a ride. She was HMS Magpie, and the number one was
friendly. He lent me shorts and a shirt after I had showered, and
sitting aft sipping pink gins we watched the arrival of the Israeli
column at a beach which is now the port of Elath. I never did
find out whether it would have seized the port of Aqaba if the
British had not arrived first, but it was a good story. I was also
told afterwards that the number one was a Lieutenant Philip
Mountbatten who married Princess Elizabeth and became the
Duke of Edinburgh.

*

I liked the Arab Legion. It was almost home from home after my
fairly recent service in the army. Most of the senior officers were
seconded from the regular British army or were former officers on
contract to the Jordanian army. They were not mercenaries. A
few could not stomach British post-war austerity and had joined
the Legion for adventure, and a tax-free income. For others the
desert exerted the powerful attraction it had done for many
Englishmen since Doughty wrote *Arabia Deserta.* The regulars on
secondment sought experience and responsibility above their
rank which could be useful when they returned to their regiments.
They were not politically motivated. They showed a polite
interest in Israel when I sallied across the line, but for most of
them it was an impersonal adversary whom they were paid to
fight or not fight according to instructions from London. On the
whole, they were typical British officers who enjoyed playing
soldiers, obeyed orders and never discussed politics or women
in the mess.

They could not have been more different from their Israeli

opposite numbers. I can remember having lunch in Jerusalem with one of Dayan's battalion commanders. He was a first-class soldier and looked it, but over the inevitable schnitzel he talked like the philosophy don he hoped to become after the war. He was also an amateur archeologist, as I was fast becoming, and he questioned me closely about Jordan's department of antiquity. He was relieved to hear that it was in capable British hands.

Later that day I crossed into Jordan for one of my periodic visits, and spent the first night at the Legion headquarters in Ramallah. I was frozen after the night ride in an open jeep, and ran to the blacked-out building as soon as the vehicle stopped. As I crossed the threshold, a hand came from behind the door proffering a large whisky. Down it quickly, urged the unseen benefactor. Champers sharp at seven.

It was very good champagne, much better than the dinner which followed. Apparently one of the advantages of service with the Legion was duty-free liquor. I was stoically prepared for an evening of drink and jollity, until I was introduced to Laish Pasha, the Legion's field commander. He looked the usual red-faced brigadier, which made the subsequent conversation doubly surprising.

He asked me if I was planning to emigrate. Britain was finished, he said, and could offer few opportunities for bright young men. I should go to America. He did not attack the Labour government or regret the passing of empire. Both were accepted as inevitable, but he argued that Britain was incapable of adjusting to her new circumstances. It would continue to decline because the politicians, the civil and military services and the press would not be able to shake off imperial attitudes. This was self evident. We were behaving still as if we were a great power although we had to pull out from Greece and were pushed out of Palestine. We should pull out of the big power game. Out of the Middle East? I asked. Most certainly. Nationalism was making the natives restless. They had already made the bases in Iraq useless, and we would not be allowed to stay for long in the Canal Zone. We could retreat to Cyprus, but apart from Enosis it would be worse than useless. We moved into the Middle East in the first place to defend our communications with India, and we should have pulled out when India became independent.

He gestured to the group standing by the fireplace, who were becoming boisterous, and signalled the mess waiter for another drink. One officer began to sing the round song about the harlot of Jerusalem, and the others joined in. They certainly did not think that, as with the legions at the decline and fall of the Roman empire, the time had come to pull back the British legions from the glacis of a crumbling empire. They probably looked forward to tours of duty in Malaya and Hongkong, the Canal Zone and the West Indies, Africa and Germany until retirement. I went thoughtfully to bed. I had spent the first year of my career as a foreign correspondent covering the decline of empire, and I would probably cover its fall. I had pondered the likely consequences, and considered emigration, but Laish, a relatively obscure officer serving in a small foreign army, was the first Briton I had met who perceived the realities of the post-war world.

It was to be a long time before I met another. The diplomats still assumed big power status for Britain. They recognized that we were losing imperial power, and a few even knew that our industrial power was also diminishing, but they could not see, or would not admit, the consequences. They were not alone. Even Nye Bevan supported the development of nuclear weapons to guarantee Britain the right to sit at the top table with the super powers. Much later, in Washington in 1964, Harold Wilson was to insist that we were still a world power. He was not amused when I said that we should stop kidding ourselves. That was in the distant future. In Ramallah that night I quickly fell asleep, and was awakened the next morning by an orderly with a silver tankard of black velvet. I was expecting tea, but even a declining empire had its moments.

I was driven to Amman next day to meet Glubb Pasha. The Legion which fought Israel was the personal creation of Lieutenant-General Sir John Bagot Glubb, and I was eager to meet, to quote Gerald Hanley, a consul at sunset. The Arab title of pasha suggested a mysterious figure, and some Israeli propagandists smeared him as a second Himmler. I met a little man, fresh-faced and with chubby cheeks which made his chin look weak. An army fatigue cap was perched squarely on the top of his graying head, and his voice was thin and high pitched. He could have been a country curate dressed up for a Christmas charade, except for the blue eyes which focussed fixedly on me when he spoke.

I was to discover that there was nothing mysterious about him. He was essentially simple, which was disconcerting at first and then impressive. He was a lucky rather than a great man. He had realized his ambitions. He had served among the Arabs for nearly 30 years, first in Iraq with the Beduin tribes at war with Ibn Saud's fanatical *Ikhwan*, and his first six years in Jordan, or Transjordan as it was then, were spent pacifying warring tribes, again along the Saudi Arabian border. He made the desert safer than Hyde Park by offering the young Bedu employment in the Legion, Transjordan's only industry. With British discipline and arms they became the best army in Arabia, and he had led them victoriously into battle. Not that he enjoyed war. He was happier teaching the tribes to behave themselves.

Glubb was simple in other ways. He ran the Legion from a small building in a market street in Amman which could have been the office of a merchant. He and his wife lived with their two adopted Arab children in a small house sparsely filled with army-issued furniture. He had the occasional drink, but lived as austerely as the Beduin. He had a natural affinity with the desert Arabs, which was not expressed in dislike or hatred for the Jews. He probably disliked town Arabs more than Israelis, and with good cause although he probably did not know it at the time. The politicians lived in the towns, and after the assassination of King Abdullah—he was killed because of his willingness to live in peace with Israel—Glubb was dismissed.

Being a Cockney, I was not prepared to believe that yokels in nightshirts chasing camels across the sand were superior to city folk, and Glubb, who probably sensed my lack of conviction, suggested that I should spend a few days with one of the tribes which had fought with Lawrence in the desert revolt. The tribe was at its winter grazing near the Saudi frontier.

I flew down next day in a de Havilland Rapide accompanied by an Arab Legion officer wearing the sheepskin-lined scarlet cloak of the Desert Patrol. We landed on the desert near a waiting jeep, and drove south. The grazing was so thin that it could not be seen except from ground level, and the tribe was scattered over a vast area. We passed in the distance small clusters of black Beduin tents, and camels decorated the skyline. We reached the sheikh's tents as night and, unbelievably, snow was falling. A bare-footed boy took us to the *majlis* tent, the Bedu equivalent of a sitting room where they gathered to chat and drink coffee. Four or five of them were sitting or lounging on carpets round a small fire of camel thorn. Two hook-spouted coffee pots, blackened and battered, stood by the fire. We were welcomed ceremoniously, and invited to sit. I accepted gratefully. I was frozen in spite of my American fur-lined flying jacket, and the fire and the company had worked up a warm fug. Unaccustomed to squatting cross-legged, I leaned against a camel saddle and thought of the scotch bottle in my musette bag, but the Legion officer had warned me not to drink in their company. The Bedu were very religious, and would no more countenance alcohol than an orthodox Jew would break bread with somebody eating bacon. I settled for a proffered glass of tea, sweetened and thickened with condensed milk.

I cannot report that I enjoyed my long weekend in the desert although our hosts were attentive. They were small men with soft women's hands. Their eyes were alive with curiosity, and no wonder. They must have exhausted the possibilities of conversation in that empty desert long ago, and at least we were two fresh faces from the outside world. They spoke softly but with what appeared to be much rhetorical embellishment, and my companion translated. The conversation was not enthralling although something might have been lost in translation. They did not refer to the war with Israel although many of the tribe's young men were in the Legion. They just made small talk, and not as a preliminary for a more sustaining conversation. The small talk went on until they withdrew for the night. Thankfully I had a slow snort of whisky, and wrapped in one of those marvellous cloaks of the Desert Patrol fell asleep by the fire.

The remaining evenings were a repetition of the first, except one night we had a feast of mutton, rice and *peta*. I swallowed one of the sheep's eyeballs as desert courtesy apparently required. During the day we accompanied a troop of the Desert Patrol, who kept the peace in the desert. They rode camels, and we tagged behind in a jeep. The immensity of the desert was impressive although it did not compare in beauty with the empty glacier country of Iceland which I had roamed in my early army days. The changing light and shadow was attractive, but the overall effect of the desert was similar to that of space exploration which I later covered in the United States. Both were empty, voids of nothingness. What was the attraction of nothingness? With the best will in the world I could not see the point of living in the desert or exploring space when the cities offered so much. The Bedu had more natural dignity than the astronauts, but they remained a case of arrested development. I was relieved when the time came for our departure.

We spent a day at an Arab Legion fort, where I left my companion, and that night headed for Ma'an where a plane was to collect me on the following day. The moonlight was very thin, and we soon lost our way. We then followed the accepted desert practice of driving in ever increasing circles until we found the track, which I was told later was first made by Lawrence's armoured cars. The driver paused for a moment, and then turned right. I looked up at the sky, located the north star and decided that we were driving in the wrong direction. At the speed we were travelling we would soon fall into the Wadi as Sirhan across the Saudi frontier.

I was in a quandary. How could I, a Cockney, tell the driver, a true son of the desert, that he was driving in the wrong direction? I was also cold and tired, and after taking another look at the north star above our port beam, I told the driver to stop. He probably thought I wanted to pee, and stopped willingly enough. He was a sergeant, and spoke a little English, and when I told him to turn round he became rebellious. I could see why. He was a Bedu on his own desert and I was an ignorant foreigner. I was apologetic, but determined. I pointed to the north star, and argued that Ma'an had to be behind us. He was not persuaded, and eventually, and ashamedly, I had to play the role of the colonial master. Turn the bloody thing round, I said in a hard voice. He shot me a look of distilled hatred, but obeyed. We did not speak for hours, and when dawn broke I was beginning to wonder if I had mistaken the north star. Then we breasted a low rise, and there was the town. He dropped me at the Ma'an hotel, and drove off with a muttered *salaam aleikum*, and I went into the hotel and ordered a large cold beer, a hot bath, and breakfast in that order. The man behind the reception desk was as silent as the driver, but the beer quickly appeared and the hot bath was announced as I was considering the advisability of having a second bottle. The bath was huge and wonderfully hot, and the breakfast an indescribable dish of eggs, bacon, sausages, fresh rolls and a large pot of strong coffee. My faith in Arabs, if not in the Beduin, was fully restored, and I flew back to Amman in the best of humours.

I returned to Jerusalem with Glubb Pasha, who was on an inspection of troop positions, and on the way visited a refugee camp outside Jericho. I had seen other camps, but this was terribly depressing and not only because Glubb, who was bilingual, was a patient interpreter. Thousands of men, women and children were crowded into rows of makeshift huts, which were covered by a pervading cloud of hopelessness. It was unnerving because I, a typical western optimist, could not accept, let alone understand, this kind of hopelessness, but they had been there for months and it looked as if they would be there for ever. I spoke to many families, some of whom could speak English, and their stories were similar. After the Dier Yassin pogrom, they joined the new Diaspora in fear of their lives. But unlike the ancestors of Israelis they were unprepared to become wandering Arabs. Palestinian Arabs were better educated than most, and opportunities beckoned in Kuwait and elsewhere in the oil states for the adventurous. Many did emigrate, but the majority were determined to stay in what amounted to ghettos until their ingathering of the exiles. According to the UN representative in charge, their numbers were increasing because there had been more births than deaths and emigrants.

In my experience, Jews are a most generous and humane people. In the west they have long been in the forefront of the struggle against injustice and inequality, but whenever I tried to discuss the Arab refugee question Israelis were either defensive or prevaricating. Mr. Moshe Sharett, the foreign minister, lost his temper when I tried to discuss it in an interview. The parallel with the history of the Jewish people was too close for comfort, but the final tragedy was unparalleled. Whatever the diplomats said then or since, the concept of a Jewish state would be destroyed if the Arab refugees were allowed to return. Palestinian Arabs had to be excluded from their homes forever if Israel was to survive.

In the early months I had not appreciated the enormity of this injustice. I assumed, with most Israelis, that the refugees would be resettled in Arab countries. Arabs had always seen themselves as one nation united by language, religion and culture. The national frontiers imposed by the Allies after the first world war were unnatural barriers which should not prevent Palestinians settling in the Lebanon, Syria, Jordan or anywhere in the Arab world. There was plenty of land and aid would be forthcoming from the western world. The refugees would get tired of waiting in refugee camps, and solve the problem by seeking a new life elsewhere. The injustice would be assuaged over the years once the Arab governments accepted the consequences of military defeat.

This comforting assumption was blasted when the United Nations Conciliation Commission met in Beirut. I crossed the line to cover it, and spent many hours talking to Arab delegates. They sat in the lobby of the St. Georges hotel fuddling their beads, and most of them were approachable. I tried to discuss the refugee question from every possible angle, but the answers were always the same. There would be no resettlement. The refugees would stay in the camps until they returned to their homes. This became Arab policy thereafter. It was cruel policy, and mitigated at least in diplomatic debate the injustice upon which the future of Israel depended, but both sides were guilty in varying degrees of *Realpolitik*.

In retrospect that Beirut meeting was the beginning of all that came after. The Arab refusal to accept the consequences of defeat led inevitably to the 1956 war, the Six Day war, the Yom Kippur war, Palestinian terrorism and the oil boycott. No less dismaying, the first generation of *sabras* were denied the opportunity of coming to terms with their neighbours. Israel became an embattled state increasingly militaristic in outlook and internal organization.

It might have been otherwise. Three of the Arab frontline states were prepared to come to terms with Israel. Syria remained a dour and introverted state but its frontier with Israel was narrow and of little importance. The Lebanon, Jordan and Egypt could have established a *modus vivendi* with their Jewish neighbour. That was made evident during my visits to Beirut, Amman and Cairo, but Arab defeat and unchecked nationalism produced Nasser and when he died the Palestinian terrorists born and raised in the camps were to keep hatred alive as did the *Irgun* and the IRA before them.

*

I was not obsessed by such dark thoughts at the time. I was, thank God, a reporter and not a leader writer. I was learning that some problems could not be resolved by diplomacy or conciliation, that rational thought and compassion were almost always the first victims of clashes of national interests. The division of India and the massacre of one million refugees and the division of Palestine and the Arab refugees had occurred within months of each other. I had reported both in my first year as a foreign correspondent, and I suspected that more violence and injustice was in store for me. I could not agonize over the casualties of the post-colonial era and remain sane. In any case, good reporting could help them more than breast-beating in editorials.

This was how I tried to resolve the dilemma most foreign correspondents have to face at some time in their careers unless they work only in safe places such as Paris and Washington. I was not always successful in applying what amounted to a self-discipline, but I was generally helped by my youthful optimism, misleading though it was. Despite the evidence, I wanted to believe that somehow right and justice would prevail in the end. Life went on. New stories presented themselves, and I pursued them with vigour and increasing confidence. I was beginning secretly to believe that I would make a good reporter. And life was fun. I was still in my twenties and very much in love. Tensions also appeared to relax in the Middle East when the refugees disappeared from the front pages.

This was most noticeable in Israel where the majority believed that their new state was secure and their troubles over. The first British ambassador arrived, and despite Britain's declining influence in the world its recognition of Israel was seen to be the final international stamp of approval. Many Israelis rediscovered an affection for the former mandatory power, and our social life improved immensely. Pat found a furnished flat, which belonged to an academic on a sabbatical in the United States, and we set up together the first of our many homes. I could also relax a little and enjoy some of life's normal pleasures although food rationing was more severe than in wartime Britain, and the lack of housing caused all kinds of problems.

For instance, one condition attached to the lease at the flat was that the owner's nephew could sleep in the second kitchen when he was on leave from the army. We had two kitchens because the flat was actually two knocked into one, and we had two of everything. Clearly we did not need a second kitchen, and we were assured that the nephew would use it very occasionally. We reluctantly agreed and forgot about him until one night when we gave a party. It was a good party and as good parties go it went on and on, until David Woodward from the British embassy came to me red-faced and deeply embarrassed. He had gone into the second kitchen thinking it was a lavatory, and had pee-d on the nephew asleep on a cot.

Peace had its surprises and excitements. We spent a weekend in Jerusalem, and left Tel Aviv early on the Friday morning because nothing was supposed to happen on the sabbath. We checked into the Salvia, and at lunch met an old acquaintance who came to the table to help finish the wine. He asked me if I had heard of the Dead Sea scrolls, which he said were of immense antiquity and importance. They were discovered in a cave above the Dead Sea just before the war by Beduin, who sold them to Dr. Sukenik of the Hebrew University and Archbishop Samuel, Metropolitan of the Syrian Orthodox Church in the Old City. Dr. Sukenik had worked on them throughout the siege, and was now preparing to announce his findings to the world.

I called on Sukenik that afternoon. He spoke Hebrew, German and imperfect English, and we conversed in a mixture of German and English. It was difficult for me because I knew literally nothing about the subject under discussion. Gradually and painfully, I began to understand that the scrolls were the find of the century.

I walked down to the empty PIO and filed a tentative five-hundred-word story and a service message asking if they were interested. Within the hour the answer came back marked urgent. The scrolls were indeed the find of the century, and I was to drop everything until I had the complete story. I returned to Sukenik, and this time I was not so ignorant. I got in touch with the Assyrian bishop at St. James', and over the weekend wrote and filed thousands of words on the discovery of the Dead Sea scrolls. Looking back, it was my greatest scoop although the story was more than two thousand years old. I used a five-letter word beginning with b the next time one of my colleagues said that nothing happened on the sabbath.

Pat and I travelled widely together on stories, to Cyprus, Athens and Istanbul as well as Cairo, Amman, Damascus and Beirut, until she was with child. We were very happy. In India, a fortune teller had come out of the heat haze one day at Amballa, and had told my fortune for five rupees. Among other things, he had told me that I would have six children, and we both wanted to get started. We decided that she should have the child in London, where her family lived, but she would first go with me to Eritrea, a former Italian colony whose political future was in dispute. After a few days Pat left for London, by way of Khartum where she picked up the BOAC flying boat at the confluence of the two Niles, and I promised to rejoin her before the baby's arrival. I then went hunting *shifta*, as the local freedom fighters were called, and except that the local beer was awful had an amusing and fairly profitable time.

Then the foreign news editor asked me to go to Damascus, where there had been another *coup d'Etat*. That was not so amusing, if only because I wondered if I was still known as Britain's master spy. The story written and filed, I thankfully drove over the mountain down to Beirut, and advanced my departure for London to the morrow. I was having a boisterous farewell drink in the bar of the St. George with friends that evening when a telegram arrived announcing that the baby had died in childbirth.

4 War and Half Peace

A few days after Pat came out of hospital Ian Morrison, *The Times* war correspondent in Korea, was killed when his jeep went up on a mine. An old friend of mine, Colonel Unni Nayar of the Indian army and Christopher Buckley of *The Daily Telegraph* were killed with him. We heard the news from the BBC as we were eating breakfast, and neither of us said very much. The war was only in its third week, which somehow made the news more shocking. Morrison was the son of China Morrison, the legendary Peking correspondent of *The Times*, and had been South-east Asia correspondent based in Singapore since covering the Pacific war for us. He was a slight, handsome man, and the hero of Han Suyin's bestseller *A Many Splendoured Thing*. I regretted his death, but grieved more for Unni Nayar. We had been very good friends.

Pat broke into my reverie. She supposed that I wanted to replace Morrison. She spoke calmly and without apparent emotion, and next day I received a hand-written letter from the editor, William Casey. He assumed that I had heard the dreadful news. The posts of South-east Asia correspondent and Korea correspondent were open. Best wishes, William. Typical, I thought. Too damned nice to make it easy by ordering me to Korea. I liked what I had seen of Singapore at the end of the war, and the South-east Asian job was one of the best, but I could not sit there while a war was being fought. I was on my way to Korea before the end of August.

Korea was divided after the second world war, and the communists installed Kim Il-Sung in the north. Syngman Rhee returned to the south with the blessing and support of the United States. It was an uneasy situation, and made worse by Dean Acheson, the American Secretary of State, who announced early in 1950 that South Korea was not within the American defence perimeter. Whether or not this was seen by Kim Il-Sung as an open invitation to invade, his army crossed the frontier in late June. The UN Security Council called for a ceasefire and withdrawal of forces, and requested all members to assist in the defence of South Korea. The resolution made the war unusually significant. Many optimists hoped that it was a step towards a new world order in which the peace would be maintained by the joint action of all peace-loving nations. Others were more concerned about the possible strategic significance of the invasion. The cold war was being waged in Europe, and the invasion suggested a new Sino-Soviet offensive. The two large communist powers were seen to be determined to dominate the Euro-Asian landmass.

The United States was the first to respond, and warships and planes were sent to support the retreating South Koreans. American troops garrisoned in Japan were landed in early July, but the North Korean offensive continued unabated and they could only fight a delaying action. The assumption was that they would be forced to retreat to Pusan at the south-eastern tip of the Korean peninsula, and might be pushed into the sea.

I did not want to miss such a wonderful story, but had to fly by way of Washington. A general on MacArthur's staff had taken a dislike to Lumby, *The Times* man who covered the Italian campaign, and whatever the reasons, the grudge still lingered. Morrison had flown into Korea without checking in at the US army headquarters in Tokyo, but the general was determined to prevent the accreditation of his successor. I was advised to pick up my ID card from the Pentagon in Washington. This was my first experience of Americans as a correspondent, and my next was no happier. It was a long flight from Britain to Korea, much longer by way of Washington, San Francisco and Midway, and I had taken a long book with me to while away the hours. It was the Penguin edition of Andrew Rothstein's *History of the USSR*. I was clutching it in my hot, little hand when I landed at New York, and the immigration officer, an Irish-American, asked if I was a commie. The McCarthy witchhunts were well under way, and I refused to answer. He said that I could not enter the United States.

I was tired, and beginning to regret leaving Pat so soon after the death of the baby, and had no difficulty in simulating rage. Fine, I said. I won't have to go to fucking Korea. British war correspondent refused US entry. What a story, I added. He looked nonplussed, and called a superior who inspected my visa. It had been issued free which suggested that I was in good standing with the American embassy in London, unless that had also been taken over by the communists. He apologised, waved me through, and suggested that I put the book in my pocket.

Despite that nasty beginning, it was love at first sight. I spent only two days in Washington, but immediately felt at home. San Francisco was all that it was cracked up to be, and when we took off for Midway I promised myself that I would take on Washington once my wanderlust was appeased.

The Press Club in Tokyo was filled with old friends from India and the Middle East. We were rivals, but our welcomes were genuine. It was good to be among friends. Too good. My one night in Tokyo was riotous, and when I was poured into the American air transport next day I realized that I had forgotten to buy a uniform. I went to war in a gray flannel suit, shantung shirt, foulard tie and suede shoes. I did not mind. The American combat uniform looked like a locomotive engineer's overalls, not a suitable garb for a dashing war correspondent or an appropriate shift to die in. In any case, I told myself, the war would not last long enough to warrant buying a uniform.

That was certainly my first impression when we landed at Taegu. The pilot was so eager to get in and out quickly that he scraped the side of the control tower and damaged the wing. The advancing North Koreans were still a few miles away, but some of the troops at the airfield were badly frightened. I asked one young kid what was happening, and he said that the lieutenant had told them to bug out because the gooks were coming. He had abandoned or lost his rifle, and was too frightened to be ashamed. There seemed to be many like him, and despite the protestations of the crew chief they scrambled aboard the plane.

The town of Taegu looked as if it was being abandoned. The streets were full of civilian refugees and soldiers who looked like deserters. The divisional headquarters was in a state of chaos. Six-by-six trucks were being loaded in the yard outside, and the revving up of their heavy motors raised the level of hysteria. Inside the building troops were packing up files and wireless equipment, and an officer stood by an open door urging them to hurry. I wandered unchallenged down corridors where normally the strictest security would be maintained. It was eerie, like being an invisible man. It was also rather frightening. Without discipline, military retreats become mindless and terribly destructive. The soldier who throws away his rifle tends also to jettison all sense of decency and honour. Any stranger is a potential enemy; and there I was half a world away from home, my gray flannel suit conspicuous in a world of olive drab, and with only a little plastic card to prove my identity.

Actually the situation, as I was to discover, was not quite as desperate as it looked. The retreat was not yet a rout. The South Koreans were caving in on the right flank, but most of the American units were retreating in a more or less orderly fashion. They were doing well in the circumstances. They had slowed down the North Korean invasion, and given General MacArthur time to prepare the counter-offensive I had heard mentioned in Tokyo. The deserters were garrison troops who had signed on for occupation duty in Japan because of the massage parlours. The divisional headquarters was moved down to Pusan, but a command unit remained. The retreating US 8th Army launched its own counter-attacks in an effort to stabilize the front.

I covered one, the crossing of the Naktong river, which was very messy. For some unknown reason, the boats were at the end of the long convoy of vehicles, and it took most of the night to get them forward. I inadvertently moved too far ahead, and found myself nearly on the river bank. I could not move back, because of the press of vehicles which had churned the ground into mud. I had fortunately exchanged my civvies for a uniform, but the mud came over the top of my combat boots. I spent a miserable night perched on the edge of a crowded jeep while the artillery barrage slid wetly overhead. At least that was how it sounded, and I had plenty of time that night to choose my words. The enemy responded with mortar fire at dawn, and I took shelter behind a command car while the young troops, poor blighters, moved down to the water's edge. Few of them in the first boats made the opposite bank.

MacArthur's counter-offensive came in September at Inchon, where thousands of troops were landed, and Kimpo airfield was quickly seized. Fierce fighting was raging around the perimeter when I flew up from the south, and we were fired at as we came into land. I saw a line of bullet holes apparently dancing across the starboard wing, but the pilot got the plane down and we baled out quickly. Transports were already arriving from Japan, providing a superb display of American industrial power and efficiency. The C119 Flying Boxcars came in at the rate of about one every five minutes, bringing in troops, ammunition and supplies. No other country could have mounted such an operation. By the fourth day they were landing dental chairs and coca-cola-making machines, but no hard liquor. Except for beer, the US 8th army was dry.

A bridgehead was secured across the river, and we advanced quickly towards Seoul, the South Korean capital. It could not have been more different than Taegu. Morale was high, especially among the Marines. They were tough, well-trained troops un-cluttered with the equipment that seemed to slow down the army troops, but even they were slowed down when we got into Seoul. The North Koreans were also tough, and no form of combat is more bloody than street-fighting. Nearly every doorway was the scene of a skirmish and every street inter-section a minor battle. Casualties began to mount, but they did not erode the Marines' *elan* and discipline. It was a privilege to be one of their company.

It was also an ordeal. War correspondents are not the favourite clients of life assurance companies, but compared with frontline troops, especially infantrymen, they have an easy and safe time of it. They do not have to go into battle, despite the memoirs of some of them, and of course invariably they have to leave the battle before nightfall to file their messages. There is after all no point in exposing yourself to shot and shell if you cannot share your experiences with the readers. The ordeal at Seoul was compounded by bad communications. Indeed, in the early months, the Korean war was positively unAmerican in that communications were bad and personal transport non-existent. The battle for Seoul lasted more than a week, and each evening I had to hitch-hike to Kimpo and fly back to Japan to file my story. Flying out presented no problems because most of the C119s flew back empty. I used to climb aboard, and type my story squatting on the floor. As the trip lasted about four hours I had plenty of time. At Ashiya, I handed my story to an air force public relations sergeant

who got it on to the wire to London, and then went to the
officers' club where I washed down the dust of Seoul with half a
shaker of dry martini and ate a T-bone or plank steak. On my way
out I bought two bottles of Ballantine's whisky, a good scotch and
especially favoured because of the stout carton in which it was
packaged, and about midnight lined up for the return flight.

We used to sit in a waiting room, dozing or drinking, until
called by the PR sergeant. He was a former reporter of the
Providence Journal of Rhode Island, who behaved as if his sacred
duty was to get us back to Korea. We hardly appreciated him at
the time because we were terrified by those return flights. The
planes were loaded of course, and often overloaded with ammunition or petrol. Only one correspondent was put aboard each
plane, and the knowledge that crashes were not infrequent made
the trip more lonely. I would sit on the cargo and doze until we
landed at Kimpo at about dawn. I would eat breakfast at the mess
there and hitchhike back to the front to begin another day's
work.

It was very wearing, but one night stands out in my memory.
About a score of us were waiting at Ashiya, and trying not to look
at the line of C119s lumbering by. Rosenkrantz, a friendly and
popular UP photographer, was called, and he picked up his
heavy Speed Graphic camera and walked to the plane. It rumbled
down the runway, took off, swerved and exploded in flames.
Apart from the initial ejaculations of horror and anger, I do not
recall a word being said until the sergeant came into the room
and said, Mr. Heren, your plane is ready. I was still stunned by
the crash, which might have helped. I picked up my typewriter,
waved to the silent group, and like a zombie walked out into the
night. The crew chief, a young sergeant who looked as scared as I
felt, reached down for my typewriter and musette bag and I
stumbled up the ladder. The plane was filled with 40-gallon
drums of aviation spirit. The sergeant slammed the door shut
before I could change my mind, and went forward to the flight
deck as the plane jerked forward for takeoff. I managed to say
four Hail Marys before the pilot pulled her off the ground.
The wing became yellowy-pink as we banked over Rosenkrantz's
funeral pyre and roared into the night.

That was not the only accident on the Kimpo-Ashiya run
during that dreadful week. Faber of the *New York Times* lost a leg

when his plane crashed on takeoff. The death toll among correspondents was, I think, the highest since William Howard
Russell of *The Times* went off to cover the Crimean War. It was
worse for the flight crews of course. They and their planes were
over-worked and overloaded, and they knew it. They kept going
partly because of discipline but also, I think, because the operation
appealed to the American soul. It was magnificent. Day after
day, night after night, the planes took off every few minutes.
The offensive could not have been maintained without such
a time table, which in turn could not have been maintained
without the American response to mechanical and organizational
challenge.

The price exacted by mechanical failure and pilot fatigue was
probably not high statistically, and failure was not always
disastrous. Another night I was sitting with Denis Warner of
the *Daily Telegraph* when my name was called. The intense rivalry
between our two papers made friendship impossible, but in war it
is better not to travel alone and I said I would wait for him at
Kimpo before moving up to the front. Warner was late arriving,
and was hardly recognizable. He was a big, heavy Australian with
reddish hair and a suggestion of immense latent energy. That
morning he looked pale and shrunken, and no wonder. The plane
he was assigned to was loaded with aerial bombs, and halfway
over the Sea of Japan one of the two engines failed. They began
to lose altitude, and the crew chief came aft to jettison the
cargo. The fusilage of the Flying Boxcar was suspended between
two booms supporting the tail, and the cargo doors were at the
back. The two of them began rolling the bombs over the edge
into the void below, and the plane lost less height. Naturally,
they worked with a will. It was hard to get the 250-pounders
moving, but there was no stopping them when they rolled
towards the open doors. Warner knew this when the cuff of his
field jacket got caught on a nose cone, and was dragged towards
the door despite his weight. At the last moment he managed to
unzip the jacket and wriggle free as it disappeared towards the
ocean with his passport, ID card and travellers' cheques.

The plane returned to Ashiya, and the landing on one engine
must have been almost as frightening but they made it. Warner
thankfully disembarked, but his relief was short lived. That
sergeant from the *Providence Journal* was waiting. 'Mr. Warner,

your plane is waiting,' he called. The weakly-protesting Australian was led to a C119 loaded with petrol, and flown to Kimpo.

We who commuted regularly between Kimpo and Ashiya had reason for believing that we were not armchair critics, but the ordeal of the Marines fighting in the streets of Seoul was infinitely worse. This was why I always bought two bottles of scotch. I shared the first with my companions, and I presented the second to the Marines who were fighting on a miserable diet of C rations and coffee. One morning I gave a bottle to Colonel Puller, the C.O. of the 5th Regiment of the US 1st Marine Division. He was a legendary field commander with many Navy Crosses and more wounds, and was known as Chesty Puller because one bad wound had left him with an aluminium plate instead of a rib cage. He thanked me, and said, 'Get out of those doggy clothes, boy, and get a real uniform.' From then on I wore a Marine uniform, including the long cloth gaiters laced halfway up the leg.

One day I thumbed a ride to Seoul in an empty truck driven by a gray-haired sergeant. He beamed at me through steel-rimmed spectacles, and when I asked him why the vehicle was empty, he said that he belonged to a morticians' unit. He was going forward to pick up the night's dead. He was garrulous, and we chatted as he drove past Chesty Puller's regimental command unit and up a main street. Broken overhead tramwires festooned part of the carriageway, which was cluttered with the debris of war. Nothing could have been more desolate. We then passed a battalion command unit, and I got worried because the sounds of war were very close. We continued to move slowly up a slope, and just before the crest I spotted a company commander peering round a corner with his wireless operator behind him. The operator waved us back, and not a second too soon. We were driving into the frontline. I shouted to the driver, jumped out of the cab, and skidded and fell on something soft. It was human flesh ground into the tram lines. I got up horrified as a Russian-built T34 tank advanced from the other side of the rise, and ran to a hole in the middle of the road. Leaning against the forward parapet were three or four Marines with a bazooka, and behind them with cameras at the ready, was Dave Duncan of *Life* magazine. 'Welcome aboard,' he said and raised his canon as the Marines fired.

We survived, as did the mortician sergeant. He apologized profusely, and later that day sought me out at the press camp in an abandoned schoolhouse. I was drinking a warm coke without pleasure when he dumped on a desk a carton of canned beer. It was ice-cold, I could feel the chill radiating from the cardboard as we tore it open. The pleasure was indescribable, and I did not try. I opened a second can and asked where he got the ice from. From the unit, he said evasively. Eventually I caught on. There is rarely a corner of some foreign field which is for ever the United States. The American dead are always shipped home in special caskets, and in warm weather a great deal of ice was required. I stopped drinking for only a minute or two, and until we moved north I always had cold beer to drink. It almost made the confrontation with the tank worthwhile.

*

With the capture of Seoul, South Korea was cleared of the invader. The United Nations forces had achieved their objective within a few months, largely because of American troops and logistical support, and I thought of going home. Just a few more stories to tie up loose ends, and then back to Pat. I flew to Tokyo and discovered to my dismay that the war was not over. According to rumour, we were to advance across the 38th parallel into North Korea and reunite the country under Syngman Rhee.

I did manage to interview General MacArthur before going back, and could not but be impressed. He was tall with a good soldier's face, and was dressed informally in an officers' shirt and slacks. He was a living myth, and knew it. He played the part of the great soldier and proconsul splendidly, but before the end of the interview I began to wonder how much was real and how much play-acting. Not that I objected to the role he projected with such certainty and grace. Good generals have to be larger than life, but he did not fit into any known American mould. I decided that he was born in the wrong country and century. He should have been a nineteenth-century Englishman and the viceroy of India. He had the presence, the reputation and the administrative skill, but more than that he exuded Victorian confidence and a sense of mission. He was determined to impose a *Pax Americana* in the Pacific basin, not only for the greater glory of the United States and himself but also because he believed it would be good for the natives.

He discussed the Korean campaign, the Pacific, world strategy and the future of Japan, but not the rumoured advance into North Korea. We returned to global strategy, and although I did not anticipate his eventual dismissal by President Truman I was not surprised when the former haberdasher gave him his marching orders. He was too big for his well-polished shoes. American generals know how to play politics. The shrewd ones take advantage of the constitutional separation of powers, and play Congress off against the executive to further their own ends. More than one general has become President, and in the autumn of 1950 MacArthur might well have been thinking of contesting the 1952 presidential election. But apart from any political ambition, he behaved, to use Truman's phrase, as if the buck stopped at his desk and not in the White House. The illusion of grandeur was apparent, and not all of it was illusion. He did wield great power as supreme commander and proconsul, and with little reference to Washington because of the myth and the support he enjoyed in Congress. His great authority persuaded Truman to agree to what became a disastrous campaign. It proved fatal for thousands of soldiers, for Truman's presidency and finally for MacArthur. Illusion became more powerful than reality, which Truman proved when he fired him.

I withdrew from his presence, feeling like one of those early English adventurers kowtowing as they backed out of the divan of the Great Moghul in Delhi, to discover that some of his authority had rubbed off on me. His entourage treated me with great respect, and I took quick advantage of my transitory importance. I asked for a briefing on North Korea, and was soon ushered into the office of an intelligence colonel.

He said that the invasion would be a walkover. The army was badly battered and demoralized, and the civilian population longed to be liberated. I asked about the Chinese north of the Yalu river, and he gave me an indulgent smile. They had not yet recovered from the revolution, and large sections of the country were still opposed to communist rule. The army was not well equipped, and much of it was pinned down by Chiang Kai-shek's KMT forces on Taiwan which were ready to return to the mainland. I said that Chou En-lai had been making threatening noises, and the Indian ambassador in Peking, Sardar Panikkar, had warned that the Chinese would fight if the United Nations forces advanced to the Yalu. This was shrugged off. I can tell you, he said, that the Chinese have only a few thousand troops on the frontier, and are incapable of bringing up reinforcements without our knowledge. He patted me on the shoulder, and said that I would be home by Christmas, a promise repeated by MacArthur when he ordered the troops to advance.

I was not convinced, but clearly could not go home. I returned to Korea, retrieved the jeep which we had bought for $400 from a thieving but friendly transportation sergeant, and when D Day came we drove into North Korea unopposed in an eerie silence.

The advance was not a pushover. I almost got killed in one short, sharp fight, but the enemy was incapable of stopping the drive to Pyongyang, the capital. The US 1st Cavalry Division was in the lead, and morale was high. One of its regiments, Gary Owen's Own, had been wiped out with Custer at the Little Big Horn river, and in the curious way with soldiers this made them feel superior. General Hobart Gay, the commanding general who usually went armed with a double-barrelled shotgun, was a quiet intelligent man and we became friendly. I went to his caravan the night before we attacked Pyongyang, and he gave me a bourbon while Tommy Thompson of the *Daily Telegraph* showed him on the map how to take the capital. It was a cheek, I suppose, but Gay took it in good part. I was willing to leave tactics to the soldiers, but was worried about deadlines and communications. Gay promised the use of a telephone line, and said that I would have to go in with the first battalion if I wanted to be certain of making the paper.

The final approach march was made after dark, and with headlights blazing. Never could an army have been so confident, and it was wonderfully exhilarating. I was driving the jeep, and we belted along behind the leading battalion. At one stage we were waved over to let the general pass. He waved his shotgun, and I shouted good luck as if we were out on a farmers' shoot. With little or no opposition we crossed the river and took the city.

Gay was as good as his word. A telephone was made available, and we drew lots for who would file first. I was seventh or eighth, and the waiting was relieved by vodka and caviar looted from the abandoned Soviet legation. My call eventually came through on a very bad line. I could hardly hear the copytaker in Tokyo and dictated 1,200 words more or less blind. It made the paper, but I did not know that at the time. There was nothing to do except drown my anxiety, and I filled my canteen cup to the brim with vodka and smeared about two ounces of caviar on an army biscuit. Ralph Izzard of the *Mail* was not so fortunate. He got through to a colleague, Ward Price, at Tokyo's Maranuchi hotel where Price had been celebrating peace for some hours. He invited Izzard to the party, and Ralph patiently explained that he was in Pyongyang, P-y-o-n-g-y-a-n-g, and would Price take his story. I saw him blanch, and asked what was wrong. Stuttering more than usual, he said that Price told him the war was over and not to be so tedious. He had then hung up. The last story of the war, he whispered, and the blighter hung up.

It was not the last story, alas. Troops in pursuit of North Koreans fleeing northwards captured some Chinese prisoners, which wiped the smiles from our collective face. At 1st Cav. headquarters not even military discipline could disguise the anxiety. Intelligence reports were sparse, and they had no contact with X Corps which was advancing up the east coast. One officer tried to make a joke of it, and announced with mock solemnity that the 8th army had sent out patrols but had failed to make contact with X Corps. We laughed nervously. The map showed the danger of our situation. In his haste to end the war quickly MacArthur had sent columns up each coastal belt, and in between was a vast expanse of uncovered territory. The flanks of both columns were completely exposed. What to do, somebody asked, if the Chinese come down the middle?

The question was quickly answered. The Chinese did come down the middle, and we withdrew. There was no alternative with such long and exposed flanks, but the mysterious chemistry which governs the collective spirit of men in times of acute danger and stress turned the retreat into a rout. It was Taegu all over again, but much worse. We came back to the press camp and found it abandoned. We drove out to the airfield, where an agitated air force captain said that the planes preparing to take off would be the last out of Pyongyang. We had no idea how far the Chinese had advanced. There was the possibility that our retreat had already been cut off, and we clambered aboard a DC4. I had two bottles of vodka in my bag and a can of caviar in my field jacket pocket, but I could have wept with vexation as we took off. There by the runway was our abandoned $400 jeep, and in the back, plain to see, were cases of vodka and caviar.

We landed at a temporary field north of the parallel for no apparent reason, and I walked over to the road where traffic was streaming south. I stood in the classic pose of the hitchhiker, and eventually a command car stopped. A colonel of the 1st Cav. said jump in, and I jumped in. There was no conversation or chitchat. Everybody looked straight ahead, and I could feel them urging the column forward. Night fell, and we pulled off the road to refuel. A sergeant issued C rations, and we stood eating the cold food from the cans with plastic spoons. As I recall, mine was chicken and rice. The colonel who had been talking to division over the radio, said it was time to move down the pike and nobody had to be urged to climb aboard. By this time the traffic had thinned out, and when we moved off the vehicles we were leading formed a compact group. I dozed off, one of the things I was good at.

It was dawn when I awakened, and the convoy was pulling off the road on to the narrow shoulder. The road was raised above the paddy fields and to the left was a low line of hills. I felt horribly exposed, and said as much to the colonel. He said not to worry. He had just talked to division, and the latest air reconnaissance reports confirmed that the enemy were miles behind. The division was reforming, and we would move into defensive positions later that day.

Reassured, I took the neat little packet of toilet paper from a C ration case and scrambled down into the paddy for my morning exercise, another thing I was good at even on a diet of C rations and vodka. I was crouching and wishing I had a newspaper to read when heavy machinegun fire sprayed across the road from the other side. I heard shouts, scuffling, and the starting of engines. Grit was scattered as the vehicles jerked off down the road, and there was I alone in the paddy literally with my trousers down.

The firing stopped, and there was silence except for the distant sound of the departing convoy. I zipped up my trousers and was about to scramble back on to the road when I realized my dilemma. If I stood on the road I would be a sitting duck for the machine gunner, if he was still there, and if I showed myself when a vehicle appeared I might be mistaken for one of the enemy and shot. I sat on the bank and smoked a couple of cigarettes while occasional vehicles thundered by above. There was no shooting, and when the sound of approaching vehicles was still distant I scrambled quickly on to the road and waved my arms energetically. The jeep at the head of a small convoy slowed down, and a Thomson sub-machinegun was aimed at me. I was bearded, but in uniform and obviously not Chinese or Korean, and I thankfully rejoined the US army.

Later I made my way to divisional headquarters where a press camp had already been set up with customary American efficiency. A lieutenant welcomed me like a long lost brother, and produced my typewriter and bag. He added that the guy who left them said that they had lost me in the retreat. It was hardly a fair report of what had happened, and I ate my supper morosely. Then I remembered the vodka, and to the others said, 'scrummy tuck in the dorm.' This was the password among British correspondents, unintelligible to Americans, meaning that liquor was available. It was not that we were unfriendly, but a bottle could satisfy only so many. We sauntered one by one into a classroom—press camps were nearly always established in school houses—and I passed round the bottle.

The situation was still fluid, to use one of the military commentators' favourite clichés, and brooding over my recent experience I remembered the observation of an old soldier: only disciplined troops survive in a retreat. It was not proven, disciplined troops were too often left behind to fight rearguard actions, but it was basically sound. I thought of joining one of the British brigades, which were very good, but were inclined to be stuffy. Unlike American generals, British brigade majors were reluctant to discuss the day's battle with correspondents let alone future intentions. I decided upon the US Marines, and made my way over to the east coast.

It was a bad error of judgement on my part. Winter was approaching, and the wind was coming out of Manchuria with flurries of snow. I had forgotten how cold it could be in those latitudes. The army parkas and winter underwear were first class, but nothing could keep out that cold. The war was also going badly for the United Nations forces again. The Chinese had withdrawn after their initial attack, and MacArthur had ordered the Marines forward again. They had recovered much of the lost ground when the Chinese responded in even greater force. On the map at least the Marines were trapped, and the only alternative to surrender was a fighting withdrawal to the sea. I therefore joined not another retreat to safety or a stabilized defensive line, but a desperate rearguard action.

The Marines fought with the doggedness of disciplined fighting men, and each phase of the withdrawal was planned. The disengaging troops marched in battle order on both sides of the road while their armour, guns and transport moved slowly southwards on the hardtop. Oddly enough, for a time I felt secure. I was with if not one of a body of men held together by discipline and *esprit de corps*. We were also in the shit together and nothing could be more sustaining, but there was something more. Many of the trucks were filled with Marine dead, and frozen arms and legs made grotesque silhouettes against the gray sky. Even in this desperate situation the Marines did not leave their dead behind. The withdrawal began to resemble a mobile charnel house, or so it seemed in subsequent nightmares. At Wonsan, the bodies were stacked like cordwood waiting to be taken off by allied ships. It was macabre, like a Henry Moore sketch, but reassuring for the troops; final proof that they would not be left behind, alive, dead or wounded. So I thought at the time, and still do. Who would want to be left behind as manure for some foreign field?

I was thinking like a Marine, but of course I was not in spite of my gaiters and the faded corps insignia on my left breast pocket. I was a war correspondent, and a useless one because there was no way of sharing my experience with the readers. I was dead tired, and so cold I could only think that the beach was the end of the war—at least for me. I cannot remember making an objective decision. Perhaps I bugged out as did those young frightened soldiers at Taegu so long ago. It was only four months but seemed a lifetime. That could have been the deciding factor, but whatever the reason one day I got on a boat and was ferried out to a waiting British ship. An officer led me to a shower and lent me clean clothes. I ate some dinner, and then drank scotches until sleep came. When I woke up hours later we were underway. We landed at Yokohama, and within fortyeight hours I was on a plane flying home.

Eighteen war correspondents were killed in Korea, most of them in the early months during the initial retreat, the advance to the Yalu and the second retreat after the Chinese intervention. Our casualty rate was proportionally higher than that of the armed forces, partly because of the air crashes. Another reason was the complete freedom of movement allowed us by the American army. This is not a complaint. I for one was grateful for the army maintaining American standards of press freedom, which are alas unequalled elsewhere including Britain. A correspondent was allowed to go wherever he wanted to go. The army fed him, generally found a place for him to sleep, and if he got killed provided a coffin and the appropriate national flag. Apart from communications, no correspondent could have asked for more. The army remained helpful and accommodating in the retreats as well as the advance. There was even no press censorship until some boneheads repeatedly reported troop movements and other restricted information of no interest to anybody except the enemy.

Korea was a miserable story nevertheless. The war achieved little except to preserve the sovereignty of South Korea. That was guaranteed after the capture of Seoul, and when the ceasefire was eventually negotiated three years later the United Nations forces were still along the parallel. MacArthur's miscalculation or vanity cost thousands of lives and dashed hopes that United Nations could maintain the peace by international collective security. Other factors were involved of course, but after Korea no military power was again prepared to fight for and by the principles of the UN Charter. Troops were subsequently provided to act as observers and umpires in disputes but not to wage war.

Heaven knows that the concept of fighting for the United Nations was difficult for most men to grasp. The blue and white flag of international conscience could not replace Old Glory, the Union Jack, or any of the other national flags. The nation states had deeper roots in the loyalty of their soldiers than political scientists had supposed. Nor did the allied armies get on well with each other, except for the British, Australian and New Zealand contingents in the Commonwealth Division. It was a good division in which the troops could take pride, but there was more to it than that. The affinities between the men, the sense of being with one's kith and kin, was still strong. Even the Common-wealth correspondents tended to travel and eat and drink together although I had good American friends.

I did not meet a single soldier belonging to the twelve nations who fought in Korea who believed in fighting for the United Nations. The concept was too big, too theoretical, and what I saw of the UN organization did not make me a convinced supporter. For instance, soon after the Inchon landings I came upon a civil prison filled with South Koreans of both sexes and all ages. The UN flag flew over it, but inside I saw a young civilian being beaten with a rifle butt by a South Korean military policeman. I remonstrated, and was told that they were collaborators. The cells were crammed with men and women, some holding babies. The black hole of Calcutta could not have been more crowded. My fury perplexed the South Korean police, and they produced a UN official. He said that it was none of his business. South Korea was a sovereign state, and the UN could not interfere in its internal affairs. I angrily asked if this was what we were supposed to be fighting for, and he shrugged his shoulders. 'The North Koreans were much worse', he added. They might have been. I had no way of knowing, and nor did he, but we were supposed to be the good guys.

*

Southeast Asia, my next assignment, was another world. There was none of the harshness of Korea or the poverty of India. The lands were green and languorous. The local people were easy going and physically attractive. They smiled easily and most of them moved with grace. Expatriate communities could be found nearly everywhere, from Chiang Mai in northern Thailand to Makasser in the Celebes. It was Somerset Maugham country, but with a difference. While the Union Jack and the French tricolor still flew over vast areas, the struggle for political independence had already been won in Indonesia and was well under way in Indo-China and Malaya.

Not that the white expatriates in Singapore appeared to be aware of it. The Korean war had led to a rubber and tin boom, and in turn to undreamed affluence for the business community. They lived in great style, and still maintained their colonial prerogatives and colour bar. Most of the clubs still refused to accept non-whites, and any talk of political independence was frowned upon. I was to be accused of being a communist for suggesting that political independence was inevitable, and representations were made to my editor. They were ignored of course, but it was mildly astonishing that in the early fifties British colonial officials and businessmen still believed that the old colonial empire would survive, and that *The Times* would withdraw its correspondent because he thought differently.

I was nevertheless happy to be back in Singapore, where I had lived for some weeks at the end of the second world war, because it was a bustling seaport inhabited largely by overseas Chinese. They had all the virtues I most admire, including industry, cleanliness, resilience and love of family. If that sounds too solemn or Victorian, they were also good fun. They loved laughter, parties and good food. They were also the best living argument against communism and planned societies. I was to discover that the Chinese in China were dull and earnest, but in the relative freedom of the Nanyang, as they described Southeast Asia and Hongkong, they remained my favourite people after Cockneys.

Singapore was also a very comfortable place as a base. While I was by nature an anti-colonialist, the colonial way of life could be very pleasant. We rented a bungalow in Kampong Loyang, a Malay village near Changi. It was large and well furnished, and the garden, which had a tennis as well as a badminton court, swept down to a private bathing beach. A staff of five went with the bungalow; the number one boy, a cook, a gardener, a driver and his wife who cleaned and did the laundry. Pat was taken aback by such affluence, and said, let us enjoy it while we may but remember that we will have to return to reality one day.

Pat's advice was sound, and we enjoyed Kampong Loyang all the more because my new parish was huge and demanded a great deal of travelling. I was on the road, with or without Pat, for about six months of the year, and the kampong was a nice place to come home to, especially when we were met at the airport by Abdul, the Malay driver. The parish included Indo-China, Indonesia, Sarawak and Thailand as well as Malaya and odd places such as British North Borneo. In those days Thailand had a *coup d'état* at regular intervals, but French Indo-China and Malaya were the two big running stories. The British were fighting what they chose to describe as the Emergency, a police action against the guerrillas in the Malayan jungles. The war against the Vietminh in Indo-China was more serious because the defeat of the French looked probable long before Dien Bien Phu.

They had only themselves to blame. Unlike Britain, which in theory had always assumed the eventual independence of its colonial territories and in practice had gone part of the way in preparing its subjects peoples to assume power, the French had done little or nothing until it was too late. Even the counters in Saigon's main post office were manned by Frenchmen who sold stamps to the natives. Worse, they needed to prove themselves. Their defeat and occupation by the Germans in metropolitan France and the surrender of Indo-China to the Japanese made them determined to win the war before considering a political settlement. They had also put down deep roots which made the final departure more painful to contemplate. Like the Dutch and the Portuguese, they were only too happy to bed the local girls, which made for easier personal relationships. Saigon was a real French town, provincial perhaps, but with good restaurants, an opera house, tree-lined boulevards and sidewalk cafés. In comparison, New Delhi, although much grander, was lifeless. The Indian capital was built to express imperial grandeur rather than as a place to live in. The expatriate ICS officials knew they would go home to die. To that extent it was easier for the British to relinquish power in India.

The Indo-China war was being lost before I left Korea, but the defeat was delayed by General Jean de Lattre de Tassigny, a great soldier in the romantic Gallic tradition. He was also very shrewd, and willing to learn—even from the British. He might have reversed what was regarded as the tide of history if he had not died from cancer. We first met in his enormous office at the palace, and discussed the fighting. Our conversation did not go too well until suddenly his face showed exaggerated surprise and respect. It was as if he was acting the role of an excitable and voluble Frenchman, which he probably was. But you understand war, he said. Forget what we have discussed. He then turned to a large wall map, and described and explained the terrain, the military positions and the enemy's capabilities as if he was an art critic enthusing over a great picture. He gave me a fundamental understanding of the war which stood me in good stead years later when the Americans got involved and I was covering the Washington end.

I was invited to stay for lunch, and met his wife and their son, a young army lieutenant. Over coffee, de Lattre announced that he was about to tour the three associated states of Indo-China, and invited me along. I jumped at the opportunity because correspondents were not allowed to roam freely in Indo-China as they were in Korea, but de Lattre warned me that it would not be a scoop. The raised eyebrows placed parenthesis round the unfamiliar word. He said that he had already invited Graham Jenkins of Reuters. I invited you because you are *The Times*. I have invited Graham because I love him.

Jenkins was a dour Australian and a very good journalist, but with the possible exception of his mother I could not imagine anybody loving him. He was completely devoted to his job and slept with a teleprinter in his bedroom at the Continental hotel. He more than shared my fundamental scepticism—why is this lying bastard lying to me?—and this became evident when we met at the airport to fly off with de Lattre. We were dressed for the field, combat boots and field jackets, and his suspicions were aroused when a number of black, tin uniform boxes were loaded on the waiting plane. The ADCs were also smartly dressed in white tropical uniforms, and Jenkins asked why the fancy gear if we were going to war. The naval aide, a bright lieutenant with amused eyes, reminded him that the general was the high commissioner as well as the commander in chief. The war was intensely political. Like the British in Malaya, the French were fighting for the hearts and minds of the people. The general would be meeting Bao Dai, the Vietnamese head of state, King Sisavang Vong of Laos and Norodom Sihanouk, the king of Cambodia, as well as military commanders in the field. Protocol require a certain amount of pomp, but we would find it very instructive.

We did indeed, because these royal gentlemen were in effect the French political response to Ho Chi Minh and the Vietminh guerrillas. A modern war of national liberation supported by the new communist regime in China was being fought in the name of three puppets who looked as if they should be performing in *The King and I*. It was not de Lattre's idea. The three new associated states were invented in 1949 by politicians in Paris. Malcolm MacDonald, the British Commissioner General for

Southeast Asia, chose to see the elevation of Bao Dai, the former emperor of Annam, as a great act of statesmanship, but it was cruel farce. Bao Dai was interested only in girls and tiger shooting, and would have preferred to live in the south of France except there were no tigers along the corniche. He lived instead in the hill resort of Dalat, which was rather like the British prime minister moving to the Lake District. Alas, his elevation was more than farce. It was one of the many tragic mistakes which made the war the longest in modern history, from 1946 when the Vietminh first took to the jungle until 30 years later when the American ambassador was rescued by helicopter.

Dalat was our first stop, and we were received by a guard of honour large enough to fight a brigade action in the distant Delta. The pomp was overwhelming, and after I was shown to my room I was presented with a large engraved card about half a metre square inviting me to a state banquet that evening. I sought out the obliging naval ADC, and asked if there was a Moss Bros where I could hire white tie and tails. Such an outfitter did not exist in Dalat, but he said not to worry. The court had been informed that we were war correspondents, and our clothes would not be an embarrassment. We were wearing an honourable uniform. Perhaps, but the room in which we were presented to Bao Dai was filled with French and Vietnamese officials in brilliant uniforms and their ladies looked as if they had just flown in from the latest Paris fashion shows. I took a goblet of champagne and retreated into a corner thinking that only a few weeks earlier I had been retreating with those truckloads of dead Marines through a blizzard to Wonsan. Before I could reach a conclusion which no doubt would have been obvious and trite, an ADC hurried across and said that the general wanted me. I gulped down the champers and followed him through the crowd which divided as if I was suffering from leprosy, and de Lattre introduced me to the former emperor and now the defender of civilization against the communist hordes. He was a chunky man with a smooth expressionless face. The black eyes stared at me without any hint of recognition or interest. I bowed, partly in the hope that he would not see the Marine Corps insignia on my field jacket and very much aware that stencilled across its back was the legend, Heren, London Times. De Lattre told Bao Dai that I had recently arrived from Korea and would like to interview him after dinner, and I thought I detected a flicker of apprehension in those black eyes before I was dismissed.

The banquet was superb. Course followed course in a wonderful symphony of French and Vietnamese cooking, and I tucked in. The wines were no less superb, especially the vintage champagne which was served with the gateau, an immense creation decorated with the French and Vietnamese flags in coloured icing. This was paraded round the room to genteel applause.

I was enjoying myself, and joined in. Even the French wife sitting on my left, who earlier had only spoken to the man on her left, thawed out a little and said how much she admired Bao Dai. He knew how to maintain standards and—this as an afterthought —he had already brought great stability to Vietnam, and she regretted that her husband had been posted to Pondicherry.

This was one of the tiny little French colonies in India over which the tricolor still flew four years after the British quit India. They were anachronisms, but the French seemed supremely unaware of this. I assured the lady that Pondicherry was a charming place with wonderful beaches. She was not persuaded, until I told her that although the Indian princes had lost much of their power the rich ones still knew how to maintain standards. I was listing the high livers when the banquet finally finished, and I was led to a small room for the interview with Bao Dai.

It was delicately furnished in bamboo and yards of green silk curtaining which almost made a tent of the room. There were no chairs, and I was wondering how the interview would be conducted when the curtaining on one side of the room silently opened and revealed Bao Dai standing on a low dais. I bowed again, and was about to pose my first question when one of his courtiers appeared holding a cushion on which was a paperback book. Bao Dai, without the slightest hint of animation on his face, gave me the book, and the curtain slid together. The interview had ended without either of us saying a word. The book was about tiger hunting.

De Lattre roared with laughter when I told him about it on the plane next day, and said he looked forward to reading my account of it. I went back to the rear of the plane and sat next to a man who had earlier been introduced to me as the chief of the Sûreté. I asked if the high commission subscribed to *The Times*, and he thought not. There was no need. Copies of my stories were filed in my dossier. He mentioned this matter-of-factly but with a suspicion of a smile. I was beginning to think that the French in Indo-China were a humorous lot, and asked what on earth he had on me that was worth filing in an intelligence dossier. Quite a lot apparently although I had been in Indo-China for less than a week. He had a look at it when he heard I was to be on the trip. As he recalled, there were the routine police reports on my movements, and a more interesting one on a meeting with Vietminh sympathizers in the Southern Cross bar. He wondered how I had got on to them so quickly, and then warned me not to take them too seriously. They were only café guerrillas, and enjoyed being taken by correspondents to the Southern Cross. It was one of the very few places in Saigon which served scotch whisky, and was too expensive for them.

He said that it would have been even expensive for me except for the Singapore cheque I had cashed on the black market in Cholon. I had indeed cashed a largish cheque in Saigon's neighbouring Chinese city because the official rate of exchange was daylight robbery, but he told me not to worry. There was no intention of bringing a currency charge against me. Then why bother? Well, not yet, he said. I was safe because the general liked me, but . . . But what? I persisted. The Sûreté man was now enjoying himself thoroughly. The general would not be in Indo-China forever, he might change his view of me, or I might prove to be an unfriendly correspondent. It would be a political act to expel a correspondent of *The Times* because of his reports, but not because he had cashed cheques on the black market.

There was another banquet that night in Luang Prabang, the royal capital of Laos, and then we flew on to Pnom Penh, the Cambodian capital. There the guard of honour was provided by native troops and King Sihanouk was at the airport. He wore traditional dress which included what looked like baggy bloomers. They were bright blue, and apparently he had a different colour for each day of the week. Unlike Bao Dai, he had an animated face with alert eyes, and was bubbling over with energy. He was deep in conversation with the general before they got into a limousine with white silk seat covers. Jenkins and I followed in an open car, and I was charmed by the countryside and the small groups of people who had gathered to see the king and the general. Sihanouk was obviously popular. We stopped outside one small village, and he showed us a water pump which had recently been installed. He spoke knowledgeably about farming, and explained with enthusiasm how he hoped to improve yields with the help of the American aid programme. It was clear that the French were unenthusiastic about American aid, but as I was to confirm later it was effective in Cambodia perhaps because it was modest in conception and was mainly intended to increase rice production. I did not meet Graham Greene's quiet American in Saigon but there was more than one ugly American quietly getting on with the job in Cambodia.

We were hot and sticky when we arrived at the palace, and groaned when we saw the cards inviting us to our third banquet in three days. We decided to play hookey, and drove to an open air café down by the river. The beer was cold, and the suggestion of a cooling breeze was coming off the Mekong when the naval ADC arrived. He had been looking all over town for us. The general would be most disappointed if we missed the banquet. We returned obediently to the palace, and duty proved to be not overly onerous. After dinner we strolled over to an open air pavilion to see the royal Cambodian dancers. Sihanouk sat with the general and Madame de Lattre, and Jenkins and I were behind them. There was no moon and the breeze from the river was as fragile as the music and the girl dancers. One of the dancers, a girl who looked no more than fourteen, fluttered her eyelashes at Sihanouk, and we all laughed at his embarrassment. I benignly wished Sihanouk well. He was a reformer in his own way, and his tragedy was that the politicians in Paris, and afterwards in Washington, did not take him seriously.

Our royal progress continued the next day, when we flew to Angkor Wat. The curator, an intelligent Frenchman, showed us the ruins and we picnicked by the lake. At least de Lattre said it was a picnic, but the champagne was cold and the luncheon superb. An orchestra hidden behind some flowering shrubs played tinkling Cambodian music, and de Lattre expounded on the glories which were once the Khmer empire. Judging by his comparisons, he had obviously read Gibbon, and I asked if the French Union would go the way of all empires. He said rather sombrely that it probably would. He suddenly looked tired. The trip had not been just a succession of banquets for him. He had conferred with military commanders and government officials, and his conclusions were apparently bleak. We flew back to Saigon in silence.

*

De Lattre had a strong sense of history, which might have explained his sudden fit of depression that day. Angkor Wat, a galleried temple complex, is one of the greatest, perhaps the greatest monument to a forgotten civilization, and the general had inspected the depredations of the encroaching jungle in silence. He had been powerfully impressed by the destructiveness of the roots of a single tree which had displaced large blocks of masonry. The comparison with the Vietminh was unavoidable. A group of guerrillas dressed in black pyjamas and armed with burp guns was emerging from the jungle to erode and undermine French civilization.

This sense of history was part of the complex character which made him a great general and a natural leader of men. He was an aristocrat not unlike de Tocqueville who had distrusted democracy but regarded it as inevitable. More than a century later the question was whether communist imperialism was no less inevitable. After Mao's victory in China, much of the Euro-Asian landmass was under communist domination and in the early post-war years there was reason to believe that the remainder would submit or be overrun. The Greek civil war, the blockade of Berlin, the invasion of Korea, and the guerrilla wars in Indo-China, Malaya and the Philippines suggested a coordinated plan of communist expansion. As a Frenchman, de Lattre could understand the intellectual attractions of communism, and as a soldier he respected the courage and tenacity of the Vietminh. Before leaving Paris to assume command in Indo-China he had addressed a group of students who reflected the scepticism and divided loyalties of their generation. He had told them that the future was theirs, and they should not avoid their responsibilities. If they did not want to work or fight for France they should join the Vietminh.

De Lattre also had that elusive quality known as charisma. He could assert his personality and dominate men by some mysterious chemistry. It was theatre, but not entirely. Whenever required, his eyes flashed, his back straightened, and his voice became declamatory. His critics said that he was vain and too

fond of pomp, but his men always responded. I was with him one
day when he inspected a battalion of the Foreign Legion which
was due to go into action in the Delta. The men were dressed in
the usual jungle green, but they wore their Legion kepis and the
NCOs epaulettes and bright cummerbunds. They held themselves
with the forbidding arrogance of professional fighting men, and I
found myself standing to attention when the French national
anthem was played with great verve. De Lattre's demeanour also
changed. He was no longer the paternalistic general con-
descending to his troops, but a commander ready to lead his men
into battle. He stood rigidly to attention, his saluting hand
quivering and the brim of his kepi only a few millimetres from
the tricolor and the bayonets of the colour guard. Such was the
tension, that if he had sounded the advance we would have gone
through Indo-China like shit through a blanket—to use the old
army phrase—and I would not have been in the rear.

The orders were given in German, and I noticed that most of
the men were blond under their sun tan. A company commander,
a Frenchman from Alsace, introduced some of the NCOs to de
Lattre, and said that four out of five in his company were Germans. Most of them were former *Wehrmacht* men, and some had
been in the *Waffen SS*. One platoon sergeant had fought in most of
Hitler's campaigns, from the western front, Greece and the
Western Desert to Russia. He had marched in the victory parade
when Paris surrendered and had parachuted into Crete. In the
final retreat from Russia he led his squad across Czechoslovakia
with the firm intention of defending the *Heimat* when he was
captured by Americans in Bavaria. And now he was defending
western civilization against the yellow hordes on the crumbling
glacis of empire, I added. Why not?, the comapany commader
asked. He is a professional soldier. De Lattre, who by then was
probably accustomed to my line of thinking, said, he is a soldier
of France.

The sergeant blushed with pleasure. There could be no finer
accolade. De Lattre had fought in the first world war as a
cavalryman, and had killed two Uhlans with his sword and was
wounded by the lance of a third. He commanded a division in
1940 and the First French Army in the 1944 invasion. He
proved to be a superb tactician capable of accomplishing great
things with slender resources, and this was again apparent in

Indo-China. De Lattre's assumption of command coincided with the Vietminh's first full-scale orthodox attack. Their divisions were newly equipped with Chinese weapons, and supplied from bases on Chinese soil, which were safe from attack. The pressure was so heavy that the French ordered the evacuation of Hanoi. The *coup de grâce* was about to be delivered by the Vietminh commander, Nguyen Van Giap, or so it seemed before de Lattre's arrival. He countermanded the evacuation order, and despite the inferior numbers of the French forces the enemy was fought to a standstill. Giap tried again later in the Red River Delta, and his men were again routed with heavy losses.

The Vietminh returned to guerrilla warfare, and de Lattre developed the strategic combination of strong points to defend villages and communications and mobile columns to root out the guerrillas. He flew to Washington and persuaded the Americans to overcome their distaste of colonial regimes and increase their military aid. He went to Malaya to inspect the system of protected villages which had proved fairly effective against guerrilla infiltration. He increased the strength of the Vietnamese army to eight divisions in his first year, a policy of Veitnamization which the Americans belatedly copied in the sixties.

Improvements in the general security were evident when I returned to Indo-China, and de Lattre was the man responsible. He spent most of his days in the field, and the rapport he struck up with the troops was extraordinary. He could be heroic and kind, but his senior officers were pushed hard and some resented it. The Vietnamization programme, with its promise of real independence, was also resented by General Salan, who I think was chief of staff. He was a small man, good looking in a soft way with brown spaniel eyes which somehow always looked hurt. He also resented de Lattre's relationship with Jenkins and me, probably because we were Anlgo-Saxons. We were representatives of a world and a future he hated. Years later he led the revolt in Algeria, which was another attempt to deny the future.

De Lattre used us of course. Indo-China then attracted very few American correspondents, and those who came were so much against colonialism in an unthinking way that they appeared not to understand what de Lattre was trying to do. Jenkins and I were therefore two of his main contacts with the Anglo-Saxon world whose help and understanding he needed. De Lattre was still very much the Frenchman, who almost certainly believed that France was the centre of civilization, but he knew that he could not hope to achieve his objectives without American help and at least understanding in London.

The calculation was obvious. He was also learning English, and wanted practice, but he seemed to enjoy our company. Certainly he showed more than the usual sympathy when I had dengue fever in Hanoi. Dengue is not particularly dangerous, but very painful and debilitating. I was marooned in my hotel room, and alone except for the daily visit of a Vietnamese doctor who prescribed aspirin and lots of fluids. De Lattre sent a senior army doctor to take care of me, although he too could only prescribe aspirin, and Madame de Lattre called. She looked like the usual formidable French matron, but brought iced soup and a supply of fresh limes.

Despite the improved security, de Lattre could not work wonders in the short time available. The chief of Sûreté might have had cause to sneer at the so-called cafe guerrillas in Saigon, but in Hanoi I met many young Vietnamese intellectuals who strongly supported the Vietminh. Most of them were Marxists if not communists, and while they had respect bordering on reverence for French culture they had a contempt for the French Union. They wanted to do well by their country, and rightly or wrongly believed that Ho Chi Minh was their only choice. We used to have long discussions, usually in a French restaurant near the lake where the food was superb. Two foreign consuls with long service in Hanoi said that they represented the vast majority of students in Hanoi and Haiphong. The French could not win their hearts and minds, and de Lattre knew it.

The French forces were also very thin on the ground, and large areas of the country were in effect policed by private armies belonging to curious sects such as the Cao Daists. Its theology was obscure, perhaps non-existent. The sect's pope communicated directly to God with the help of an ouija board. This was explained to me by the assembled college of cardinals one hot afternoon while we sipped warm champagne and nibbled sweet biscuits. With a direct line to the Deity theology was unnecessary, one of them said with a smile as he expertly opened another warm bottle without loosing too much champagne. Another cardinal demurred politely. Brushing the ash of a

Gauloise cigarette from his rather spotty white gown, he said that they practised the teachings of all the great men elected to their calendar of saints. Victor Hugo was one, and Winston Churchill would be beatified and canonized as soon as he had passed on.

The architecture of their cathedral was as much an admixture as was the Cao Daist faith, except that while the latter was essentially gentle the cathedral had the effect of rock music played at full volume. It made me cringe, but it was the only aggressive aspect of the Cao Daists. The commanding officer of the armed forces was a little man who wore a French army forage cap and heavy horn-rimmed spectacles. He looked like a student in fancy dress. I was solemnly sworn in as a honorary captain—I still have the badge they wore to distinguish themselves, an enamelled shield made in Lyons with the motto *pro deo et patria*— and was asked to inspect the troops. They were an undisciplined shower armed with guns which looked like relics of the Franco-Prussian war.

The loyalty of these private armies was suspect, but they helped to fill up blank spaces on de Lattre's map. I suspected that they made themselves scarce when the Vietminh visited their villages at night. Certainly they provided scant protection when they occupied the little forts built every few kilometres along the main roads. It was in one of those that Greene's journalist anti-hero in the *Quiet American* was nearly killed. My experience was different. Some of the larger forts were commanded by French NCOs, and my car broke down near one of them about the time Greene was in Indo-China for *Life* magazine. The native troops were apprehensive although it was broad daylight, but the young NCO was most civil. We had aperitifs, and the lunch was an omelette, a delicious stew with rice and then salad and cheese. The wine was issued vino, shipped from France in tankers, but he fed me better than some senior officers' messes in the British army.

If the private sectarian armies were at the bottom of the fighting heap, the Foreign Legion was almost certainly at the top. I accompanied a battalion on an operation in a coastal area south of Hue, and the parade-ground *élan* I witnessed earlier was translated into bold manoeuvre and dash. No field commander could hope for better troops. Some Vietminh guerrillas were flushed, and the operation developed into a sharp little battle. With very few casualties, the enemy group was fought until it surrendered. They looked like peasants in their black pyjamas, but they were well armed. They looked frightened as do most troops immediately after capture, but they were obviously disciplined.

They were held for interrogation while the battalion reformed, took care of its casualties, and had a meal. I ate with the officers of one company, and noticed that the mess sergeant had brought some fish and chickens from a nearby village. One of the officers explained that the Legion was provided with basic rations and a messing allowance for fresh food and extras. I asked if it was adequate. More than adequate, he said. The men take rather than buy supplies from the villages. They have plenty left over for drinks. I could see the attraction of such an arrangement for the legionaries, but it was hardly designed to win the hearts and minds of the Vietnamese people.

I afterwards watched an intelligence officer interrogate the prisoners. They were cuffed and roughly handled but not badly treated. They said little or nothing, and eventually, with their hands tied behind their backs, they were flown back to base in helicopters. The intelligence officer said that they rarely talked, which was one reason why the war was so difficult. There was very little intelligence of their positions and movements, and this meant that the French had to fight more or less blindfolded. The Vietminh were as tough as the Legion in their own way. They were not supermen, as some people in Paris were beginning to believe, but they were well trained and highly motivated. They were nationalists. He compared them with the French underground during the German occupation, but the Vietminh were better organized and had the advantage of their supply bases in China.

De Lattre conceded that he could not defeat the Vietminh by force of arms while they could seek Chinese support. To that extent the situation was similar to the Greek civil war where the rebels were supported and given sanctuary by Yugoslavia. He could only win politically, and his tour of the three capitals confirmed his fear that nation-building would be a slow and painful business. He knew also that he was dying of cancer. It was a well-kept secret between him, his wife and the doctors, but it must have been a constant factor in his calculations. Then his son Bernard was killed in action. Bernard had begun his military career by fighting with the French resistance when he was only sixteen, and had chosen to serve with a Vietnamese unit. He was a dashing young man, and very close to his mother and father. It was a cruel blow, and not long afterwards de Lattre returned to Paris to die.

I did not know the reason for his departure of course, but accepted an invitation to attend the farewell reception. It was laid on with overwhelming pomp. The avenue leading to the palace was lined with Foreign Legion troops wearing full uniform and holding flaming torches, and for once I was suitably dressed. I drank champagne, and chatted with some staff officers who were looking forward to a less strenuous life during the general's absence. It was his practice to spend his days in the field, and his nights working at headquarters. This meant that his staff often worked an eighteen-hour day, and a few of them occasionally went to an opium divan to relax in the small hours. It was a very smart place, and served only the best Calcutta white. I went along a couple of times because it was the only opportunity to talk to them. I smoked a couple of pipes, and although I preferred to relax with a glass of whisky the smoking did loosen one or two tongues.

Eventually it was time to leave, and I joined the line of people waiting to bid their adieus. De Lattre was in great form, and his face broke into a smile when he saw me. Louis, he said, do you remember when we first met and I said that you could accompany me because you were *The Times*, but that I had invited Graham Jenkins because I loved him? I nodded, and he said I have learned to love you too. We must travel together when I return. He kissed me on both cheeks, and that was the last I saw of him.

*

The war in Malaya against the communist terrorists had been going on for nearly two years when we arrived in Singapore in early 1951. Not that any traveller passing through would have noticed. Reports in the local press were sparse, and in conversation the price of rubber and tin demanded much more attention. The emergency, as it was known, was mentioned only as a threat to the newly-found affluence, to the high rubber and tin prices which depended upon the continued killings in Korea.

British conscript soldiers were expected to keep the enemy at bay in Malaya while the *tuans* made their piles, and their piles were that much bigger because local income tax was derisory and the overburdened British taxpayer, still meekly enduring postwar austerity, paid for the troops. Yet the death of a British soldier in the jungles of Johore or Selangor got no more space in the local papers than reports of damage done to rubber trees. It might not have been a classic case of capitalist and colonial exploitation, despite the evidence, but it was very nasty. The social consequences were even nastier. *Tuans* and *Memsahibs* of all degrees behaved as if they were 19th-century empire-builders while greed and avarice were reflected in low wages, conspicuous consumption and opulent living. It was enough to make anybody who did not know better become a commie.

I think it was Noël Coward who said that Singapore was first-class place for second-rate people, and apparently in the old days Oxbridge men who were not good enough for the Indian Civil Service joined the Malayan Civil Service. Coward's generalization was no doubt unfair, as irresistible remarks often are. Some of my best friends in Singapore or Malaya were Britons, and I did not write that with tongue in cheek, but they were very different from the British in India. The ICS was wholly dedicated to India and the public good. Many of its officials were loyal to their own personal vision of India rather than to Britain. Indians in the forefront of the independence movement respected them for their contributions to Indian life. When the revisionist historians look back at British imperialism they will almost certainly agree.

We met dedicated MCS men, but they were rarely as close to the local people. One reason was that the eleven Malay rulers retained a large measure of authority, and in the administration of internal affairs Britain was mainly represented by a resident or adviser as in the Indian princely states. Another was the Chinese, who made up two-fifths of the population of Malaya. They were more or less ignored. They lived largely outside the administrative structure as did the Jews in Palestine. The MCS had a Protector of Chinese, but the office served only to emphasize the separateness of the Chinese community. The MCS favoured the Malays and regarded the Chinese as intruders although the economy depended upon them and to a lesser extent upon the Indians. These were mainly Tamils from southern India who had been brought in as contract labour when the rubber estates were first planted because the Malays, like the Red Indians in America, would not work on plantations. This was an old British imperial practice, first adopted after the abolition of slavery. Plantations could not be run profitably without an assured supply of cheap labour, and during the Victorian period poor Indians were exported to Africa, the Caribbean, Ceylon and Fiji as well as Malaya. They went willingly enough because the only alternative was starvation. They were protected by labour and health regulations, but many lived in a state of semi-peonage. To some extent this was unavoidable. The rubber estates were large, and those who lived and worked on them were isolated. They depended upon the planter for living accommodation, then rows of primitive shacks known as lines, shops and schools. Some were completely dependent upon the planter until they organized trade unions. Even then their pay was miserable.

The Chinese were very different. Even the lowliest coolie seemed to know that he came from the Middle Kingdom, and was therefore superior to the high-nosed, red-haired barbarians from Britain, who of course were convinced of their own superiority. This did not make for an easy relationship, although the Chinese were conditioned by the unhappy condition of their homeland to publicly acknowledge British authority. Behind that bland facade they pursued their own lives. They were in many ways more exclusive than the British. In Singapore they were an *imperium in imperio*, at least commercially and socially, and were resented throughout the peninsula. The Malays were frightened by their energy and business acumen, and the British were both jealous and uneasy. Most of them managed to hide their emotions by inflating their own egos, and by excluding the Chinese from their clubs, from business whenever they could, and officially by siding with the Malays. The fiction was maintained that the Chinese were *Gastarbeiter*, as the Germans subsequently named their foreign labour, although there were Chinese in Malaya long before Raffles founded Singapore. The well-established Chinese of the old Straits Settlements were intensely loyal, and once referred to themselves as the King's Chinese. Arguably they were more loyal than the Malays, whose first loyalty was to their rulers.

The racial antipathies, resentments and hatreds meant that the

British did not have to divide to rule, but they did. Malay fears and resentments were respected and occasionally encouraged. Chinese separateness was exaggerated. This enabled the British to see themselves as impartial proconsuls maintaining the peace for the benefit of lesser races, but this was proved to be nonsense when later Dato Abdul Rahman of the United Malay National Organization and Sir Cheng-lock Tan of the Malayan Chinese Association came together to work for independence.

To be fair to Britain, there was nothing to prevent the Chinese and Indians from making money, and many of them did well. The rich Chinese merchants were richer than the *tuans* who were mostly hired hands of London-based companies. The obvious example was Mr. Aw Boon Haw, the Tiger Balm king. The ointment allegedly had magical powers, and the fact was that even European sceptics used it to relieve headaches. The best food in Singapore was served in Club Street, a short turning filled with private Chinese eating clubs. I still treasure the memory of them. Nevertheless, Singapore was unashamedly organized for the benefit of the British community. They were officially conceded a special status denied to them in India, and they were well represented in London where the banks, shipping lines and rubber and tin companies had their head offices. Their boards, upon which retired MCS officials invariably sat, were powerful pressure groups, and in 1946 their support of Malay opposition helped to persuade the British government to drop the proposed Malayan Union which would have ended racial discrimination in politics and citizenship and reduced the authority of the Malay rulers.

They actually did this while Britain was preparing to quit India. They succeeded in turning back the clock while living literally in the middle of a region over which the revolutionary monsoon of change was blowing. Like the white settlers in Rhodesia two decades later, they believed they could maintain a way of life briefly enjoyed by the middle and upper-middle classes in Britain from the industrial revolution to the first world war. The colonial administration, which eventually had to answer to Westminster, prevented them from taking racial prejudice and commercial advantage too far, but they were apparently unaware of the fundamental change brought about by the defeat of Britain by Japan in 1942 and the subsequent occupation. They could not perceive that Asians no longer regarded them as supermen. Instead, they returned after the war assuming that nothing had changed, except for rubber and tin prices. Affluence made most of them more insufferable.

Not that Pat and I were young angrys. In any case, Singapore was just a base, and we lived as far from the city as we could without falling into the South China Sea. Kampong Loyang could only be reached by a roughly-metalled track which disappeared into the sand on the outskirts of the village. It was a typical Malay fishing kampong of simple but graceful wooden houses built on stilts and shaded by palm trees. The bungalow was beyond the village and the villas owned by wealthy Singapore Chinese merchants, who came down at the weekend to play mahjong. The constant clatter of the tiles competed with the sound of crickets if not the bullfrogs in the creek. For the rest of the week we had the place to ourselves, and after the months in Korea I was glad to become accustomed to the slow tempo of Malayan life.

It did not come easily. I had recurrences of nightmares similar to those in India when I relived the mass killings in the Punjab. My bearer in Delhi, a hillman from beyond Simla, would awaken me, and then find himself plastered against the opposite wall with me thrashing about on top of him. He eventually learned to put down the *chota huzri*, or small breakfast of tea, banana and thinly-sliced bread and butter, on a distant table. He would then retreat to a corner, prod me with a length of bamboo and watch me bound out of bed like a mesmerized Kung Fu fighter.

In Kampong Loyang I relived Taegu, those awful flights between Kimpo and Ashiya, being left in the paddy with my trousers down and the retreat with the Marines down from the Yalu and the reservoirs. Those frozen arms and legs would pass through my mind unendingly until I awakened shaking and sweating, often holding Pat in what is normally described as a vice-like grip. She was very good about it, and her mothering was immensely comforting. I could argue that the soundest foundation for a good marriage is to send the man off to the wars and give him a good wife to take care of him afterwards.

I find the nightmares difficult to explain. I was tough. I grew up poor in London, and although I like music and poetry none of my friends would have called me sensitive. In my early days I got rid of the usual frustrations and hangups by losing my temper—which I always recovered quickly—getting tight or whoring. The act of writing, or self-expression, also provided great relief. A psychiatrist could no doubt produce a class explanation, but I do not think it was that. It could have been something more atavistic. I always knew when the moon was full because I felt uneasy and touchy. The small hairs on the back of my neck would stiffen and my brow would tighten. I had premonitions. I recall this with reluctance, but on more than one occasion over the years I received advance intimations through those short hairs of great and often terrible news. For instance, the night Robert Kennedy was killed—but I will get to that later.

What was clear in Singapore in 1951 was that I was living an unusual life. Apart from nearly seven years of army service, I had witnessed too much killing and upheaval. I had been cut off from my roots, from those mean but friendly East End streets, although more than twenty years later when I was asked to write a book about them I wrote it in three months and made only two identified errors. I had also been separated too often and too long from Pat, whom I first met before going out east in the big war. The death of our first child must have hurt more than I had imagined. Whatever the reason, Kampong Loyang was an ideal place in which to get rid of the nightmares and recuperate.

We lived an open-air life because of the warm climate. Singapore is only one degree north of the equator, and the temperature varies only a few degrees between winter and summer, midday and midnight. The high humidity bothered a lot of people, but I wore a sarong most of the time and swam two or three times a day. Loyang was also cooler than Singapore city because it was on the Straits of Johore, and a breeze blew off the water in the evening. We ate on the verandah, which had a built-in bar where I mixed the drinks. But not gin *pahits*. I had looked forward to them for years after reading Somerset Maugham and was disappointed to discover that they were only pedestrian pink gins. Instead, the *mali*, or gardener, would shin up one of our thirty-odd palm trees, with a machette stuck in his sarong, and cut down two or three coconuts, and we would drink gin and fresh coconut juice in tall frosted glasses. It was a splendid drink, much superior to the gin and fresh camel's milk I had to drink afterwards in the Horn of Africa.

We did not ignore the city, which had many attractions. Between my travels we would often drive, or be driven in during the morning to meet other itinerant correspondents on the verandah of the Cricket Club, which had a splendid view of the Padang and the inner harbour. At mid-morning the bar would be full of BAs (young business assistants) swilling BGAs (brandy and ginger ale). They all wore white shirts and slacks, the Singapore equivalent of city gents' suits, and most of them seemed to be overweight. At home they would have been clerks, content with a cup of coffee in a Jolyons, but in Singapore their pinko-gray faces made them *tuans*.

I joined the Cricket Club because we needed a meeting place, but we refused to join the other clubs in part because of the colour bar. It offended us for obvious reasons, and we had many Asian friends. One was Lee Kuan Yew, who afterwards became prime minister of Singapore. He had joined a law firm after coming down from Cambridge, and I might have been responsible for his subsequent political career although he had always been politically conscious. A newly-organized trade union needed a legal adviser, it had little money, and I suggested to Harry, as he was known in those days, that he should do his duty. He did, and never looked back. Another friend was Rajaratnam, who then worked for the *Singapore Standard* and afterwards became Singapore's foreign minister. He had a nice Hungarian wife who frequently entertained us at their house in Chancery Lane.

Looking back, I chose my friends well, but of course we were of the same age and politically involved, and apart from the Chinese food, neither Pat nor I were attracted by Singapore's social life. Occasionally our rubber-rich Chinese hosts were overwhelming. They would lay on immense quantities of wine and spirits, and during a very festive evening Schloss Johannisberg, Mouton Rothschild, 5-star brandy and other assorted drinks could be poured by slap-happy waiters into the same glass. At the end of the evening they would appear from the kitchen, and with broad smiles display all the bottles we had emptied. We also ate in Bugis Street, an empty space filled with tables and chairs and lined with food stalls. We would select the dishes from the stalls and wash them down with cold Tiger beer. Afterwards we would hold hands in one of the air-conditioned cinemas.

We liked roaming the streets, and there was a good bookshop in Raffles Square. We did not avoid the British, but I did not play golf or tennis having decided long ago that chasing little balls was no pastime for a man, and their social life was too pompous and status-ridden. Its apex was Government House, a vast barn of a place, and we were occasionally invited because I was a correspondent of *The Times*. It was more formal than Buckingham Palace, and the dinner parties would have been stupifyingly tedious except that we always giggled. The meals were of the brown-windsor-soup, meat-and-two-veg variety, served with great solemnity. The women wore long dresses, and the men black ties, dinner jackets or white bum freezers and cummerbunds. It could be insufferably hot, and conversation was reduced to the irreducible minimum. Politics, books or music were never discussed, at least not in my hearing and my attempts always ended in failure. I might have been a bit off-putting. I was not MSC, Chartered Bank, Straits Steam, Butterfield and Swire or any of the other trading houses. I did not belong to the posh clubs, and could not prattle about the latest tennis championship. I was not affluent, was only a journalist and therefore of no account but suspect.

For me, the highlight of any evening at Government House was when the men rose to join the ladies after dinner. A major domo would appear at the door, and bang the floor with his staff of office. Led by the governor and his guest of honour, we would troop down the stairs two by two, and before rejoining the *Mems* in the drawing room would be led into an enormous lavatory with more than enough pee-holes for everybody. We would solemnly relieve ourslves, while maintaining strict precedence and would not zip up until the Governor had finished. I enjoyed this little ceremony, although not so much as the one at Government House in Khartum. There a major domo also appeared, and the Governor-General again led his male guests from the dining room in solemn array, but we went through the tall french windows and pee-ed on a bed of cannas at the edge of the garden high above the confluence of the Blue and White Niles. The cannas were among the best in Africa, no doubt because they had been so watered since Gordon's time.

Government House was not the only summit for ambitious wives to conquer. In the immediate post-war years Britain's official overseas representation increased in direct proportion to the diminution of imperial power. In my parish, the largest addition was Mr. Malcolm MacDonald, the Commissioner-General for Southeast Asia. An enormous inter-departmental bureaucracy was established in Phoenix Park near Singapore, and across the causeway in Johore MacDonald lived at Bukit Serene, a swank villa with more mod con than Singapore's Government House. MacDonald was a bit of a mystery. The son of a tragic political failure, and himself a political failure, he was not a favourite of the Labour party and was disliked by Winston Churchill. He should have sunk without trace. Instead, he served in a number of appointed posts, including high commissioner in Canada, before being appointed a kind of diplomatic and colonial overlord in Southeast Asia.

Whatever he and his bureaucrats were supposed to do, they achieved very little. His support for Bao Dai suggested that the Foreign Office men at Phoenix Park had given him bum advice, but that was to be expected. The lack of political progress in Britain's Southeast Asian colonies hardly matched the anti-colonial impulse of the Labour government, but none of this diminished MacDonald's reputation.

One thing had to be said, he was a good front man. He made the right kind of liberal speeches to Asian audiences, and there were always more Chinese, Malays and Indians at his parties than British. He managed to conjure up a fresh image of Britain despite the contrary evidence in Singapore. He was also very informal, and male guests were urged to remove their jackets. Bukit Serene became a haven of informality where the twain actually did meet. The *memsahibs*, who had hoped for a touch of high diplomacy to leaven their colonial and commercial lives, were not amused. Their gossip was malicious and often salacious, and their anger once overflowed into the correspondence columns of *The Straits Times*.

The occasion was the visit of a symphony orchestra which broke its journey to Australia and made a one-night stand in Singapore. It was a big social event, and MacDonald suggested to a few of us that he should seize the opportunity to make a stand for progress and bodily comfort. We would attend wearing the required black ties and dinner jackets, and remove them when he gave the signal. We were all confident that this would lead to a general unrobing and the belated passing of the tie-bound past. Not a bit of it. MacDonald took his place in the front row, and we were scattered throughout the audience. After the playing of the King, he stood up again and leisurely removed his jacket. We followed. There was a gasp of surprise, a burst of conversation and then a kind of buzzing silence. Not a man got up to remove his jacket, and the man sitting next to me muttered something about political upstarts and it not being done.

Their outrage and anger showed no sign of diminishing, and at the end of the week I launched a counter-attack. In a letter to *The Straits Times*, I noted that in tropical waters officers of the Royal Navy wore Red Sea rig, comprising black trousers, cummerbund and a short sleeved-shirt. If this was good enough for the Royal Navy it was certainly good enough for Singapore's chamber of commerce. They were not amused, and my reputation as a dangerous socialist was confirmed.

*

To be fair to Singapore's business community, the Malayan emergency was not an exciting war. It was very difficult to report, and only occasionally made the front pages. There was none of the drama of the Vietnam war. The British did not try to defeat the enemy by destroying the country it was defending for the rubber companies. Instead, they fought an intelligent police operation. At one period thousands of troops were deployed, but mainly on patrols—or jungle-bashing as it was called. Artillery was rarely used. The air force did little bombing, and only in the jungle. The strategic plan, known as the Briggs Plan after Lieutenant-General Sir Harold Briggs, the first director of operations, could hardly have been improved upon. The only drawback was that its application was to take many years.

The enemy was the so-called Malayan People's Anti-Japanese Army, a communist-led group first raised to fight the Japanese during the second world war, when it was supported and supplied by Britain. The men were almost entirely Chinese and could not therefore claim to be the liberators of oppressed Malays. Oppressed or not, the Malays hated their guts simply because they were Chinese. Divide and rule became divide and conquer, and was all the more effective because the racial divisions were unfortunately real.

The MPAJA could only survive in the jungle with the support of the local Chinese, most of whom were former supporters of Chiang Kai-Shek, members of the Malayan Chinese Association or apolitical. Many of the youngsters in Singapore admired the new communist regime in Peking if only because it promised to make China great again, but they could give little help to the MPAJA in the jungle. There was no evidence that Peking supported them apart from propaganda broadcasts, which left the squatters. These were Chinese families who had cleared patches on the edge of the jungle to grow food during the Japanese occupation. They claimed squatters' rights after the war. Most of them became market gardeners, but the men also worked on the rubber estates. They had been largely ignored by the colonial administration, and without police protection were vulnerable to the MPAJA, or its Min Yuen, the organization outside the jungle which used intimidation and violence in their collection of food, medical supplies and information.

This was perceived very early by Sir Henry Gurney, the high commissioner of Malaya, and part of the Briggs Plan was to separate the squatters from the MPAJA. Hence the new villages in which the squatters were resettled behind barbed wire and with police protection. The new villages might easily have become concentration camps, but the fundamental decency of most of the British officials involved, and the need to guarantee labour for the rubber estates, saved the operation from disaster. Schools and medical clinics were established in the new villages, and eventually most of the squatters were better off than they had been on their patches.

The second part of the plan was for the army to hunt down the MPAJA. This was much more difficult. The communist guerrillas were few in numbers, never more than 7,000 at the outside, and the jungle in which they found security covered about half of the Malayan peninsula. Good intelligence was vital if the patrols were to have any success, and although it was available there was at first little coordination. Most of the patrols were fruitless during the early years, although they probably kept the enemy on the move. They were also arduous because of the climate and the terrain, and the men had to carry everything—food, water and ammunition—on their backs. The troops were mainly young national servicemen from all walks of life in Britain, and none of them had walked through a jungle before. They survived because of the discipline, but they spent too little time in Malaya to become good jungle fighters. By the time the best of them had adjusted themselves to the utterly alien world of the jungle they went home to be demobilized and return to factories and offices.

Spencer Chapman, who stayed behind in Malaya after the British surrender in 1942, wrote a book entitled *The Jungle is Neutral*. It was too class conscious to be taken seriously, which might explain why he was never regarded as a second T. E. Lawrence. He apparently believed that only public school men could survive in the jungle, and that working class blokes would quickly crack up. This was nonsense of the kind which used to make me ashamed to carry a British passport. Apparently Chapman failed to realize that North America, Australia, New Zealand and South Africa were not pioneered and settled by Old Etonians. Daniel Boone did not wear an old school tie. Davy Crockett never heard of the Headmasters' Conference and whatever snotty-nosed school Chapman attended. And both did more than Mr. Chapman in Malaya, but I digress.

Chapman was correct to the extent that the jungle was neutral. It neither attracted nor repelled me. It varied enormously, but the prevailing sensation was of isolation, of being cut off from the world. I never had that sensation in the desert or the higher Himalayas, where I was physically more isolated, presumably because they had horizons and were open to the sky. I rarely saw the sky in the jungle. The thickness of the roof was such that at best the sunlight percolated through the layers of foliage as it does through the stained-glass windows of cathedrals. That was the second sensation, and it could be over-powering on rubber estates as well as in the jungle. We tended to talk in whispers, obviously for fear of revealing our whereabouts to the enemy but also because of the sensation of being in a holy place. The jungle floor also varied. Rarely was it as dense as those studio jungles in which Errol Flynn once fought the fiendish Japanese. More often than not it was free of undergrowth because of the lack of sunlight, and the carpet of decayed vegetation was easy and soft to walk on. The jungle was eerie, rather like what I suppose the ocean bed is for an exploring diver, but not frightening except for the fear of being ambushed.

The only Briton I knew who felt at home in the jungle was a

Protector of Aborigines. He was married to one, a girl with a pretty face made incongruous by lipstick who loved to drive fast cars. She was literally just down from the trees, a Stone Age person suddenly exposed to the consumer society of the 1950s, but she drove with the skill, sensitivity and sureness of a Stirling Moss. The jungle proved neutral for the husband. He fell through the raised roof of an aborigine longhouse, and was impaled on a bamboo stake. He must have been in terrible pain. They tried to carry him out of the inner jungle to a doctor, but he died on the way. They buried him where he died, and aboriginal superstition prevented them from disclosing the burial place. More than twenty years later, in Hongkong, a former MCS official told me how he finally persuaded them to lead him to the unmarked grave.

Gurkha and colonial troops adjusted quicker than the British to the jungle if only because they were less bothered by the climate; but among the imperial battalions who served in Malaya only the Fijians seemed to enjoy it. They were big chaps physically, well over six foot and immensely strong. The day before I went in with one of their patrols I drank a number of pink gins and ate an immense curry tiffin in the officers' mess. I was ready for a siesta, but the officers were due to play rugby against the other ranks. They were one man short, and I felt obliged to fill the gap in the forward line. The Fijians were impervious to heat, gin and vast quantities of curry. I was not. The game was a ghastly experience, and worse followed. I was in an advanced state of dehydration and was happy to drink ice-cold Australian beer, but it went on and on and on until about ten at night they jumped into jeeps and drove to Batu Pahat for a Chinese dinner. I dragged myself to bed with aching limbs and an extended bladder. It was a disturbed night. Nobody knows what I do for *The Times*, I can remember moaning to myself as I pee-ed through the verandah railings for the third time. I finally fell into an exhausted sleep only to be awakened after a few minutes, or so it seemed, by the commander. It was still dark, but the whites of his eyes beamed down at me from somewhere near the ceiling. Blinking my dry, bloodshot eyes I thought bitterly that he looked as if he had never drunk a drop of gin or beer in his life. He was fully accoutred for battle, and radiated good health, clean living and inexhaustible energy. If you hurry, he said, you will be in time for a cup of tea. And don't forget to shave. We must set an example for the men.

In the pre-dawn chill I sat shivering in the back of a weapons carrier sipping the life-giving tea until we reached the start point on the edge of the jungle. The company commander inspected the waiting men, and then with a hand signal we plunged in. The going was rough at first, as it always was on the jungle edge. My hangover pounded away like a truck engine missing on two cylinders, but gradually the going became easier and the hangover faded with the exercise. My mouth tasted like the bottom of a birdcage, but I was again the alert, or reasonably alert reporter.

For all their sense of fun, the Fijians did their job very seriously. The point man, who moved in advance of the main patrol, was always covered, as was the rear. Caution slowed our progress, but unlike British troops the Fijians rarely fell out for a smoke. They rested and ate lightly at noon, again well covered, and we continued until it was almost dark. The company commander found a suitable camp site against an outcrop of rock which provided some cover, posted sentries and then ordered a brew-up. Sipping tea, I watched the cook prepare supper from a 14-day pack. This was an intelligent attempt on the part of an army to vary the troops' diet in the field, but the Fijian cook emptied every can into the stewpots. He filled my messtin with a mixture of steak and kidney pudding, lamb stew and macaroni. It's the bulk that counts, he said.

After supper I wrapped myself in a poncho, and tried to sleep. I was tired, but the jungle was loud with noises I could not identify. The fire had been put out, and night was blacker than the Fijian faces. Their whispering suggested that they were nervous, and the company commander spoke to them softly. I dozed off, and was awakened by shots and shouting. Dawn was breaking, and in the half light I could see the company commander directing his troops. I stayed where I was, unwilling to get in the way until the commander asked me to help the Bren-gunner. He threw me some magazines from his pouches, and leaving a New Zealand sergeant in charge of the camp disappeared into the jungle with two men.

They returned about one hour later with the sentry who had fired the shots. He had seen two men wearing the black shirts and trousers of Chinese coolies, and had waited assuming that more men would follow them. None did, and he pursued the two and fired when one of them turned and spotted him. He was sure that he had hit one of them, but the commander and his men found no trace of a wounded man. The commander could not understand why two bandits—as the troops generally called the MPAJA—were alone in the jungle, and assumed that they had come from a nearby camp. The remainder of the patrol was spent finding it; three or four *bashas*, or huts, a cleared space which had obviously been used as a parade or exercise ground, but no evidence of recent occupation except for some Chinese pamphlets.

That patrol was more interesting than most, but gradually the effectiveness of the security forces was improved. Sea Dyaks, the legendary head hunters of Sarawak, were brought in as trackers. A couple of men from the Special Branch in London arrived to improve the coordination of intelligence. Previously it had only been used for tactical purposes. Patrols acted on information received, and that was that. The two experts put it to strategic use. Information was no longer discarded after action had been taken. Instead they used it to construct a mosaic of MPAJA movements, and the deployment of their forces slowly emerged on the maps. The war still moved at the cautious pace of the jungle patrols, and I campaigned for helicopters. Few were available in those days, but a Royal Navy flight eventually arrived. They were too few to lift many patrols in and out of the deep jungle, but they were invaluable for rescuing the sick and wounded.

I had first flown in choppers in Korea, where they were mainly used as communications aircraft, and flying them in the Malayan jungle was an entirely new experience. They could obviously only land in clearings, and as the machine lowered itself down through the hole in the jungle roof the rotar blades sucked the branches inwards and shut out the sky. It could be rather alarming. When the jungle floor was littered with dead timber, the chopper would hover a few feet from the ground and the passengers climbed down a rope ladder. This was always alarming because of the noise and the moving foliage. It looked as if the jungle had come alive like Tolkien's forest. The naval pilots, who became very expert, were agreeable men with the easy self-confidence of the senior service, and on a couple of occasions flew me home after an operation. Coming out of the sky and alighting on my own front lawn caused a sensation in the kampong, and forever afterwards I was treated with the greatest respect.

The war was going reasonably well by the middle of 1951, although very few people realized it. Operations mainly took place in the jungle far from public—and press—view. The planters living on lonely rubber estates were incommoded by security requirements. Barbed-wire fences, often floodlit at night, surrounded their bungalows. Most of them went armed and drove armoured cars, but normal traffic was rarely interrupted. Pat and I travelled alone in our car all over the peninsula, and trusted only upon speed to see ourselves safely through tricky areas. Only once were we fired at, and Pat was unaware of the incident. We were driving through the Slim river area, perhaps the most dangerous region in Malaya, when a burst of Sten-gun fire punctured one of the rear wheels. I kept moving. Pat asked why I did not stop to change the wheel, and I said that it was too hot. I would ride on the rim until we reached the next village. This we did, and I found three bullets inside the ruined tyre.

Wherever we travelled I found increasing confidence among the security forces but even they did not know how well they were doing. They could only judge by the number of incidents. These increased because of their improved efficiency, but a pessimist, and there were many, could also see the increase as evidence of growing enemy strength. To that extent the war looked indecisive, and in October 1951 the high commissioner was ambushed and killed. Gurney died bravely by drawing the fire from his wife, who survived, but his death caused an uproar in Malaya and Britain. Strong action was called for, and General Sir Gerald Templer was appointed high commissioner.

In fact, the war had already been won, but nobody outside the jungle knew that the victory flags could be hung out until an enemy document was captured early in 1952. It was dated September 1951, one month before the assassination of Gurney, and it was a directive from the Politburo of the Malayan Communist party which in effect conceded defeat. It admitted that violence had not won popular support, and the state and district committees were ordered to end hostilities. The Min Yuen was also ordered to stop intimidation and sabotage. More attention was to be given to urban organization. In other words, the Politburo wanted to come in from the cold.

The report was not published, presumably because of the imminent arrival of Templer, but General Sir Rob Lockhart, the deputy director of operations, showed me a copy. It was top secret, and could not be taken from his office. I sat in an ante-room throughout a long hot afternoon reading the translation which ran to about 30,000 words. The language was unusually obscure even for such a document, and the ideological jargon self-serving, but there was no doubt that the leadership had admitted defeat. It should have been obvious to them at least two years earlier. Their campaign had been a failure in every possible way, but they had believed that the Vietminh would defeat the French in Indo-China earlier than they did and that South Korea would be overrun and united with the communist north. This expectation of communist victory throughout Asia had kept them going.

The war was to drag on because the MPAJA did not have radio transmitters. The directive had to be delivered to the state and district committees by messengers, and in many instances this took months, but the graph showing the number of terrorist incidents proved that the directive had taken effect. The number declined from over 6,100 in 1951 to 1,100 by the end of 1953.

I wrote my little scoop after promising not to reveal the source, and to my surprise it caused widespread anger rather than general jubilation. The search for the leak was as extensive as anything attempted by President Nixon's plumbers many years later. It did not matter that my report was correct. Templer was furious. From then onwards I was regarded as one of the enemy.

Templer was an Ulsterman, an ambitious regular soldier who from no fault of his was denied the opportunity of proving himself as one of the great captains of the second world war. He made a joke of it, claiming that he was wounded more than once but never by enemy action. The first time he was watching a demonstration of close aerial support at Warminster, and a Polish pilot, who had been on the town the night before, shot up the reviewing stand instead of the target. Templer was wounded in the neck, and denied his chance of glory in the desert war.

No doubt that was annoying as well as painful, but worse was to follow. He was the only general in military history, at least according to my researches, to have been wounded by a grand

piano. It happened in Italy after he had gallantly accepted demotion to command a division in action. The piano, apparently
looted, was in the back of an army lorry which Templer's staff
car was trying to pass. As usual, he was impatient. His driver
repeatedly sounded his horn until the lorry pulled over onto the
verge and blew up on a mine. The piano landed on the unfortunate general, and put him out of the war. That must have
hurt as much as the piano, although his back was broken. He was
often in pain, but that did not entirely explain his irascibility. He
was the kind of man who could not tolerate opposition. Absolute
obedience was demanded, and disobedience was instantly pun-
ished. Most of his subordinates feared or disliked him. Malaya
was his last chance of glory, and he was determined to seize it.

Templer accepted the conventional wisdom that the struggle
in Malaya was for the hearts and minds of the people, but he
ordered the mass punishment of villages. He had the countryman's
sympathy for peasants, but disliked politicians despite the role
they would have to play in any settlement. His contempt for the
press was unconcealed. Che Abdul Aziz Bin Ashak was a member
of the legislative council and the Kuala Lumpur correspondent of
Utusan Melayu, the country's most important Malay newspaper,
but Templer called him a rat, and a rotten journalist whose name
stank in Southeast Asia. Strong stuff, but a gentle purr compared
to what was reserved for me.

One member of the Malayan war council told me that I had
been accused of being a communist. I sighed wearily into my
martini. Was I to go through life eternally damned as a commie
and a spy, I asked rhetorically. But it was no joke. Efforts were
made to have me removed. The editor defended me. This was no
more than I expected as a *Times* man, but it was a tricky moment
for such an attack. Sir William Haley had just been appointed
editor, and did not know me. We did not have bylines in those
days. I was known to him only as Our Own Correspondent, which
must have made me a shadowy figure. I was not an Establishment
man. I had often caused trouble for the paper because of my
refusal to give proper obeisance to sacred cows, and there were
many in those days. The Tories had just returned to power, and
independence for Malaya was not high on their list of priorities.
The Singapore business community suddenly had greater influence in Whitehall. I was in a very exposed position. Not that

I had done much except to report the MPAJA's admission of defeat at an inopportune moment and had always assumed that the promise of political independence was the key to victory. But I was regarded as a trouble-maker in Singapore and Kuala Lumpur, and that was sufficient reason for getting rid of me.

Haley wrote me a friendly note, and asked me to explain the situation as I saw it. I did as requested, on one-and-a-half sheets of paper. He came back quickly, and thanked me for a good letter. His instinct to defend one of his men in the field against most serious charges was apparently reinforced. As far as he was concerned that was the end of the affair. Templer could scream until he was blue in the face, but I would remain the Southeast Asian correspondent of *The Times* until the editor decided to post me elsewhere.

This of course was the other side of the coin, the reason why I continued to work for the paper despite the poor pay, but it was not the end of the affair for Templer. Later he mounted a brigade operation in the jungle to capture a reported communist headquarters. It was rather like Nixon's invasion of Cambodia except on a much smaller scale. The British had forced the politburo of the Malayan communist party to admit defeat by eschewing such military extravagances, but no matter. Unbeknown to Templer, I covered the operation and filed factual reports daily. By the end of the third or fourth day it was clear that the operation was a failure. I thought nothing more of it. For me it was just another second-rate story I was required to file, but not for Templer.

Soon afterwards I went up to Kuala Lumpur to report a meeting of the legislative council. Again I was doing no more than my reluctant duty. The Legco, as it was known locally, was a bit of a joke. The official and non-elected members were in the majority. Many of them were MCS men who appeared in full dress uniform, which included a solar topee with plumes. Templer, dressed in the tropical garb of a full general, presided and was attended by two ADCs. He glowered down at the council, and in so doing destroyed the fiction of democracy in action.

I was prepared to accept an official majority in the Legco. At least it was a step towards full representation, and could hardly be reversed. The Legco was a half-way house to independence, which was inevitable once the Malays and Chinese decided to work together, but Templer's glowering military presence made it a charade. The insult was compounded by the occasional smirks of the two ADCs, who stood behind him as if they were bodyguards. Fortunately, the business of Legco was never allowed to interfere with the luncheon engagements of the official members, and it was over before gin time. Afterwards I was talking to some Malayan politicians in the lobby when Templer approached with his ADCs. He held his sword in one hand, and with the other he was waving an airmail edition of *The Times*. He was working himself into a paddy as he approached, and was almost speechless with fury when he arrived. The Malayans, accustomed to the ill tempers of *tuans* over the decades, drew back. Still waving the paper, and with his face contorted, Templer shouted, What do you know about war? You, you . . . I realized that he was referring to my report of the failure of his brigade action. I was aware of the Malayans watching me, and I was vaguely ashamed that the King's representative should behave so atrociously in public. I was also fed up with his behaviour and assaults on my professional integrity. I snarled back, At least I have been in fucking battle. I regretted the words as I mouthed them. They were unfair, but he had asked for it. I thought he was going to strike me, but after a moment which seemed an eternity he stalked away followed by his gaping ADCs. At least the smirks had been wiped off their faces.

I never understood why he carried on so. I was then an anonymous journalist, known only to my colleagues and the people I reported. My story of the MPAJA's admission of defeat was soon forgotten. He was eventually given full credit for ending the war, and went home to serve as the Chief of the Imperial General Staff. He was promoted field marshal, and did sterling work in establishing the National Army Museum. His admirers said that he was a real soldier, and I believed them. He had guts. At an advanced age he fought off a would-be mugger in a London street. Whatever the reason, it rankled for years, for nearly 20 years to be precise.

In 1971, after I had returned to London, Pat and I were invited to dinner by the Malayan high commissioner. We were late as usual because of Pat. As I was fond of saying, she was only punctual when producing babies, but hosts were willing to believe that it was because of the exigencies of journalism. We arrived on the heels of the guest of honour, Sir Alec Douglas Home, who was then the foreign secretary, and his wife. We knew each other, and went in together. I naturally receded into the background as our host approached, but Templer, who had already arrived, saw me. He glared with the same intensity as he did in the Malayan legislative council nearly two decades earlier, and I half expected him to throw his gin and tonic at me.

I am told that before we went into dinner his wife, who looked a very nice and competent woman, suggested to him that it really was time to forget old grudges. She was even supposed to have said that I looked a nice young man. True or false, he managed to make conversation over the dinner table, and I went home relieved to know that if the British army ever staged a *coup d'état* I would not be immediately arrested as a danger to law and order.

I recall the incident to prove once and for all that *The Times* is not the mouthpiece of the British government, and that its correspondents do not always hobnob with the high and mighty.

5 Somerset Maugham and Sunburned Englishmen

In the summer of 1953, Pat and I, and our young son Patrick, left Southeast Asia for home aboard the *Glenorchie*, a splendid British freighter which had just finished trading along the Chinese coast. France did not admit defeat in Indo-China until the following year, and Britain was to rule Malaya for another four years, but European colonialism was in retreat and the new superpower was moving in. Not that Americans were much in evidence. In Malaya they only had a consulate-general because of its colonial status, and the legation in Saigon had yet to play an influential role. The minister was a Francophile and politically naive. The military aid and advisory group was relatively small. Known as MAAGs, these groups came packaged with American military aid programmes. There was more than 40 of them scattered around the world to instruct the recipient armies in the use of arms and equipment provided.

The Saigon MAAG was nevertheless of historic significance in that it was the first American military presence in Indo-China. Eventually it was to be expanded to an army of 500,000 and lead to a terrible defeat of American arms, but neither I nor anybody imagined that that would happen. The French were too assertive and the Americans too discreet. In *The Quiet American*, Graham Greene was to see some sinister significance in the air-conditioned lavatories at the American legation, but I rather enjoyed them. My first experience of a cool crap convinced me that lavatories should be high on everybody's list of air-conditioning priorities, but again I digress. There was nothing sinister about the American presence in Indo-China in the early fifties. American imperialism, or whatever anybody wanted to call it, was only evident in Thailand.

That free-and-easy land appealed to Americans. It had never been colonized, and it was an attractive country with a surplus of rice, pretty and complaisant girls and government officials willing to cooperate when adequately recompensed. The Central Intelligence Agency was very much in evidence in Bangkok. The CIA men congregated in the Bamboo Bar in their seersucker suits, which became a kind of uniform for them. Clearly they regarded Bangkok as the beachhead for the counterattack against communism, as was Berlin in central Europe and Beirut in the Middle East. (Oddly enough, Philby, the British spy who worked for the Russians, also wore seersucker when he drank at Beirut's Normandie Bar before disappearing behind the iron curtain).

The CIA openly ran a trading company in Beirut with an amiable but shrewd agent in charge. The United States had a contract to rearm the Thai para-military police, and this was used as a cloak to deliver arms to groups of alleged freedom fighters along the periphery of China. Among them were some Nationalist Chinese troops who had fled to the Shan states of Burma after the communist victory. Like the KMT troops in Taiwan, they were supposed to be preparing to invade China, but most of them were too busy cultivating poppies for the opium trade. The Shan states were in the so-called Golden Triangle, one of the world's largest opium-producing regions. According to subsequent reports, the CIA used the opium traders of the region for their own nefarious business, and this could probably be traced back to that early period.

Arms for the KMT troops were shipped from Bangkok to Chiang Mai, and then flown across the border into the Shan states. They could do this with impunity as long as the Thai officials were adequately bribed because the Burmese government had no control over its hill tracts. They had been lawless since the Japanese invasion a decade earlier, and the enthusiasm of the hill folk for guns and independence had first been fed by Force 136, the British cloak-and-dagger force. The inefficient government in Rangoon dealt with the situation by largely ignoring it. Foreign correspondents were rarely given visas, and were never allowed near the area. I flew in from Chiang Mai aboard a CIA transport loaded with arms and equipment, took a quick look round and decided that it would be unwise to stay long. The Nationalist Chinese looked and acted more like bandits than soldiers. Their continuing presence, and presumably CIA involvement, eventually provoked the Burmese to complain to the United Nations, and my reports provided much of the evidence for their complaint.

The KMT carried on their opium trade for many years until even the romantics back in Washington admitted they were not fit soldiers for the crusade against the anti-Christ. Their evacuation to Taiwan was arranged eventually, but in the early fifties only a few people questioned the activities of the CIA. The American ambassador in Bangkok was one. He objected to not knowing of what went on in his own embassy, but he was dismissed as an old fuddy-duddy diplomat who did not understand that an unusual situation required unusual methods.

The general situation was in fact disturbing, and there was little the CIA or any other western agency could do about it. Apart from Senator Joe McCarthy's rantings in Washington, at the time even calm and well-informed diplomats could not rule out Chinese expansionism after Korea. The overseas Chinese were seen by some as a potential fifth column. Much was at stake, including most of the world's supply of rubber and much of its tin. A vast area of the earth's surface, from India to Australia, was seen to be threatened. Stability was as necessary for the emerging nations as it was for world order. Observers such as myself had long argued that political independence was the only solution, but it had not brought stability to Burma and Indonesia. Apart from the failure of the Rangoon government to maintain law and order, its half-baked socialist policies—I write as a man who could not vote Tory—had quickly ruined the economy. Indonesia's economy was in no less a shambles, and outside the villages the megalomania of Soekarno led to the virtual collapse of the country. The political atmosphere became malevolent. The Eurasians and the Chinese were expelled. Towards the end I always felt uneasy in Jakarta, and apparently there was little improvement after I left.

I can remember standing on the deck of the *Glenorchie* as we left Singapore for the last time, and thinking that Joseph Conrad had got it right. I felt the powerful sense of foreboding that filled his books about Southeast Asia. Despite the charm of the lands and the people, there did seem to be an incipient savagery waiting to erupt. That over-dramatic response was alas confirmed later. In the mid-sixties there was a bloodbath in Indonesia in which, according to conservative estimates, more than 500,000 men, women and children were butchered. In the mid-seventies the victorious Khmer Rouge in Cambodia were just as ruthless dealing with their own internal opposition. These once peaceful lands had become barbarous, and the ideologies in whose name hundreds of thousands of innocent people were murdered could not be held wholly responsible. Only the former British possessions escaped. Malays occasionally ran amok (which is a Malay word), but law and order prevailed. The different communities maintained the civilities. It was just possible that the old colonial life depicted by Somerset Maugham has as much to do with it as the systems of law and administration left behind by the British.

Maugham certainly portrayed another aspect of the old colonial Southeast Asia. When I was there, the life of the British expatriates outside Singapore, especially the rubber planters, had not changed much since his day, and I was always being reminded of him. Indeed, he became a consuming hobby as had archeology in the Middle East. He was a very good reporter, and it was said that some of the situations so sharply observed in his short stories were given different locations to avoid libel or embarrassment for others. A story which took place in, say, Penang, was written against the background of Malacca, and my hobby was to establish their true backgrounds.

It was not easy, and I quickly discovered that Maugham was not fondly remembered even by those who could not have been in Southeast Asia when he travelled through. He was thought to be a cad who had abused the hospitality of his hosts. I did meet one old gentleman, the secretary of the Chiang Mai club in northern Thailand, who remembered him clearly. The Chinese hotel where I was staying resounded with Chinese operatic music all day and much of the night. I liked gongs, but not at two in the morning, and the British consul suggested I should stay at the British club. It was down by the river, was cool and pleasant, and above all, quiet. We drove down to meet the secretary, who had spent all his adult life in the teak forests and, perhaps because of his Thai wife, had chosen to retire in Chiang Mai. He had beautiful manners, and called for gin *pahits*. He was agreeable to my staying at the club for a few days and, assuming that I was a member of the embassy in Bangkok, asked after the ambassador. He was appalled when I said that I was a journalist. 'Not a scribbling chap like that bounder, Somerset Maugham,' he ejaculated. It took another couple of gins before the consul managed to sooth him down.

On another occasion in Malaya I arranged to stay with a rubber planter who ran a large estate in Selangor. One of its boundaries marched with the jungle, there had been several incidents, and the bungalow was a long way from the public road. I lost my way, and night was falling as I drove up the unmetalled estate road. The bungalow stood on a knoll, which had been cleared of trees because they could have given cover to attackers, and the high barbed-wire fence was brightly lighted. A young Malay policeman closed the gate behind me, and I drove up to the bungalow where the planter was waiting on the verandah. He was tall, wiry and gray-haired, and his white shirt and slacks were spotless. He had obviously just had his after-work bath. He greeted me with the usual mixture of shyness and tentativeness, and suggested a drink before I had my bath. He poured two thick ones, said cheers, and presumably as a conversational gambit assumed that I thought he was a typical whisky-swilling planter. My protesting denial was ignored, and we almost killed the whisky bottle before I finally persuaded him that such a ridiculous idea had never entered my head.

The bungalow was a sprawling building, raised on stilts with the bathrooms underneath. They were of the old-fashioned variety, with concrete floors, large casks of water and wooden scoops for splashing oneself. I preferred them to the usual bathrooms. The bungalow was sparsely but pleasantly furnished with a few good pieces of chinoiserie in the living room. One long wall was lined with books, most of them mildewy because of the humidity. It was a pleasant surprise. Planters' bungalows were too often pretentious. I was also to discover that he kept a very good cook.

The planter was another surprise. He was a cultivated man who had read most of the books on those long shelves, but as most lonely people do he talked a great deal about himself. He began tentatively over the dinner table and continued far into the evening on the verandah where the number one boy had left a tray of drinks. I was interested—how else do you find out about people?—and at the back of my mind wondered once again why people spoke so easily to journalists. Alone, away from their usual surroundings, or their wives or husbands, they could speak with an embarrassing absence of reticence. Presumably they believed that they had a story to tell. Whatever the reason, I was willing to believe that I heard as many real confessions as the average Catholic confessor.

The planter said that he had been in Malaya for 30 years, and had gone broke in the thirties when the bottom fell out of the rubber market. He had cycled down to Singapore, and slept on the beach with other down-and-out planters. Later he was interned by the Japanese during the war, had afterwards thought of going home but decided to begin again for the third time. I thought he was trying to justify his present affluence, but he rambled on and recalled how he came back from town one day to find his wife in bed with a young planter from down the road. He got up and gave himself another drink, and said that he must sound like some character in a Somerset Maugham story. In retrospect he could not blame her. They had probably been married too long, and rubber estates could be damned lonely for women. He stood at the verandah rail looking up at the distant hills, and said there was also something about Malaya which made people step out of character and do odd or crazy things. Malays ran amok for inexplicable reasons. Chinese gambled away their life savings at one sitting. The Europeans could behave as if they had never read the Ten Commandments or *Vitai Lampada*. Did they still teach that in school, he asked.

The emergency had a strange effect upon the Europeans. Some of them enjoyed it, especially those who had been interned and missed the war. The guns and armoured cars were lovely toys, and Saturday night at the club could be very jolly. There was a lot more drinking and womanizing. But it got others down. Planters could be sitting ducks on estates such as this, despite the barbed wire. It was not just a matter of carrying on under difficult and occasionally dangerous circumstances. A planter was as much involved in fighting the terrorists as the army or police. The daily inspection of the estate was rather like a jungle patrol, and there were probably more terrorists and Min Yuen to be found on the outlying estates than in the jungle. Planters were expected to ensure that their labour did not take any food and money with them when they went out to work. It was rough on the labour having to work all day without a bite to eat, and some resented it. An over-diligent planter could attract the attention of the terrorists. Not many had been killed, but a lot of them had had their trees slashed.

I asked if all the planters applied the emergency regulations with diligence, and he shrugged his shoulders. Some turned a blind eye, or left it to their conductors. They could over-sleep and not leave their bungalows until the labour had gone off to work. At least one had been arrested and put on trial for consorting with the enemy. He paused, but really needed no urging to tell the story.

He had gone to stay for a few days with an old friend in the next state. He had looked forward to spending the evenings playing bridge at the local club, but there was talk of nothing else but the forthcoming trial. The club was also swarming with lawyers, including a Singapore lawyer well known for his courtroom rhetoric who had been retained by the accused.

The life of that small expatriate community revolved round the courtroom for the several days the trial lasted, and he spent most of the mornings in court. Sitting under the slowly-rotating ceiling fans and fingering the unaccustomed collar and necktie he felt obliged to wear, my host thought that the accused looked vaguely familiar. He was in his late forties, and was tanned to the colour of old leather. He was muscular and wore heavy shoes, which suggested that he spent more time out in the rubber than in the office. But there were dozens, perhaps hundreds of such Englishmen in Malaya, and my host stopped trying to place him when he became aware of the tension in the courtroom. All the seats were taken by Europeans, the *mems* wearing smart hats and dresses as if for a social occasion, and the men muttering among themselves. They thought it ridiculous to bring a European to court on such a damn-fool charge. Some of them were angry, but in spite of their indignation not one showed any sympathy for the accused.

Apparently he had been in the area for about a year, and his estate was isolated. That could have explained why he had gone to the club so infrequently, but it was discovered that he was living with a Eurasian woman. Nobody would have minded if he had been discreet. He was not the first, and would certainly not be the last planter to sleep with a local girl, but she did not disappear into the servants' quarters when visitors came. Instead, one of them said at the club bar the first night, she queened it as if she was as good as you or me. Even that might have been accepted in time because she was such a pretty and vivacious girl. She was Anglo-Chinese and looked ravishing but demure in her cheongsam. She spoke good English and was nicely behaved. The older planters could feel protective and randy and their wives patronizing. She almost crossed the racial and cultural divide until a visitor from Singapore recognized her as a former prostitute. He said that the accused had found her in a monsoon drain, full of drugs. The story had been all over town. That had put her beyond the pale of course, but the accused would not go anywhere without her which meant that the couple were seldom seen about locally, although from time to time they were reported to have spent weekends in Penang or Kuala Lumpur.

I suspected by this time that my planter really thought that he was another Somerset Maugham. He savoured the interesting details with evident satisfaction, but his story had the ring of truth about it. What the hell, I said to myself as I helped myself to yet another drink. I can at least check the public details in the files of the local papers.

My host said that much of the trial was actually rather boring. The prosecution witnesses were Tamil rubber tappers, and their testimony had to be translated. It took time, but what emerged was damning. It was alleged that after trees had been slashed and one of the estate trucks ambushed, the accused told them that he did not want any more trouble. He allegedly ordered them to take food and money to give to the terrorists when they went out to work, and an estate clerk said that money was taken from the company safe for that purpose. Counsel submitted that the accused had literally bought himself protection.

There was an uneasy stir in court. Apart from their sense of tribal solidarity, many of the planters present were probably guilty of a few sins of omission. The thought that the authorities might be cracking down worried many more as became evident in the club bar that night. Then it was the turn of the defending counsel. He questioned the tappers closely, asking again and again if they spoke English, and if not how did the accused tell them to help the enemy. The planters in the public section of the court knew how they communicated with their labour. Not one of them spoke Malayalam, the Tamil language, and all of them depended upon their conductors, or foremen, to translate. The accused's conductor was not in court. He had gone to India on holiday soon after the accused was arrested, and could not be traced.

Then the forensic skill of the Singapore lawyer was used to the full. He had the tappers denying themselves and each other, and thoroughly confused the prosecuting counsel, who was young and inexperienced as were most trial lawyers in the colonial legal service. He finally submitted that there was no case because the accused could not communicate with his labour without his conductor. What the conductor said in Malayalam to the labour was double dutch to his client. The conductor might have told them to help the terrorists, and the tappers no doubt thought that he was translating the instructions of the accused, but there was no case because the prosecution had failed to produce the key witness.

The accused was found not guilty. The verdict, however, brought only a sense of relief rather than jubilation in the club that night. The planters felt that they had been vindicated as a class, but the accused disappeared with his Eurasian popsy. There was a rumour that they were emigrating to Australia. The Singapore lawyer was, nevertheless, treated as a hero, and somebody ordered champagne. Later that evening, the planter said, the lawyer joined him on the verandah and asked him where he came from. Was he ever in Johore, the lawyer asked. Yes, soon after the war. Then he remembered. The accused had been on the estate next to his. He remembered him as a bright chap who had probably spent too many weekends in Singapore. He supposed that was when he met the Eurasian girl. He thought back. There was something else which distinguished him from the other planters, and then he got it. But he spoke very good Malayalam, he spluttered. The lawyer nodded. We were very worried after he had recognized you in the courtroom, he said. You could have destroyed our case.

The planter smiled when he finished his story, and asked if it was good enough for Maugham. It was indeed. We had a nightcap, but he was in no mood for more talk and said he was for bed. He would have to be up before dawn. I finished my drink and went to my room. It was fairly cool, but I could not sleep. I supposed it was the story, and I wrote my notes. I turned off the light at last, pulled my sarong up over my shoulders, and was just drifting off when I heard the patter of bare feet along the corridor. A door opened, and there was some muttered conversation, a girlish giggle and then the door closed. I wondered if the planter also spoke Malayalam. Certainly he was a Maugham character.

*

Our next post was to have been Rome, but somebody in Printing House Square remembered that I was a Roman Catholic and that was the end of that. I was not the only Catholic in the office, but collectively *The Times* was apparently still suspicious of Popery. I protested that I knew more dirty jokes about the Pope than any C of E, and was more than ready for the second Reformation, but to no avail. Secretly I was rather relieved. I was still in my early thirties, and reluctant to wear a collar and tie every day. I would have liked to have gone to Hongkong, with the hope of getting back into China, or to the Middle East but only the Indian sub-continent was open, and I was happy enough to return. I had been stationed in India for a while during the war, and had learned to speak Urdu, and of course I covered independence, partition and the massacres in the Punjab. I wanted to see if India and Pakistan were making a go of it after six years of independence, and in any case I liked the sub-continent.

I probably liked it for the wrong reasons. Politics and material progress, the stuff that made the columns of *The Times*, were of course important, and I was genuinely interested, but above all I loved the sights, sounds and smells of India. The Red Fort emerging from the early morning mist and the Taj Mahal at moonlight, especially under an October moon, were obvious attractions, but Calcutta's Maidan, the Mall in Simla, the Shalimar Gardens in Lahore, Chandni Chauk in Old Delhi, the Negem Bagh in Kashmir and a thousand and one other places gave me as much pleasure, as did Indian trains. Kipling was partly responsible. Driving up the Grand Trunk road or travelling aboard the Frontier Mail was always an adventure, but there was

more to it than literary associations. Life in India could be
wonderfully sensual. We used to sit in the garden in the evening,
relaxed and refreshed after our baths, and watch the birds fly
home to roost in the trees by the Jumna, and the warm night
would envelop us like a huge silken sari. From beyond the Kashmir gate the sounds of life in the Old City would pulsate through
the trees. The throb of drums would announce yet another
wedding, and occasionally we would walk through the gate to
watch the boy bridegroom, dressed like a maharajah, proudly
riding a horse and accompanied by a brass band, Indian drummers
and his admiring relatives.

The murderous mobs I remembered in the Punjab were on
such nights gentle and smiling. Terrible poverty was evident, as it
always was in India, but when we succeeded in suspending our
western standards and consciences we were aware of a social
and emotional equilibrium. Those vast crowds, only to be found in
Asia, milled around perhaps because they had nothing better to do,
but we had a feeling of humanity in balance that we never had in
Britain, Europe or the United States.

Perhaps poverty was the great leavener. Few people in those
crowds could have earned as much as a clerk or production-line
worker in Britain. I always filled a pocket with annas to give to the
beggers, and as far as I could see the more affluent Indians—a
very relative term—gave paise, or fractions of farthings. Clearly
it was not up to the standards of a welfare state, but poorish
people did give something to the very poor, and made a harsh
life a little more humane. I was nevertheless more bothered by the
terrible poverty than was Pat. Not that she was insensitive to it,
but rather she accepted or became part of the equilibrium.
Perhaps she was wise enough to realize that there was little the
government could do to alleviate the poverty, at least in the
lifetime of the poor, but that personal charity could at least help
a few poor souls. What I did know was that for her the poor were
those emaciated and diseased people we met, and not the
statistical fodder I wrote about.

She accepted India for what it was. Two or three times a week
with a few of her Indian girlfriends she would dispense powdered
milk to poor mothers and children in a small park outside the
Kashmir gate. I remember that park for the green pigeon which
darted in and out of the trees, their green turning from pea to

Atlantic blue-green as they flew from the sunlight into the shade. I thought it was worthy but inconsequential for Pat and her friends to hand out powdered milk to the poor, but she communed with them, made physical contact, holding the kids on her lap and talking to their mothers in an elementary but expressive Hindi which soon improved.

Pat, a rather private and fastidious person, learned sooner than I did that physical contact was essential in communicating with ordinary Indians. Perhaps it was the climate, possibly the amount of flesh exposed outside official and polite society: the bare flesh under the sari or chola, above and below the *dhoti*, the bare feet, the hands which looked all the more naked because of their gesticulations. Whatever it was, Indians wanted to make physical contact, even the women who were supposed to be more demure than their western sisters. Not that I found them demure. India probably has a higher proportion of good-looking women than any other country, and I could not associate demureness with dark eyes made larger and more provocative by kohl and pneumatic bosoms barely restrained by skimpy cholas.

This physical coming together was not necessarily sexual, hetero- or in any other way. A close friend of mine was Frank Moreas, an Indian journalist and editor of great distinction. He was of Goanese extraction, and had a simple Portuguese peasant's face, a very dark Indian skin and a sharp well-stocked mind. Alas, he drank too much, and probably drank himself into his early death. We were very good friends, and years after I had left India and was in Washington, he phoned me from the Mayflower hotel. In his soft, tentative-rather-than-stuttering voice, he said he was passing through, and could we have a drink together. I dropped everything, and met him in the hotel bar. We had a couple of whiskies, or *burra pegs* as he called them to the complete mystification of the bartender. Afterwards we walked down the long lobby of the Mayflower towards the Massachusetts Avenue entrance, and his hand reached out for mine. I knew, or thought I knew, what the tourists sitting in the lobby thought of two grown men walking hand-in-hand. One old lady with blue hair looked doubly aghast; not only were two men walking hand-in-hand, but one was white—well, pinko gray—and the other black—black as the ace of spades, as my old mother would say. The vice squad might have had a beady eye on me, but I was glad to hold his hand. It meant, or rather I hoped it meant, that he, an Indian, accepted me as a friend.

This was only part of the sensuality of India. I loved the smell and the feel of the earth. The Indo-Gangetic plain must be one of the most intensely populated areas in the world, and over-cultivation and the sun had broken down the earth almost to the consistancy of sand. Walking in the Punjab, the soles of my shoes sinking into the earth, I felt closer to the earth than at any other time. I went hunting as often as I could because I liked shooting for the pot, but the shotgun was also the best passport for a European when he ventured into the countryside. Peasants the world over are suspicious of strangers, and after six years of independence the villagers within motoring distance of Delhi were doubly wary of foreign aid officials, experts and do-gooders who were convinced that they could improve the peasants' lot. They asked too many questions, and the villagers probably were suspicious of their intentions, but for longer than anybody could remember, sahibs had shot over their land. The guns and the killings of duck, partridge, quail and the occasional deer did not offend their Hindu susceptabilities. Rather they welcomed the removal of birds and animals which fed off their crops, and the opportunity of earning a few annas as beaters.

Only once did we run into trouble. I generally went hunting with Harold Milks of the Associated Press and another American, the son of a missionary who had returned to India as a representative of Coca Cola. He had been born in the Punjab, and despite his nationality and calling he was a true country-born who Kipling, or Kim, would have instantly recognized. He was bilingual in Punjabi and was completely at home in the villages. He was a superb shot, and hunted venison with a .22 to make the hunt more demanding. We normally started long before dawn, shot duck in a *jheel* beyond the airport and then partridge in the mustard fields. We would frequently stop in a village, and sitting on *charpois*, the Indian string bed, would chat with the elders and ask the youngsters if they had seen any doe.

One September MATS, the international airline of the US air force, failed to deliver the Thanksgiving turkeys for the American embassy, and Milks organized a shoot for peahens, which were known as Punjabi turkey. Fully grown, they weighed about 10 to 12lbs, and if roasted slowly made an eatable substitute. About 50 peahens were required, and some embassy men joined in the hunt. It was no sport. We moved down both sides of an irrigation ditch in the early dawn and shot them out of the trees where they roosted. We had to be quick and careful because the peacock is a sacred bird for some Hindus, and we were followed by bearers and drivers who stuffed the carcasses into mailbags and loaded them into the trunks of the cars. All went well until an assistant military attaché winged one bird which flew off squawking towards a village pursued by the attaché. We shouted to him to come back, but he was too excited by the chase to hear. The Coca Cola man and I followed, and found him on the edge of the village with pump gun raised and waiting for the wounded bird to settle. To our horror it flew into a little temple and perched on a bell. We shouted, stop, stop, but the attaché fired, missed the bird and hit the bell. It was not a Big Ben, but it aroused the village, and we were soon surrounded by an angry crowd. It took 50 rupees, a case of Coca Cola and a lot of soft-soaping in Punjabi and Urdu to placate them.

I finally swore that I would never kill an animal again after a bear hunt in the Karakorams. We were spending a vacation on a house boat in the Vale of Kashmir, and Milks arrived to shoot bear. He had a spare rifle with him, and I went along. Before setting off on the trek we had drinks with George Middleton, the British deputy high commissioner in Delhi, and he urged us to kill the bear with the first shot. If you wound it, he said, it will cry like a baby. We set off, and reached the tree line in the late afternoon of the second day. A clump of mulberry trees stood on a false crest, and we took up positions behind outcrops of rock.

Just before sunset three brown Himalayan bears gambolled down the side of the mountain, and standing on their hind legs began to eat. They looked like children's teddy bears, and reluctantly I raised the borrowed rifle, which had a telescopic sight, and aimed at the nearest bear. As I was about to fire the sun went down behind the mountain, and I could not see through the 'scope. Shoot, sahib, shoot, urged the *shikari* crouching behind. I squinted under the 'scope, with my nose against the bolt of the rifle, and fired. I hit the bear, but only wounded it, and to my horror it scampered away crying like a baby. I followed, dabbing at my nose blooded by the bolt when the rifle recoiled, and trailed him for at least two hours. Fortunately it was a starlit night, and the baby whimpering was my terrible guide. I was almost whimpering myself when the bear was briefly skylined on another false crest, and I fired off most of the magazine and finally killed it. They were my last shots. I sold my guns, and thereafter went hunting armed only with a camera.

*

I did not learn anything of obvious interest for the paper on those trips, but I did get a feel of the country. I had some idea of how four out of five Indians lived—which meant about 400 million people—and despite all the nonsense spoken about the simple life they were to be pitied. Not only the Untouchables and landless labourers, the hungry, the lame and the congenitally ill, but most of the peasants with some land and a mudhut of their own. Theirs was a miserable life because of its emptiness. It was as empty as the glaring and cloudless sky above, apart from work, the occasional festival, what pleasure husbands and wives could derive from each other and their families, and the company of neighbours. Stated thus, it does not sound too bad. What other pleasures does industrialized man enjoy? One could argue that average western man would count himself fortunate if he really enjoyed his work, his family and his neighbours. Modern simple-lifers have argued the case very persuasively, but they could not have spent much time in an Indian village, or for that matter a Beduin tent or an African kraal.

The industrial slum-dweller in the west might lead a mean life by middle-class standards, but he has newspapers, radio and television, public libraries, pubs, package tours and football, to mention only a few diversions. There is always or nearly always an escape, for his children if not for himself. He has schools and hospitals as well as bingo halls. No less important, his lavatory might be an outside privy, but he still has a chain to pull. Modern progress has achieved a great deal for ordinary people, as I know from personal experience, but this has been denied to the Indian villager. He does not even have enough work to fill his days, let alone enough food, education, social services and diversions. His life is largely empty. Moreover, if he is an Untouchable he is enslaved to a degree beyond the comprehension of Marxists, or for that matter of Beduin tribesmen and African villagers.

Gandhi understood this, the emptiness of Indian village life and the total degradation of Untouchables predestined in a land largely without lavatories to perform tasks considered unclean by caste Hindus. Hence his preoccupation with human excrement, and the disposal thereof. In the *ashram*, he and his disciples emptied each other's chamber pots, but he could not persuade other Hindus because Untouchability is the bedrock of the caste system. Hence also his devotion to the spinning-wheel, home-made cloth and cottage industries to take up some of the slack in what elsewhere would be described as under-employment in the villages. But again his teachings were largely ignored. Even disciples such as Birla, in whose Delhi garden Gandhi was assassinated, sneered at such programmes as a return to the Middle Ages. So they were for industrialists, but not for Indian villagers.

He was remembered as the Mahatma, or 'great soul', but despite the monuments and pilgrimages, Gandhism was a spent force when I returned to India in 1953. Congress politicians, including Pandit Nehru, continued to wear the Gandhi cap and make the expected obeisances on appointed days, but his teachings were forgotten.

Many years later, Chakravarti Rajagopalacheri, who had been a close associate of Gandhi and a governor-general of India, said, 'The glamour of modern technology, money and power is so seductive that no one—I mean no one—can resist it. And it may be that because of Gandhi we got our freedom before we were ready, before we had developed our character to match the responsibility. The handful of Gandhians who still believe in his philosophy of a simple life in a simple society are mostly cranks'.

The man who led India away from Gandhi was Pandit Nehru, the prime minister, a many-gifted man who probably could not have done otherwise for all his personal respect for the Mahatma. Nehru was a patrician, fastidious and arrogant, and more at home with the Mountbattens than his fellow Congress politicians. Educated at Harrow and Cambridge, he was more of a sun-burned Englishman than an Indian despite his pride of race and sense of history. He was a rational, modern man impatient with the mumbo-jumbo of Hinduism and the intellectual cant of some of Gandhi's followers. He had led the struggle for independence with Gandhi, but he campaigned against British imperialism and not the political, judicial and economic systems it had introduced into India. He was a parliamentarian with great faith in the Westminster form of government. He was also convinced that India could only escape its prison of poverty by rapid industrialization.

It was inevitable that he would reject Gandhi's philosophy of a simple life in a simple society. I found it difficult to argue with his decision, but he did condemn those 400 million villagers to at least another generation of poverty and hopelessness. He did many of the right things. Untouchability was declared unconstitutional, irrigation projects were launched and village improvement schemes implemented. It looked good on paper. Much of the world applauded, and I echoed the applause, but the Untouchables remained untouchable and the lot of the villager remained more or less hopeless because a higher priority was given to steel mills than to fertilizer plants.

Nehru's intentions were wholly admirable, and the first five year plan generally reflected the conventional wisdom of the times, but he seemed reluctant or incapable of thinking through the consequences of his decisions. The development of India as he planned it depended upon foreign aid, which largely meant American aid, and he did not like Americans. They were partly to blame. By the early fifties the United States was convinced, and many other governments shared the conviction, that it was the only hope for the world. The second world war could not have been won without American arms and men, and afterwards the western world was saved from economic collapse and Soviet imperialism by American aid and military might. No revisionist historian can disprove these simple facts, but power corrupts and blunts human sensibilities. American officials and businessmen overseas could be brash. Their own success convinced them that they knew all the answers. Their ridiculous fear of communism, as opposed to Soviet imperialism, sadly influenced their collective judgement. They also tried to do too many things in too short a time.

The United States nevertheless did a great deal for India with foreign aid, technical and agricultural know-how, and massive supplies of food grains, without which perhaps millions of Indians would have died of starvation over the years. Much of that aid continued despite the endemic anti-Americanism in India. For instance, during Lyndon Johnson's Administration, India was threatened with widespread famine as a result of poor monsoon rains and Nehru's initial failure to devote more resources to food production. Wheat was quickly sent, but there were still desperate shortages in 1967. In February of that year Johnson announced in a special message to Congress an immediate and interim allocation of 2 million tons of grain, and an additional commitment of 3 million tons was also requested. Altogether the United States provided nearly 15 million tons compared with about a quarter of a million tons from the Soviet Union. The Russians were profusely thanked, but not the Americans.

They were of course rarely thanked for their generosity, but Nehru, unlike the British, West German, Japanese and other recipient governments, was not prepared to meet the Americans halfway. I could partly understand this antipathy. India had recently got rid of one imperial power and did not want to be dominated by another, but this was not the only factor. Nehru personally disliked Americans. They offended him. He shared the contempt and resentment of upper-class Britons for the upstarts. There are patrician families in the United States, and many more cultivated people than in any other country I know, but of course the United States presents an egalitarian face to the world. It was perhaps unfortunate that Harry Truman was president when Nehru came to power. I had an immense admiration for him, and now regard him as a superior American president of the second rank, but he could be cocky and brash. He was once a haberdasher, and I was certain that was how Nehru saw him. Nehru had the arrogance of a patrician, and it was not reserved only for Americans. He also shared the British establishment's contempt for the press. He was not easy to meet, and even more difficult to interview. He regarded my questions as a bore at best and otherwise as an impertinence. He was not prepared to believe that occasionally they could have been of some pertinence if only because I reflected the views, or some of the views, of the west. He could be infuriating, but at that stage of India's development foreign correspondents, including *The Times* correspondent, were much less important than the United States.

Another factor was Nehru's foreign ambitions. I think that he misunderstood American intentions, although John Foster Dulles, who became secretary of state in 1953, made misunderstanding understandable. His assumption that those who were not with him were against him irritated most of America's allies, but for Nehru it confirmed his suspicion of imperialism, American style. He was not prepared to have Indian foreign policy dictated or influenced by Washington, but there was more to it than his anti-Americanism. He was determined to be a world leader, or more specifically the leader of the third world. I happen to believe that in refusing to accept a bi-polar world he played a useful role in world diplomacy, but his ambition for third world leadership was fundamentally as objectionable as Dulles' assumption of righteousness. In both cases it was moral arrogance, although Nehru was doubly certain of the rightness of his cause and his own omniscience. Hindus, even those who strove for the good things of western life, had long condemned the west for alleged materialism and had claimed moral superiority for themselves. Presumably it was some kind of defence mechanism developed over the centuries of Moghul and British occupation. There could be no other explanation because their religion produced such barbarities as *suttee*, the caste system and Untouchability; but whatever the reason Nehru assumed the alleged moral superiority of his race, and as a Kashmiri brahmin probably claimed a double ration.

He was in fact no more or less moral than the average decent and well-disposed person, and his foreign policy record was no proof of Indian moral superiority. He ought not to have accepted the accession of Kashmir from the Hindu maharajah, but having done so he should have held a referendum among its largely-Muslim population to decide their political future. His refusal was a personal decision swayed by personal considerations. He acted like a maharajah and not the democrat he was. His roots were in Kashmir, and Sheikh Abdullah, the Kashmiri political leader who was imprisoned by the former ruler, was a personal friend. In 1947, soon after the accession of the state, foreign correspondents used to sing a little ditty to the tune of *O, What a Beautiful Morning*. One of the verses went like this.

> We met the good Sheikh Abdullah
> And found him a very nice fellah.
> But to his remarks he added an addendum
> That this year there'll be no referendum.

Abdullah changed his mind and was clapped in jail again, and eventually spent more time as a political prisoner of democratic India than he did under the despotic maharajah.

The Kashmir problem soured relations with Pakistan, which had never been good. Many Indians refused to accept the partition of the sub-continent, and I suspected that Nehru was one of them. Certainly he was a great deal less patient with Pakistan than with countries whose governments should have offended his democratic sensibilities. One would have thought that relations with the neighbouring state would have been his first priority, if only because of the problems they inherited after partition, but Pakistan and the United States were the two countries he disliked most. In 1953 came what was seen as overwhelming evidence of their joint enmity to India and all what Nehru stood for. The agent was Richard Milhous Nixon, who of course was much later forced to resign the presidency of the United States to avoid impeachment. He was then Eisenhower's vice-president, and he came seeking allies in the struggle against communism.

Nixon had then just celebrated his 40th birthday, and looked younger than his years. He was uncertain of himself, and clearly distrustful of everybody he met. Years later, after his resignation, Henry Kissinger told me that Nixon was almost physically afraid of meeting strangers. He recalled that when a distinguished stranger came to the White House, a prime minister or president, he had to prepare what amounted to a script for the meeting, and more often than not Nixon was white with fear and nervous tension. I first met him in Delhi at a press reception given by the American ambassador, Sherman Cooper, and can remember being struck first by the dark intensity of his eyes and by his inability to converse. His conversation was staccato, and more disjointed than the word normally suggests. Most of the questions posed to him went unanswered. It was not diplomatic evasiveness. He did not, or could not, listen. He appeared to be programmed to speak on only two subjects, American football and the home-towns of his questioners. Afterwards, Cooper, a Republican senator temporarily out of office, jokingly asked me why I did not like his vice-president. I protested weakly, but Cooper said, I saw you wipe your hand on the back of your pants after shaking hands with him. I had indeed, because it was cold and sweaty as if he was in a blue funk.

Nixon re-enforced Nehru's dislike and contempt for Americans. The diplomatic niceties were just barely observed, and Nixon flew on to Pakistan. I flew ahead of him, and watched his arrival in Karachi. It could not have been more different. The guard of honour at the airport was superb. The discipline and high standard of Britain's old Indian army had been maintained, and a drill sergeant from Caterham would have been forced to admit that the troops on parade outshone the Brigade of Guards. Nixon's eyes glittered when they presented arms, and the national anthems were played. The United States got itself a new ally, and Pakistan got massive military aid from the United States, at that very moment. Bullshit had baffled brains once again.

The wisdom of the military aid agreement was at least questionable, but Mohammad Ali was an indifferent prime minister and had a second-rate mind. He had served as ambassador to Washington, and his naive enthusiasm for the American way of life—or rather its goodies—reminded me of a first-generation immigrant. As for the Americans, they were primarily concerned with the defence of the Middle East, and wanted to strengthen Pakistan in order that it could support Turkey. Little or no consideration was given to the possible consequences in the Indian sub-continent. As far as the Pentagon was concerned, it was just another piece of real estate with no internal dynamics of its own. That said, Nehru's reaction was excessive. He ranted endlessly, and although India's army was much larger than Pakistan's argued that peace and the security of the sub-continent could best be guaranteed by non-violent means. Fears of a possible Chinese invasion were dismissed as baseless. Were they going to come over the Karakoram pass, he asked sarcastically. His suspicions of American intentions bordered on paranoia, and his opposition to the notion of mutual security helped to undo the little good work achieved by the Geneva conference of 1954 when the fate of Indo-China might have been peacefully settled.

The Geneva conference coincided with a meeting of the prime ministers of Burma, Ceylon, India, Indonesia and Pakistan in Colombo, and this time Nehru could not complain that the western powers were trying to decide the fate of Asia without reference to Asians. Anthony Eden, the British foreign secretary, kept them fully informed of the course of negotiations at Geneva. He also assured the Commonwealth prime ministers in Colombo that he would not be a party to any decision taken at Geneva that would conflict with the legitimate aims of Asian countries. Nehru at first responded enthusiastically, in part perhaps because he recognized Eden as one of his own kind, and the Colombo conference became an extension of Geneva.

I was made aware of this because a Sinhalese civil servant in charge of the conference secretariat, was a lifelong reader and admirer of *The Times*. Fortunately we met before the first session. I was trying only to make the usual contacts, and he assured me that he would keep me fully informed. There was no need for me to go to his office, he would come to my room at the Galle Face hotel every evening. He did, and to my amazement and gratification brought copies of the minutes of the days' meeting and of messages passed between Geneva and Colombo. It was a correspondent's dream, and for a couple of days I gave our readers better coverage of what was going on at Geneva than our man there, working under the usual conditions, could provide. I also managed to spend more time swimming from some of the best beaches in the world while my colleagues hung about conference headquarters.

Eden's purpose was clear. He knew that the withdrawal of the French would not bring peace and stability to Indo-China. He was well aware that Dulles, his American opposite number, did not view the Geneva conference with confidence, and was determined to organize a Southeast Asia defence pact. He was no less aware that Nehru opposed intervention by the United States, the Soviet Union, Britain and China. He accordingly hoped to involve India in an Indo-China settlement, and for a time it seemed that he had succeeded. On his return to Delhi, Nehru informed the Lok Sabha, the lower house of the Indian parliament, that he was prepared to participate. We cannot shed responsibilities that go with a great country, he said. It seemed that a fundamental shift in Indian foreign policy was about to take place, until Eden suggested what the responsibilities of a great country such as India might be.

Eden proposed a kind of Locarno pact for Southeast Asia, the parties to which would renounce the use of force and agree to go to the defence of each other in the event of attack. It would be confined to Asian countries, but the proposal was received in Delhi with suspicion. Some officials saw it as an adjunct to the proposed Southeast Asian Treaty Organization, but there was no reason why it could not have been a genuine Asian arrangement. It could have prevented American intervention and the Vietnam war, if Nehru had been prepared to shoulder his responsibilities, but instead he decided that the *panchsila*, or the five principles, provided better safeguards. They were respect for sovereignty, non-aggression, non-interference in the internal affairs of other countries, equality and peaceful co-existence.

Despite the Indian name, the *panchsila* were of Chinese origin, and were written into the preamble of the Sino-Indian Tibetan Treaty on the insistance of Peking. They were at best negative. Eden, when he first heard of them, said that he too was against sin. He was too diplomatic to recall, at least publicly, that China had interfered in the internal affairs of Indo-China for years by equipping and supplying Vietminh. Nehru knew this. He also knew that China had been uncompromising during the Tibetan negotiations, but he signed and thereafter quoted the *panchsila* as if they were the *Bhagavad Gita*, the sacred Hindu book.

Nehru chose the easy way out when Chou En-lai, the Chinese prime minister, unexpectedly visited Delhi on his return from Geneva. The rent-a-crowd chanted, *Hindi Chini Bhai Bhai* (India and China are brothers), but Nehru was apprehensive. Perhaps the Kashmiri brahmin suspected that the Chinese mandarin would over-shadow him, as he did later at the Bandung conference. His senior officials were no less troubled. Their agile and en-quiring Indian minds could not penetrate the bland but im-placable front of the Chinese delegation. Possibly for the first time they realized that diplomacy was not a department of polemics, but the deadly serious business of power and national will. Nothing they said could move Chou from the slogans published in the *People's Daily*. Indian jounalists, who had the pleasing custom of applauding visiting statesmen at press con-ferences, were silent when Chou answered their written questions with a repetition of those slogans. His uninvited presence was a reminder that beyond the mountains a potentially powerful country was emerging from the debris of civil war. Nehru's earlier sneer at Pakistan's fear of the Chinese coming over the Karakoram pass no longer seemed funny.

Indeed, within a year Chinese troops appeared at the Himalayan passes leading into India. My reports of minor clashes and exchanges of fire were angrily denied by Delhi. The Indian high commissioner in London accused me of all known journalistic sins plus enmity to India and a life-long dedication to communism. It was of no importance that my sources were official files which I had read in the Indian foreign ministry. They included reports from district commissioners and military commanders along the Himalayan frontier. The official who showed me the files had to deny their existance. Nehru was determined not to tangle with China.

The Chinese did in fact invade India later, and in panic Nehru called for American and British help. After rejecting and denigrating the concept of mutual security for years, he suddenly expected the United States and Britain to go to war with China in defence of India. Washington and London dutifully sent military missions and provided some aid, but their reluctance was apparent. Fortunately, the Chinese withdrew, but by that time Nehru was an exhausted man, overburdened with work, and possibly conscious at last that he was not necessarily infallible.

He must also have known that China, despite the Sino-Soviet split, had done more for its peasantry than India had done for its own despite the billions of dollars of American and other foreign aid. Unlike India, they had eschewed the glamour and seduction of modern technology and had given priority to food production. The Chinese had full bellies while Indians still went hungry. They were adequately clothed while Indians were still half-naked or in rags. They had achieved this by methods unacceptable to Nehru and social democrats generally. Nehru, to his credit, still remained faithful to the democratic process, but he lacked humility. His last hours must have been terribly sad.

*

Ralph Deakin, the then foreign news editor of *The Times* was convinced that I was the victim of a mysterious centrifugal force which propelled me to the periphery of the country or countries I was covering. Faraway places certainly had an immense attraction for me, and there were many of them in India. For instance, after reading Churchill's account of the Malakand campaign I drove and tramped over much of the terrain. On another occasion I went into Tibet from Narkanda along a narrow track thousands of feet above the valley floor. I was turned back about 30 miles beyond the frontier, but I did get some idea of the mountainous frontier which divided India and China. Deakin was not amused. He belonged to an earlier generation of foreign correspondents who believed that only the political, diplomatic and military power centres had to be covered. Nevertheless, he was responsible for the telegram which sent me off to find Sir Edmund Hillary when he was lost climbing Makalu in the higher Himalayas.

The telegram was delivered soon after we had arrived in Simla where I had hoped to enjoy two or three weeks of cool mountain air. Leaving Pat and young Patrick behind, I drove back to Delhi wondering how I was to reach Makalu. In those days Nepal was a closed country, visas were rarely issued and travellers generally had to wait two or three weeks before being informed that the applications had been refused. Fortunately I knew the Nepalese ambassador, and hoped that he would help because Hillary was a folk hero in Nepal. Alas, when I arrived at his bungalow that evening the compound was reverberating with wild lamentations. He had electrocuted himself with a faulty hand immersion heater in a lukewarm bath. I muttered my condolences, and went home to brood over a drink.

What to do? I recalled the little map of the world hanging in Deakin's office, on which Delhi was but an inch or so from eastern Nepal. He probably assumed I was already on my way, no doubt having a drink with the king of Nepal in Katmandu before moving on. I knew that the expedition had taken very few medical supplies because I had helped to arrange communications for them. It struck me that the Nepalese authorities might let me in if I arrived at the frontier with medicines urgently needed by their folk hero, and I went round to my local Indian GP for help. What would he need to take care of an unknown number of men suffering from a variety of unknown complaints at an altitude above 25,000 feet? I added that whatever they were they would have to fit into two 40-lb boxes, the regulation weight for Himalayan porters. He was a good friend, and had the supplies packed for me. The next morning I flew off to Patna with the two boxes, my bedroll, a half-case of whisky and a thousand cigarettes to catch the train for Jogbani, the railhead on the Bihar-Nepal frontier.

Patna produces very good rice but is a miserable town, I was reluctant to spend my last night in civilization in a Brahmin hotel, and the pilot suggested that I should try the local Shell Oil manager. He was a hospitable chap, a very good amateur cook, and most Europeans who passed through Patna stayed with him. At the airport I hired a tonga, a one-horse trap, and drove out to the Shell bungalow. I shouted *Ko hai*, as all unexpected guests had shouted in India since Clive, and the manager came out on to the verandah. He said that I was very welcome, but his wife was in bed with a bad attack of chicken pox. Had I had it? I had not, but I had stayed in Brahmin hotels and said that I had. He was indeed a very good cook. The pâté was especially delicious, and early next morning, with a small hamper of his goodies added to my luggage, I crossed the Ganges to the railway station and set off for beyond the periphery.

I ought to have been happy. My yearning for faraway places was to be amply satisfied, and with Deakin's sanction, but the narrow-gauge train was old and the journey very long. The pre-monsoon heat was stifling, and none of the fans worked. The Shell man's beer became warm and flat, and the only food available at the small, dusty stations was from hawkers' stalls. I always ate the local food in India, including the salads, on the theory that gyppy tummy could be best avoided if my system was adjusted to local conditions. It was one of my few theories which actually worked. I cannot remember having a stomach upset in India, but Bihar was one of the more poverty-stricken and backward states of the union and I was grateful for the Shell man's cold chicken and pâté sandwiches.

The day wore on, and in late afternoon Mount Everest gradually emerged from the heat haze until it stood startlingly and refreshingly white—as handsome as Mount Fuji but more alluring because between us reared the eastern ranges of the Himalayas. Makalu was farther to the east. At 27,790 feet it was a lesser peak, but by all accounts was a more difficult mountain to climb. The adrenalin began to run, and the warm beer was almost palatable. I had arranged to spend the night in Jogbani with a missionary, who had agreed to act as a letter box for the runners from the expedition, and looked forward to the end of the rail journey. Indian mission houses can be very pleasant, and I dreamed of sitting on the verandah after a cooling shower.

The Rev. Howard Barclay met me at the railhead with a Land

Rover. He was a young, engaging Australian, and my spirits rose higher as he chatted away while we drove into town. He knew the *burra hakim*, or governor of the province across the frontier, and was certain that I would be allowed to proceed. We were driving through mean streets, and I reflected that while frontier towns were rarely tourist attractions Jogbani was worse than most, much worse. I also assumed that we would soon leave it and head out to the mission house somewhere in the country, but instead he turned into the yard of a shophouse, and stopped. Welcome to the Jogabani mission, he said.

The Australian, I was to discover, represented an obscure fundamentalist sect, and lived with his wife and baby in the poorest part of the bazaar. The vision of a verandah and cooling shower vanished. There was no verandah, and no bath. The shophouse had four small rooms. The front room, or shop, was given over to a dispensary run by Mrs. Barclay, who was a trained nurse. Behind were two small bedrooms and a kitchen. The bath was a four-gallon, non-returnable petrol can suspended from a beam behind a screen in the yard, and the missionary said that I should pull the attached rope gently because it took time to fill up the can again. The lavatory was of the Indian crouching variety, a hole in a concrete slab. There was no electricity, and therefore no fans. The kitchen, where Mrs. Barclay was preparing supper, had a *punka* suspended from the ceiling but nobody was pulling the rope. From a teashop down the street Indian film music enveloped us at full volume.

It was grim. I thought even we Herens know where to draw the line, but there was no other place to stay. The Australian couple were also a happy pair, and they were doubly happy that night. An English missionary, a Miss Smith, had waited 17 years in Jogbani for permission to enter Nepal, and it had recently arrived. She was to leave the next morning, and to celebrate there was goat meat and rice for supper. We sat at the table, and I pulled the *punka* as Barclay poured the loving cup of strong sweet tea. Miss Smith was as happy as a young girl at her first party, and their simple niceness was almost as good as a slug of scotch and a cigarette which I realized I could not enjoy in their company. Grace was said again after the canned pineapple and custard, and automatically I crossed myself. There was a slight pause. I sensed the suspicion Protestant fundamentalists have of

Catholics, but Miss Smith recovered herself and said we all worshipped the same God, if in our different ways, and the collective good humour was quickly restored. I then went for a walk in the bazaar to fill my lungs with as much cigarette smoke as possible before retiring to the bedroom I was to share with Barclay.

The monsoon had still not broken, and it was insufferably hot in that little concrete box. The camp-bed was uncomfortable. I was dying for a drink, which made sleep more difficult, and I reluctantly resigned myself to an hour or more of conversation. Unlike most people who live in lonely places, the missionary was not really interested in the events of the world outside, in India, Europe or Australia. After two or three false starts, I tried religion, and tentatively made a reference to the 39 articles of Anglican faith. He had never heard of them. My reportorial instinct was aroused, and it was soon established that he knew little or nothing about revealed religion of any kind. The fundamentalist sect he belonged to just believed in God and the essential goodness of man. Its approach to the things of this world was no less austere. It paid the rent of the mission, and provided the Land Rover, medicines for the dispensary, and that was that. He and his wife and baby depended entirely on the income from the dispensary, which was very little. His wife charged an anna or two when the patients could afford to pay, and many of them could not. Their entire income amounted to little more than ten rupees a week, which was less than a pound, but they were absolutely happy doing, as he said more than once, the work of the Lord.

I had earlier met missionaries who lived simply and serenely, but Barclay had made only one convert in their year in Jogbani. He was unlikely to convert many more because he spoke only English, and had nothing to propagate except his simple concept of a benign God and his own goodness. It was strange, and for some reason disturbing. Even the Irish bog priests in the East End of London knew their catechism and enough Latin to say Mass. Their devotion to Our Lady was distasteful, but they did minister for a church with some intellectual content and historical significance. Barclay represented nothing except his inexplicable urge to do the work of the Lord, whatever that was. He had also chosen to do it among Indians with minds and imaginations influenced by history's most amorphous and complex religion.

I asked Barclay what he thought of Hindu pantheism, but he had never heard of it, or of Hindu henotheism, their ultimate belief in one god without claiming he was the only god. I wondered what Hindus thought of his mission. Most of them were illiterate, but Hinduism was more to them than Christianity was for most Europeans and Australians, and Barclay looked as if he had spent more time on Bondi beach than in a church. His wife was obviously doing the work of the Lord. She was a trained nurse, and ran a good dispensary in an area short of such services even by Indian standards. She had earned her inner happiness and serenity, but I could not understand Barclay's obvious sense of self-fulfilment. I eventually fell into an uneasy sleep for some reason more worried about the Australian snoring in the bed in the corner than my own immediate problem.

Next morning we drove over the frontier to the Nepalese town in Bharatnagar, saw off Miss Smith, and then called on Mr. Bhupalmansingh, the *burra hakim* of Morang province. He was a fat jovial man, and he received me with great courtesy. He expressed his high regard for Hillary Sahib, and would certainly expedite my errand of mercy. He took my passport and reached for his pen, and then paused. His round, bland face remained in the smiling position, but his eyes narrowed when turning the pages of the passport he saw my occupation was foreign correspondent. I admitted that I was a journalist, but repeated that mine was only an errand of mercy. I gestured to the Land Rover outside and to the cases in the back. We went out into the yard and the driver opened one of the cases and revealed the medicines, splints and bandages. I was asked to have the other cases opened, and his smile reached from ear to ear when he saw the scotch. I took a bottle back into the office to help him write the chit, which he pinned into my passport with a thorn. He said I could proceed on the morrow, and wished me luck. I left the bottle on his desk, and returned to Jogbani to complete the preparations for my one-man expedition into the higher Himalayas.

Preparations was perhaps too grand a word. After scouring the bazaar I managed only to buy a few tins of unknown fish, rice, dahl, a hurricane lamp and 500 Capstan cigarettes in round tins of 50. I hired three reluctant-looking coolies and a jeep with trailer to take me as far as the track went, which was not very far, and told them to be at the mission in the morning. I went back for a shower, and the monsoon broke. Slowly and hesitantly at first, and the dust on the floor of the yard quickly absorbed the big drops. Then it came down with a rush and roar, lowering the temperature and washing away the dust. I stood in the yard in my shorts with the rain pounding down on me with greater force than a shower at a pithead bath. It was wonderfully refreshing, and I felt light-headed and light-hearted as most people do at the beginning of the monsoon. In the street outside children were running around in circles, and everybody was smiling. Only later, when I had dried myself and put on a clean bushshirt, did I remember that I would be walking in that rain for the forseeable future.

We had fried eggs and chappatis for supper, and after grace Barclay said that he was ready to do the work of the Lord. I asked what exactly, and he pointed to the piano accordian in a corner. He would play and sing hymns in the bazaar. Did he have a large audience or congregation? I stumbled over the choice of words, but he did not seem to notice. Not many, generally about a dozen or so, but the children enjoyed the music. They especially liked *Abide with Me* because it was sung at Gandhi's prayer meetings. He believed this was a bridge, across which one day converts would cross to embrace Jesus.

His wife beamed, and said she had sorely missed the mission work since the birth of the baby. The baby was asleep on her lap. I had a thirst, and said she could also go off and do the work of the Lord. I was a father myself, and could look after the baby. She protested weakly, but the baby was fast asleep, and I put him in the home-made cot and draped the mosquito net. They went off like a pair of lovers, he with the accordian slung over his shoulder. I almost envied them. They loved each other, had no doubts and were genuinely happy in their work, I thought as I fetched the whisky and cigarettes. There were two books in my rucksack, Tod's *Annals and Antiquities of Rajast'han* and a randy paperback. In the circumstances, I decided Tod was more appropriate reading although that prosaic early Victorian could not disguise Rajput passions. It was very pleasant sitting there listening to the rain, rocking the cradle with my foot and sipping. For a moment, pouring myself another drink, I felt like a brute getting Mrs. Barclay out of the house so that I could have a drink, but consoled myself with the thought that she was very grateful.

The rain was steadily falling again next morning, and the
canvas canopy of the hired jeep leaked. The front tires had been
worn smooth, and the engine was firing unevenly. The coolies
looked reluctant, but I urged them into the back of the vehicle,
and waving goodbye to the Barclays we headed for Nepal. The
road or track wound northwards towards Dharan, Phushre,
Tumlingtar and Num, places I had never heard of and which I
could not find on any map. Even the *burra hakim* had been a bit
vague, but he said that I could not lose my way. I just had to
follow the Arun river. One runner from an American expedition had brought news that Hillary was in trouble and needed
medical help, and he was sure that I would meet a runner from
Hillary. It took a good Sherpa runner only about ten days to reach
Bharatnagar from the base camp in the Barun valley.

I was wearing a bushshirt and shorts, and I was soon drenched
to the skin. I wished I had an anorak, but they were then not to
be found in India, and I was beginning to have doubts about my
footwear. I regarded myself as something of a campaigner, I had
been in the army for nearly seven years and had since led an
active life. I preferred to wear heavy shoes, but I had a theory
that rubber sneakers or plimsolls were better for rock and
mountain climbing, and I was wearing a pair bought in Old Delhi
before my departure. They were already wet through, and were
beginning to look shoddy. I was wishing I had not left behind my
leather shoes at the mission house when the jeep's engine
spluttered and stopped. I got out of the jeep, and a squall drove the
rain down the valley with such force that I had to hang on to one
of the canopy staunchions. The three coolies in the back looked
thoroughly miserable, and the driver showed no inclination to
get out, but I persuaded him after the squall had passed and we
peered together under the bonnet. Cracks in the insulation of
two spark plugs explained the initial spluttering, and the ignition
system, which looked Heath-Robinsonish after a lifetime of
emergency repairs, was drenched. It was clearly impossible to
start the engine again in the open while the monsoon continued
to blow. We would have to walk, or rather start walking earlier
than I had anticipated. It took a little time to persuade the
coolies, but eventually they climbed stiffly out of the back of the
jeep. I helped them adjust their loads, and then shrugged myself
into the straps of my rucksack. I jerked my head in what I thought

was the direction of Makalu, but they just stood there eyeing the jeep as if they were willing it to start.

This is ridiculous, I told myself as the rain blotted out the mountainscape. I was already drenched to the skin, and water was squelching in my sneakers. I did not have a hat, and my hair as well as the rain got in my eyes. And I did not really know where I was going. The coolies were now looking decidedly bolshy, glancing furtively from me to the jeep. I thought I knew how they felt, and for a moment was sorry for them. Then the old army training asserted itself. Forward, I said authoritatively, and, low and behold, not only the coolies shuffled forward but I stepped out as if I was leading a platoon of trained British troops instead of the sweepings of the bazaar of Jogbani, Bihar.

Leaning forward against the straps of my rucksack, I reckoned that I had at least 120 miles to walk unless I met a runner on the way, and then quickly stopped thinking. That helped. I also began to realize that the going was not too bad. My ascent into the higher Himalayas was almost leisurely, just a steady climb like walking up the Sussex downs. The view was starker and more spectacular, except when the rain curtains swept down the valley and blotted out the world. The air was warm and incipiently muggy, but the rain kept me cool. I reached the stage when I stopped worrying about getting wet and no longer felt wet although I could feel the rain dripping off all of my extremities. I still refused to think about walking more than 120 miles, and no longer felt so miserable.

About midday, we stopped by a small stream with grassy banks, and ate lunch in the shelter of an outcrop of rock. I had a couple of hard-boiled eggs and cold *chapattis*. They were a bit rubbery, but the whisky, diluted with cold stream water helped them down. The coolies huddled together fingering cold rice from an old army messtin. The flap of my rucksack was waterproofed, but even in their round tin the cigarettes were a bit damp. I offered them to the coolies, but they preferred their own *biddis*, or conical Indian gaspers, and I smoked a couple with another whisky and water. They dozed for a while wrapped up in their shawls, and then we got moving again.

I was now moving easily in that route march slouch which has carried armies thousands of miles all over the world. Not bad, I said to myself, and began thinking cautiously of walking all the way to the base camp. I reckoned I could do it in about ten days. The eating would be plain, but I had enough scotch and cigarettes to last me the round journey. I even began to whistle, mainly *March Slav* which seemed suitable for what I regarded as my inexorable progress. I could see myself mounted on a squat Mongolian pony leading one of the hordes of Jenghiz Khan. This was an old fantasy. My paternal grandfather was a French Basque, and one theory was that the Basques were descendants of the Great Khan's hordes. This might have explained my mysterious centrifugal force, but it was a harmless if useful fantasy. William Casey, when he was editor of *The Times*, used to try to placate important readers angered by something I had written by telling them that I was a Basque. They are against all governments, not only yours, he used to say as if that explained everything.

These extraneous thoughts ran pleasurably through the back of my head, until I realized that I was alone. The coolies had stopped about 400 yards back, and were leaning against a rock smoking. I retraced my steps and asked what in the hell they thought they were doing. One of them said that we had taken the wrong turning and were way off course. The march stopped singing in my mind as he pointed in the direction where apparently we should have been walking. At about that moment a man came loping out of nowhere, put an imaginary swagger stick under his arm, came to attention, saluted with a broad smile and said what sounded like pinshuneer. He was an old pensioner of the Brigade of Gurkhas who recognized a sahib when he saw one, and was apparently delighted by what he saw.

With an even broader smile, the Gurkha confirmed what the coolie had said, and added he would be honoured if I stayed with him for the night. He gestured up the darkening mountainside as he issued the invitation. I could see nothing except mountainside, but stumbled after him for what seemed an age until we reached a hamlet of stone huts. Men, women and children tumbled out of the doorways. Everybody was smiling except me and the coolies, but I managed a half grin when he beckoned me out of the rain and into a room furnished with a *charpoy*. We had rice and dahl for supper while my clothes and sneakers were dried, and the old soldiers in the hamlet happily shared my whisky after overcoming their initial disappointment.

They would have preferred Rosa rum, which was an Indian army issue, but were polite enough to settle for my insipid scotch.

That night the ropes of the *charpoy* cut through my bedroll, and I slept only fitfully. In one dream I floated back to another faraway place, the upper reaches of the Barang river in Sarawak. I was travelling again in the *prahu* of a tribal chief known as the Admiral of the Barang. He was as jolly as my Gurkha hosts, and his badge of office was a straw beehive hat. In Kuching, where he had stayed with Tom Harrisson, the founder of Mass Observation and curator of the museum, he had drunk only champagne and boasted of his headhunting during the Japanese occupation. That night we stayed at a Dyak longhouse, and had another party. We drank local booze, and on retiring to the sleeping mat assigned to me I fell into a sleep so deep that I should not have emerged until the next morning, but something or somebody gently nudged me during the night. I turned over and felt the soft body of a girl, who, I discovered, was part of the hospitality of the Barang.

That memory of happier days was as good a way as any to pass a night on a *charpoy* in the Himalayas, but I awoke suddenly and discovered that my face was warmly wet. I licked my lips, tasted blood, and jumped to my feet, switching on a torch. In its beam I could see what looked like cockroaches scurrying away. Cor, I said, reverting to Cockney. Bleeding man-eating cockroaches. I tried to sleep again, but sleep was elusive and the girl had disappeared back into the past and up the Barang river. I lay there smoking, and watched the dawn creep through the half-open door. It was still raining.

The next day was worse. The rain came down in solid sheets, and the coolies were tiresome. We steadily gained altitude, but I began to hate the false crests. We would toil up a slope to the top only to find that we had to descend again before climbing to the next crest. Lunch was a can of fish, which I could still not identify, and a snort of whisky. Later that afternoon I finally had to admit that my theory about sneakers being the best footwear for mountaineering was painfully wrong. They gave no support to the ankles, and the soles were too pliable and not thick enough. They were already showing signs of wear, and were increasingly heavy because of the waterlogging.

We paused about teatime. We could not brew tea of course.

but I asked the coolies when we could expect to reach the next village. One of them pointed with a limp hand up the track, but did not appear to be certain. Worse, they did not seem to care. They had lost interest, and were apparently prepared to sit there until kingdom or nirvana came. I cursed under my breath, but felt sorry for them. They were not sherpas or trained mountain-eering porters, and had probably taken the job because the five rupees a day I was paying them —about seven shillings and six-pence in the old money—was much more than they could possibly earn in Jogbani. In the best sergeant-major fashion, I eventually said, on your feet, and we started to walk again.

We spent the night in a deserted hut, and got moving again at dawn. I was no longer eyeing the skyline with my usual keen hawkeyes, and as we approached yet another false crest I only belatedly saw a Union Jack flying in the distance. I thought it was a mirage, but broke into a slow trot. As I came over the crest I could see that the flag was indeed real and, to my utter relief, was flying over a neat row of army tents. The flaps of one of them had been tied back, and inside was a middle-aged military gentleman reading *The Times Weekly Edition*. He was dressed in a Viyella shirt, shorts, woollen stockings, short Fox's puttees and beautiful leather boots. He looked up, passing a trained inspecting eye over my unshaved chin and dishevelled appearance, and said, Don't bother to explain now. Sit down and have a cup of tea. I knew then that Stanley had said, Dr Livingstone, I presume, when they met in deepest, darkest Africa. He could not have said anything else. Art did copy nature.

The man in the Viyella shirt was a colonel, the commanding officer of a Gurkha unit surveying the area. He ordered whisky with the tea, and politely waited for me to explain myself. He then offered all possible help, but added I must have a bath first. We could discuss the possibilities over dinner. Did I like curry? Canned European rations were available, but he strongly recom-mended the curry. I said that the curry would be fine, asked that the coolies be taken care of, and then went off for my bath.

An hour later, the rain had stopped and we sat outside with a young subaltern drinking gin and fresh lime juice until dinner was served. The curry was indeed fine, and we sauntered over to the Gurkha sergeants' mess and drank Rosa rum. The sky had cleared, and the mountains looked magnificent although Everest and

Makalu could no longer be seen because we were too close to the intervening mountain range. The subaltern said that the *chota* monsoon had blown itself out and there would be fine weather until the main monsoon came. He was bored with the survey work and eager to join my expedition. I had a vision of myself at the head of a long column of Sherpas carrying good army rations, tents, camp beds and collapsible baths. My troubles were surely over.

But of course they were not. Two days later, when I resumed the march in fine sunny weather and wearing a pair of the colonel's shoes, I saw in the distance a man in a yellow anorak loping towards us. The distance was vast, the false crests numberless, and hours passed before we met. He cautiously stopped some distance from us, standing skylined on a ridge, looking as if he was ready to bolt if he did not like the look of us. He was a Sherpa wearing cast-off mountaineering clothes and, I noted defensively, heavy climbing boots and two pairs of socks. He had an Austrian Rucksack on his back, and carried a beautifully-made leather and canvas satchel. Engraved on a brass plate were the words, Property of The Times, London. He was Hillary's runner.

The subaltern called out to him in Gurkhali, and he smiled and relaxed. He was indeed carrying dispatches from Hillary sahib. There had been an accident, and the expedition was coming down the mountain. The subaltern told him that I was *The Times*, and he could hand over the satchel to me. The Sherpa smiled politely, but refused. He had been told to give it to the missionary sahib in Jogbani and that, he indicated, was that. He accompanied us back to the Gurkha camp, and the colonel said he could safely hand over the satchel to me, but he still refused. The satchel contained the information I wanted, and there was nothing I could do except follow him. When he resumed his lope to Jogbani next morning I was loping close behind him. We continued thus until the mission was reached and the satchel handed over to the missionary. The Sherpa only smiled when Barclay handed it over to me.

Hillary had written his reports on a couple of air letters to be posted on to London. He wrote well, and the story he told was very newsworthy. It began when Jim MacFarlane, a member of the expedition, fell into a crevasse, and Hillary hurt his ribs when rescuing him. It seemed that one of his lungs was punctured, but

Hillary set out to establish Camp 5 from which he was to launch the final assault on the summit. Any normal person would have quickly collapsed, but Hillary was built like an ox and climbed thousands of feet before he was overcome by shortage of oxygen and extreme dehydration. The assault team managed to get him down to Camp 3, he crawled part of the way, and then strapped to a stretcher it took three days for the Sherpas to bring him to the base camp. The expedition was abandoned. Hillary recovered quickly, but McFarlane could not walk because of frostbite and had to be carried on the backs of Sherpas. A seat was made from packing cases, and a team of them were bringing him back to India, each man carrying him for 20 minutes.

It was a wonderful story. I was desperate to get it on the wire to London, but there was no telegraph office in Jogbani. Then I thought of the railway, and persuaded the stationmaster to contact his boss in Patna. Would he give permission for the story to be transmitted on the railway wire, and would he be prepared to send it press collect to *Times*, London? He said he would, and the transmission began. Patna was a busy railway centre, and the interruptions were frequent. At least two hours passed until the final word was tapped out by key, and the acknowledgement was received from London. Then I thought that the paper might want a piece from me and a service message was sent. Back came the reply. It read, No, the readers of *The Times* are not interested in the adventures of its correspondents. Return Delhi soonest. Regards *Times*.

*

Back in New Delhi it could be difficult to remember that places such as Jogbani existed. The capital was insulated from India, even from Old Delhi a few miles down the road where we lived in the old civil lines. Lutyen's grand design for the city was a factor. He built it as a monument to imperialism, and for British middle and upper-class expatriates with good Oxbridge degrees and a hankering for country pursuits. Government ministers and senior civil servants lived in spacious bungalows isolated by sweeping lawns and shaded by many trees. The very quietness of the streets was un-Indian. They had tan paths for horse-riding, and I occasionally made the rounds astride Seagull, an old Indian army horse, the kind known as hundred-chippers because they

could be bought for 100 rupees, or less than £8. The secretariat
building which had become the department for external affairs
had a hitching post where I would leave the nag while talking to
officials inside. The Imperial Delhi Gymkhana Club was exactly
as I remembered it. There were many more Indian members, but
the old tribal rituals survived. Tennis was still played. Families
still congregated at the swimming pool with the *ayah* squatting
watchfully in the background, and beef was still prominent on
the cold buffet. In the evening the men still sat on the lawn
drinking *chota pegs* and there were still Saturday night dances.

It was possible to persuade oneself that independence had
changed nothing, but in fact New Delhi had become even less
Indian, and not only because of the newly-established foreign
embassies. The Indian capital was also exposed to the full force
of the great post-war explosion of government planning and
international cooperation. Officials looked outwards, and adjusted
their attitudes and life styles to organizations such as the World
Bank and their international civil servants. Many of them travelled
or served abroad, and they and their wives returned with the
unmistakable stamp upon them of favoured international civil
servants who work in air-conditioned offices and are protected
from so many of the harsh realities of life. The planning commission, which had become one of the most powerful instru-
ments of government, sent its men to Moscow to learn the
techniques of Gosplan, the Soviet planning agency. A few were so
completely converted that they were more concerned about the
integrity of the received planning techniques than the people
their planning was supposed to benefit.

Not that they had also been converted to communism. India
had long been governed by a centralized bureaucracy, and
arguably there was little difference between it and the bureaucratic
statism of the Soviet Union, despite the parliamentary democracy
inherited from Britain. Indians had taken to democracy as ducks
to water. The electoral process was a wonder to behold. Illiterate
peasants gathered in their tens and hundreds of thousands at
election meetings. It was easy to scoff. Perhaps they did not have
anything better to do, but they were genuinely involved as was
proved once again in 1977 when they voted Mrs. Indira Gandhi
out of office and got rid of her authoritarian regime. But the
system worked imperfectly largely because of the overwhelming

majority of the Congress party which made genuine debate almost impossible. Parliament was also overshadowed by the power of the bureaucracy and Nehru's unassailable position. It had little or no more real power in relation to the executive as personified by Nehru and the bureaucracy than the old legislative council had under the *raj*. The old ICS once saw itself as the iron frame holding the sub-continent together; the post-independence bureaucracy was an elite excluding what romantics might see as the real India.

A degree of efficiency was achieved. The social consequences were pleasant enough, if dull. English remained the language of government and the dinner table. The food, drinks and conversation in those spacious bungalows were internationalized. Curry, when served, was mild enough for an American with ulcers. The conversations could have been a tape recording of any one of a thousand social occasions in official London or Washington. The Oxbridge background of the senior civil servants was enhanced. It was the badge of office of the men who ruled India.

The fifties were confident years, in retrospect a brief golden age of independence. Nehru trod the national and international stage with elegance and assurance, and the civil servants shared his assurance. The twain did meet; Oxbridge, the Gosplan, the Harvard Business School in their Indian alumni, but not always painlessly. Some of the officials did not want to be reminded that they ruled a country of poverty-stricken peasants and naked fakirs, of technological backwardness and superstition. Their elitist sensibilities were offended. They could be ashamed of their own people and culture. A few retired to Britain, where they felt more at home than in their native land. Others emigrated into the international civil services of the United Nations and its agencies. The majority stayed of course, and their resentment over being the kith and kin of Untouchable sweepers and diseased beggars had odd consequences.

For instance, the schizophrenia of being a member of both an elite and a backward society led to complaints about my reporting. I was not objective because I paid too much attention to poor old Mother India and too little to the work of her modern sons. I wrote about the backward peasant and not the modernistic future being launched from the planning commission. The files of

The Times disproved the charge but they were not to be persuaded.
There was talk of censorship, which the Indian press commission
rejected. Nevertheless, their resentment festered, and 20 years
later led to a concerted third-world effort, supported by the
communist countries, to push a programme through UNESCO
that would give governments the power to control foreign reporting. Their bill of particulars had lengthened, and some
western journalists were defensive. Perhaps too much attention
was given to *coups d'état* and other violence, to natural and man-
made disasters, but the serious papers tried hard to report objectively. Certainly they reported the blemishes, weaknesses
and scandals of their own societies more extensively. The claim
that western news standards had little relevance in the third
world was questionable, but it did not concern western readers.
There was no reason why they should be denied news and
information.

The third world did not have to publish or read it. Similarly
with western news agencies. Without lowering their standards,
Reuters, AP and UPI had tried hard to meet third world requirements, if only for commercial reasons, but there was nothing
to prevent the third world from launching its own foreign news
agencies. Certainly there was no reason why they should try to
censor or control foreign news except for the split personalities
of their self-conscious elites. This was again demonstrated
during the state of emergency declared by Mrs. Indira Gandhi in
the seventies, when tens of thousands of Indians were imprisoned
without trial and the attempt was made to rewrite and debase the
Indian constitution. Peter Hazelhurst, *The Times* correspondent,
was expelled and permission to send a replacement was refused.
We nevertheless tried hard to report the situation in India as
objectively as possible, but were condemned by the ruling elite,
including the high commission in London. We would not have
been condemned if we had censored reports of the mass jailing of
Mrs. Gandhi's political opponents; in other words, if we had
treated them as non-persons. That might have been of little
relevance to third world elites, but it was of some importance to
the imprisoned. Indian newspaper publishers and Mr. Moraji
Desai, the new prime minister, afterwards thanked *The Times* for
its news coverage and support.

In the fifties, this schizophrenia did not prevent me from

enjoying India. I was fascinated watching the country trying to
escape from the dead weight of the past, even if my fascination
was misunderstood. It was no less fascinating watching the ICS
men in the field, especially the deputy commissioners at work.
Many of them were still Oxbridge men, but they were too close to
the land to harbour elitist ideas and resentments. Their job,
looking after millions of people, was arguably one of the best in
the world, and they did it largely as it was done under the *raj*.
Perhaps there was no other way. Certainly the ICS, British and
Indian, had had great experience, longer in fact than the civil
service in Britain whose establishment was inspired by the ICS.
They were indispensable in emergencies, which hardly warranted
the name because they came so frequently in India.

For instance, one autumn the Sutlej river overflowed after
heavy rains and inundated 18,000 square miles of the Punjab and
Patiala. The area was arid, and it was like snow falling in the
Sahara. About six million people were directly affected, and more
than 1,200 died because there was little high ground where they
could seek safety. It was a major disaster by any name, and I drove
to Ambala, the cantonment town where Kim had his first taste,
or distaste, of British army barrackroom life. The ICS man in
charge, Gyan Singh Kahlon, was a big confident-looking Sikh, and
he had quickly sought the help of the army and air force and had
established a joint operations headquarters. Their immediate
tasks were to rescue families in acute danger and feed those who
were marooned by the flood waters. They had a few aircraft and
helicopters, but it was useless to drop uncooked food because of
the lack of fuel. Kahlon organized the mass cooking of *chapattis*.
About 500,000 were cooked every day by prisoners in the central
gaol and even in the environs of the law courts. It was an extraordinary sight; half-naked prisoners kneading dough, often on
their sweaty chests, and languidly throwing them to be cooked on
sheets of roofing material suspended over long lines of fires. They
worked round the clock, and the night shift with their sweating
torsos shining in the firelight looked as if they were performing
some sinister ritual as their hands kneaded dough in unison.
More *chapattis* were cooked elsewhere, but not nearly enough and
Kahlon collected dried grain which could be eaten uncooked. I
feel sorry for the poor bastards, he said. But it will keep them
alive until we can do something more for them.

The emergency food was put in sacks and loaded aboard aircraft. I flew in an old Dakota at about 200 feet, and we pushed the sacks through the open door whenever we saw groups of people. Many stood on bunds and raised tracks which were below water, and they looked as if they were lining up for a water bus. Others had sought shelter in trees, and we broke open the sacks and threw down *chapattis* like so much manna from heaven. Later in the day I transferred to a helicopter, and went looking for people in grave danger. We saw a woman with her baby floating on a *charpoy* bed. The pilot pointed ahead to an irrigation headworks and came in to land, but we were too late. The bed turned over at the headworks and the woman and child disappeared in the weir race.

We were of more help later when we came upon a small village where the inhabitants had sought refuge on the roofs of their houses. The mud walls were melting under the force of the water, and we saw at least one family floating away on roof beams in the general direction of Pakistan. We took some women and children aboard, instructed the menfolk to stay together when they took to the roof beams and promised to look out for them later. Alas, more rain fell that night. I saw farmers hopelessly trying to thresh wet, half-grown cereals against logs and rocks. Herds of cattle stood half-submerged, their haunches to the wind, and overhead flapped gorged vultures. They alone were well fed.

The pathos of the scene grew as families congregated on roads that were often the only dry stretches in the area, and crouched under wet quilts waiting for the morning. I drove down the Grand Trunk Road through an avenue of men, women, children and cattle. There was nowhere for them to go, and they waited impassively blinded by the headlights and splattered by the mud thrown up by the food lorries moving up from Delhi. The wind blowing off the hills chilled even my well-covered bones. It was utterly miserable, and then came a jeep, its canopy down and Kahlon sitting next to the driver. He seemed to bulge out of the small vehicle. His bearded face radiated good will and cheerfulness, and I thought of Henry V and a little touch of Harry in the night. Behind the confident face, he was exhausted. His reddened eyes glowed like coals, but he tried to cheer up one old woman and assured the crowd that more food would be available on the morrow. He saw me and said, It's about time you went home, young man. I said, It's about time you had a drink. He looked back at his jeep, and his assistant sitting in the back was obviously eager to be left in charge. Perhaps you're right, he said. Anyway, the younger generation must be given their chance.

I drove back to his bungalow in the civil lines, and as I turned into the driveway he said, Don't expect too much. The *Mem* is somewhere supervising the *chapattis* and has taken the servants with her. Not to worry, I said. You are in the hands of a seasoned campaigner. I carried what I called my campaign bag into the bungalow, and he watched as I unpacked a can of ham, pickles, Bath Olivers, scotch, a man-sized vacuum flask of mixed dry martini and a few other essentials. He got plates and ice from the kitchen, and we drank about a half pint of martini. I could see him reviving, and he asked what we were drinking. I said it was America's great contribution to civilization, and we toasted the United States. Jai Hind, I added, and he said, the Queen, God bless her. He fell asleep over the ham.

Was it irrelevant to the needs of the third world to report such a man? The answer must surely be nonsense. Educated in Britain, trained by the *raj*, he was an Indian cheerfully working beyond the call of duty. If there had been more such as him in the old colonial empire the third world would now be a much better place.

I went to Amritsar when the Sikh leader, Master Tara Singh, was agitating for a Sikh state. I liked Sikhs. There were practical people. They drank, ate red meat, hunted and wenched. In other words, they were as uncomplicated as I was. Their women were also attractive, large jouncy creatures who looked you straight in the eye, and were liberated long before the idea reached New York and London. Master Tara Singh, however, was a bit too uncomplicated. Unkind people dismissed him as stupid. He was certainly stupid enough to try *satyagraha*, or soul force, in his campaign for a Sikh state. Stupid because non-violence is the weapon of the weak or soulful vegetarians with thin blood. A man big enough to fight Joe Louis could not be a persuasive *satyagrahi*.

He compounded the stupidity by first fasting in a sweeper's quarter as Gandhi used to do, but the line of sweepers' quarters lacked the religious solemnity which used to surround the Mahatma when he was fasting. His followers tried to keep straight faces, but the occasional giggle escaped and was followed by a wave of general hilarity. He was not receiving visitors, and I spoke to him through the door. I asked him how he was bearing up, and he said as well as could be expected. Was he drinking anything? A little orange juice. With gin in it, said somebody behind me, and there was more laughter. Later he decided to offer *satyagraha* at the Sikh temple in Amritsar, and this changed the situation. The Indian authorities knew that non-violence invariably provoked violence. The approaches to the Golden Temple were narrow, which increased the probability of trouble.

The alleys of the city were so narrow that the paint on both sides of my large American Ford were scraped. I parked it, and found my way to the command post of the local deputy commissioner who was responsible for law and order. It was on the roof of a small Hindu temple. (When I reported this a retired ICS man in Cheltenham said I must have been mistaken. No ICS man would offend the natives by using a temple for such a purpose. He had forgotten that the last generation of ICS men were natives, and did not have to be so sensitive.) The DC was reclining in a deck chair surrounded by police and army officers and an operator manning a radio transmitter and two field telephones. The sun was over the yardarm, and they were drinking *burra pegs*. The DC offered me one, and asked about London. It could have been a scene out of a movie. The temple roof and background noises were appropriately exotic. The mannered discipline of the police and army officers was almost stagey, but the star role was reserved for the DC. He was a lean man in his early fifties, and had a lazy Oxbridge voice. He smoked State Express 555s through a long holder, wore a red silk neckerchief under his tailored bush shirt, and occasionally wiped his brow with a large bandana. He looked like a sun-burned Ronald Colman, and probably knew it.

Tens of thousands of Sikhs had gathered, and outside the city a brigade of troops was standing to. Violence seemed inevitable. Scuffles occurred, but the explosive situation was successfully defused. No force was used because the DC had the training, experience and confidence to exert control. Throughout that tense day he was in complete control of the situation. The components of mass violence were separated by disciplined police, and emotions diminished and deflected by firmness and quiet humour. Not a good story, I'm afraid, the DC said that evening. He was wrong. It was a very good story. The iron frame of the

ICS, personified by one man, had withstood the test once again. Alas, it was not always so.

It was overwhelmed in Allahabad when about 2 million pilgrims congregated to celebrate the Kumbh Mela. The religious festival, held at the confluence of the Ganges and Jumna rivers where the ashes of Gandhi were scattered, always attracted an immense crowd but the numbers that year were unprecedented. Disaster struck when a procession of nagas, fakirs and saddhus of the Maha Nirvani Akhara sect, their leaders riding on elephants, was returning from a ritual bath. Their path was blocked by the crowd, and the elephants became restless. The police made a *lathi* charge, and some nagas used their trident spears. Terror suddenly struck the crowd, and it stampeded. Pilgrims standing on the strand were trapped by the fast-flowing river, and 500 of them, including children, invalids and lepers, were trampled on and killed. Another 2,000 were badly injured.

Once again my report, written soberly and, I think, with compassion, was criticized for drawing attention to an aspect of India which New Delhi did not want the world to know about. It was absurd. The naked fakirs (incidentally the word is pronounced fuckers) and saddhus were very much part of India. They had more relevance—to use the elitists' word—for Hindus than monks had for Christians. Anybody who ignored them and festivals such as the Kumbh Mela could not begin to understand India. Those millions were also India. In no other country, have I been so much aware of massed humanity, not even in China. My most abiding impression of my last visit to China was the quiet. The first evening in Shanghai was pleasantly warm, and after dinner I went for a stroll along the Bund. An occasional ship came up the river, but otherwise the silence in one of the world's largest cities was oppressively complete. The impression remains in my mind because of an earlier abiding memory, of my first arrival in Bombay aboard a trooper during the war. The crowds were so overwhelmingly large that they were a physical affront. I got used to them in the end, but that massed humanity has had more consequences for India than the overpopulation, un-employment and law and order with which New Delhi was properly concerned.

The heat of the plains was another aspect which explained a great deal. In the good old days, and when summer came to Delhi in the fifties, many patriotic Indians were inclined to believe that they were, the *raj* migrated to Simla to escape the smothering heat. Everybody who was somebody, and thousands of indispensable nobodies such as clerks, messengers and servants, packed their files, party dresses and walking boots, and took the night train to that hill station. The Viceroy exchanged a magnificent palace for a lesser one with a view, and the bureaucrats left their villas with classical porticoes for timbered cottages named Pinewood and Clovelly. The families of lesser breeds, of collectors in the districts and engineers and policemen, squeezed into lodging houses perched on the hillsides, and subalterns who had ignored the advice of their colonels to shoot in Kashmir strutted along the Mall.

Kipling wrote of the goings on of his lords and masters, and nationalists complained of the expense of this new Olympus, attaching to it a great deal of doubtful symbolism. But in the clear fine air, not unlike a hot day under the pine trees of a Surrey hill, young children quickly lost their prickly heat and sun pallor. Officials worked better in cool offices, government efficiency was maintained, and Simla prospered. The Mall was lined with smart shops and discreet civil and military tailors. All this changed with independence. Nehru rightly decided that a democratic government must share summer discomforts with the people, and the government stayed in Delhi. But the heat of the north Indian plain did not change; it was, indeed, one of life's few certainties. The monsoon might fail, but never the heat.

The coming of summer was inexorable; no light showers or variable winds could stay it. In January Kashmiri shawls covered bare midriffs, and English flowers flourished behind green lawns. Light tweeds were exchanged for gaberdines in February, but games were still played strenuously. By March cotton suits were washed every other day, and weather reports were no longer ignored. An extraordinary number of people became convinced that attendance at a health conference in Stockholm or an instructional course in London was vital for the future prosperity of India. By April the bush shirt—India's major contribution to hot weather living—was *de rigueur* as thermometers on shady verandahs edged up to the 100 mark. Flowers shrivelled, and the antique dust of the Indo-Gangetic plain seeped under doors. Sweepers poked at it half-heartedly with silly little wisps of brooms, but by breakfast time the furniture was gray again. Water-sellers offered clouded tumblers of questionable liquid, thirsty Untouchables waited near wells for the charitable to fill their pots, and the price of beer went up by four annas a bottle.

In darkened offices the ceiling fans turned briskly, the only sign of activity for many months. Production dropped, and strikes threatened textile mills built many years before by Lancashire engineers loyal to their distant cold county. The first cases of heat exhaustion were reported, and in newspaper offices leader writers grew more peevish. Cooks working over charcoal fires made even hotter curries, and stomach upsets increased in frequency. Scuffles on the floors of state assemblies were almost a daily occurrence, and relations with Pakistan deteriorated. By May most of the streets were deserted at noon, and Delhi took on an introspective appearance. Doors and windows were closed against the heat or hidden by a *kus kus*, the blanket of dried grasses wettened to cool the air passing through it. It was often an unhopeful gesture, a traditional, almost propitious act. In more prosperous houses desert coolers or air-conditioners were installed in at least one bedroom, and the fortunate inhabitants tended to become housebound.

By June the shade temperature in Delhi was above 115, and unbelievably it was hotter in forsaken towns such as Jacobabad. The dust pall darkened the sky, and I wore gloves when driving because the steering wheel was too hot to hold. Road traffic, always uncontrollable in a country where motorists and cyclists believed that police signals applied only to vehicles behind them, grew absolutely chaotic. Pointless anger came quickly, and violence was never far beneath the surface. Altercations were frequent—shrill and sudden—and English upper lips grew stiffer. The evening brought some relief. As the sun sank below the Ridge, windows and doors were opened and hot stale air was replaced by hot air. Government clerks went home and changed into *dhotis* or pyjamas, and beds were dragged out on to the pavements. Large Sikhs, wearing only very short shorts, removed their turbans and revealed little topknots tied with coloured ribbon.

By early July the bureaucrats relaxing in the garden of the Gymkhana Club hopefully read the weather report in *The*

Statesman. The monsoon was blowing over Bengal and was reaching towards Orissa and Bihar. Its daily advance was read eagerly, until that blessed day when the rains came. Drenched to the skin, passers-by laughed at each other in the street, and children ran naked in the gutters. The policeman on point duty smiled tolerantly as yet another car drove under his outstretched arm. It still took a long time to tame the heat, and after a few days of rain the humidity seemed just as unbearable. Not until the end of October did the day temperature bear comparison with an English heat wave. Even then, brick walls still radiated heat.

No Indian, no matter how sensitive to foreign comment, could ignore eight months of such discomfort. It was the one reality of India which could not be censored. It was in the summer of 1857 when the hot wind of revolt blew through the cantonments of the army to ignite the Mutiny, It was in the summer of 1947 when one million refugees were slaughtered in the Punjab. If a long enough record of daily temperatures was available, historians could probably establish that heat shaped the history of the sub-continent as much as imperial ambition, religious intolerance and political nationalism, and the Indian character as much as Hinduism. Certainly it will remain the greatest enemy of progress and development. There is little or nothing the Gosplan-trained bureaucrats can do about it. No man can do an honest day's work, or think straight, when the *loo* blows off the desert and sends temperatures up to 115 in the shade.

Heat and all those millions of people will, alas, long continue to impede the efforts to raise living standards, but they were the realities of a country we still both loved. The United States was eventually to win a larger share of my affection, but India remained Pat's favourite foreign country. We had an Indian daughter, Katey, who was born in a hospital not very far from where General Nicholson marshalled his troops for the assault on Delhi which ended the Mutiny. We had many friends, and I thought I was doing a good job despite those overly-sensitive elitists.

Then one night Patrick became feverish and we called our GP. He came again in the morning, when we discovered that Patrick could not walk. I called Mike Sachs, an American doctor and close friend attached to the WHO office in Delhi; he was about to go to the airport to meet some doctors arriving for a medical conference, and he brought them directly to our place. I was on the verandah when they finished, and Mike came out to confirm what the Indian GP had already diagnosed. Patrick, one month before his third birthday, had polio.

6   Old Enemies, New Friends and a Drahtzieher

Most people presumably have defence mechanisms to protect them from shock. Mine was not so much to dodge an issue as to assume that all would be well in the end. I suppose I was an optimist. More acquainted with death and destruction than most people, I could not easily accept defeat, failure or, in this instance, a crippling disease. This was before the discovery of the Salk vaccine, but I wanted to believe, indeed did believe, that the doctors would somehow cure Patrick. It would only be a matter of time. Pat was very different, perhaps because of her Irishness and deep Catholicism. We were not complete opposites. She laughed as easily as I did, and responded to music and good company, but she had a capacity for pain as well as fun. She accepted the prospect of both which, I suppose, helped to explain her serenity.

On that first dreadful morning Pat behaved better than I did. She comforted Patrick without frightening him with too much concern. She listened carefully to the doctors, and made a list of what had to be done. There was pitifully little. I felt in the way, and the GP took me out on to the verandah and said that Patrick would have to be removed to a hospital. We were then living in the grounds of the old Cecil Hotel near the Kashmir gate, and there was no question of a polio victim staying there although we were some distance from the main hotel. He said that the Delhi hospital was not up to western standards. It had to take care of too many poor people suffering from every known tropical disease. There were no facilities for Europeans, and Indian families tended to move into hospital with their sick. It would be better to make other arrangements. He could not think of any, but would make enquiries.

Malcolm MacDonald had just been posted to New Delhi as the British high commissioner. We had not known each other very well in Singapore, certainly we were not friends, but he immediately suggested that Patrick should be moved into his official residence. I discovered later that he had informed Alec Douglas-Home, the then Dominions secretary who was due in Delhi later that week, that he would have to stay with the deputy high commissioner. (Six years later I met Home at the United Nations when he was foreign secretary. We rode back together in his car to the Waldorf Towers, and the first thing he asked was about Patrick's state of health).

MacDonald's gesture was very decent, but India was a sovereign country, the health authorities had their standards and procedures, and Patrick had to go to the hospital. A small building in the grounds was made available, and although Katey had been born only a month earlier, Pat insisted upon staying with him. I drove them down to the hospital, and was appalled by the best the hospital could offer. It was a little brick box about twelve feet by twelve, with a concrete floor and an Indian-style lavatory. A bed and small table were the only furniture. The window was uncurtained, and a bare electric light bulb was suspended from the ceiling immediately over the bed.

Pat seemed not to notice. She quickly made up the bed, and I laid Patrick on it. He was terribly feverish, his leg seemed to have lost weight and, it was probably my imagination, already looked wasted. I tried to read to him, but he wanted Davy Crockett, then a popular song. Pat began to sing: 'Born on a mountain top in Tennessee, The greatest state in the land of the free . . .' His muddied eyes lighted, and he tried to join in the refrain: 'Davy, Davy Crockett, king of the wild frontier.'

Their ordeal lasted about ten days. I fetched food and drink, fresh clothes and bed linen from the hotel, but could not stay too long because Katey had to be looked after. We had parted company with the *ayah* because the doctor said she might have been the polio carrier, and I was without help until an Anglo-Indian widow was found. I had few callers because the prospect of a polio epidemic naturally frightened most people away. For the first time in my career I regretted being so far away from our families. This was one aspect of a foreign correspondent's life I had not previously considered. It was infinitely worse for Pat and Patrick. Day after day his condition deteriorated. His second leg was affected, and then one of his arms. We had many doctors eager to help, but there was nothing they could do. When not asleep he clung desperately to Pat. She had few visitors, and Christopher Rand of *The New Yorker* was the only regular caller.

The first time we met was in Southeast Asia, when we travelled together as deck passengers on a tramp from Kelantan to Singapore. He was a big quiet man with teeth like those of John Foster Dulles. He was also a much tormented man, but his silences had a soothing effect upon Patrick. He had grown up in Oakland, California, and worked on the *San Francisco Chronicle*. Every working day he crossed the bay, and the ships heading for the Pacific made him restless. One morning he got off the ferry, and instead of going to the office got a berth on a freighter bound for Shanghai. He worked for the old *New York Herald Tribune* in China and was a good correspondent, but he was still tormented by his private devils. He became a Taoist, which apparently gave him some peace of mind, but years later he committed suicide.

I was grateful for his silent presence in Delhi because I knew that Pat would not be alone when I was looking after Katey.

The crisis came one evening soon after I had arrived with dinner. Pat had just been aroused from an exhausted sleep, and the nurse I had managed to hire to help Pat during the day said that the doctor had ordered an iron lung. An orderly brought in an old dusty machine which had been left behind by the American army in 1945. I pointed out that the flex did not have a plug, but he was unbothered. He poked the bare wires into a wall socket, and secured them with match sticks. I was horrified. We were in India, and the hospital authorities had done their best for us. I was both grateful and half-ashamed of the preferential treatment, but the sight of those match sticks, which could be the difference between life and death, was too much. I went to the main building and phoned Mike Sachs, who said he would take care of everything.

He did. Within the hour he arrived with the American embassy doctor, a naval surgeon, and a modern iron lung still in the maker's wrappings. The surgeon said nothing could go wrong. If the hospital's power supply failed he could run the lung from a generator in his station wagon, and if that went wrong he had a pedal-operated generator. Sachs had also brought a bottle of bourbon, and suggested I should go outside and try to take it easy. There was nothing I could do. I sat outside on a *charpoy*, and watched the sunset. Pat came outside, and said that Patrick was not yet in the lung. She shared my drink and cigarette, and cushioning her from the brick wall I realized how exhausted she was. She was cold and limp. Sachs came out, and said Patrick wanted her, and I was alone again. Night fell, and I lost track of time. The only light came through the window which I had curtained, and I was aware of an occasional shadow. Then the naval surgeon came out, and said it was all over. The fever had finally passed, and Patrick was fast asleep. He would be all right, he said, and helped himself to a drink. Patrick was discharged from the hospital next day.

We had to wait three weeks before flying home, and I had a stretcher made for Patrick which was strapped across two seats. The trip was a nightmare. Katey cried or whimpered most of the time because she had been vaccinated for some reason on her bottom which became inflamed from wet nappies. The BOAC stewardesses tried to help, but the plane was full of a ship's crew being flown home from Calcutta and they took full advantage of the free drinks service. The plane was delayed at Nicosia airport in Cyprus, it was hot and stuffy and the local authorities were reluctant to permit Patrick being taken off the plane. After a long argument I eventually carried him off and bathed him in the men's lavatory. There was another delay at Frankfurt. It was November and the plane was as cold as an ice box. Patrick, who had spent all his young years in the tropics, shivered violently. I smothered him with blankets and Pat warmed him with her body.

I remembered how we had begun life together as international tramps eight years earlier, young if not fancy free, and with only a couple of bags apiece. We had set off to cover if not conquer the world together, and now we were in full retreat carrying our wounded. Pat sensed my dark mood, and comforted all three of us like some great earth mother although her measurements were only 36, 23, 36. The plane finally took off on the last leg of the journey, and an ambulance met us at Heathrow. One of Pat's sisters took care of Katey, and we went to Great Ormond Street Hospital for Sick Children. Patrick emerged five months later wearing leg braces, and I was posted to Bonn as chief correspondent in Germany.

Life had caught up with me at last. From then on, except for special assignments, I would have to wear a necktie and jacket every working day for the first time in years. There were to be other changes. For the first time I was to have an office, an assistant correspondent, a secretary and a news agency teleprinter. I was to work more or less regular office hours, but would still be available until the final edition went to press. I would have to leave telephone numbers whenever we went out to dinner or the theatre. For the first time I was to be boxed in by routine, the reporting of politics, diplomacy, east-west tensions and defence. No swans along the periphery of the world, no wars, no jungle bashes, no wild dashes from one crisis area to another, no dawn arrival in strange exotic places, no time out in Sarawak long houses, Kashmiri houseboats or on the decks of tramp steamers. I felt like a bloody civil servant. I was only 35, and I was to be denied the excitement, the fun and wonderful unpredictability to which I had become accustomed—at least so I thought. I was also to be on the end of a telephone from London, at the mercy of the half-baked ideas of a foreign news editor. Not that *The Times* bothered its foreign correspondents unduly. We were not sent news schedules every morning, or bombarded with stupid requests. The assumption was that we knew what was going on and could be trusted to report the news without being chivvied. That civilized practice was to continue, but somehow the telephone threatened to curtail my freedom. It was a potential leash.

If this was promotion, I wanted nothing of it. I considered the possibility of refusing, but there was Patrick to think about. We had been assured that the treatment for post-polio patients was very good in West Germany. Pat also suggested that we might enjoy living a more normal life. It might even be nice to settle down for a few years. We would not have to give away books, and she would have a chance to cook. The prospect was still not pleasing, but she was a very good cook. I bought myself a gray flannel suit, a couple of neckties and a set of Linguaphone records to help brush up my German. Pat bought winter woollies for the children, the first she had had to buy. The four of us took off,

Patrick in his leg braces and Katey in a carry-cot. It was not exactly like old times, but we were together again.

*

In the mid-fifties, even after sovereignty had been granted by the occupying powers, West Germany still had the atmosphere and attitudes of an occupied country. The temperature of the Cold War was still below freezing. Despite the death of Stalin, the Soviet Union still seemed to be motivated by imperial ambition. President Kennedy's alleged missile gap was still in the future, but Sputnik had persuaded Americans that they were lagging behind in missile technology. John Foster Dulles still encouraged the mad dream that eastern Europe would be liberated. He was still determined not to negotiate until the United States had achieved overwhelming military superiority. The *Bundeswehr* was still training its first divisions, and western defence planners were mesmerized by the reported deployment in East Germany of 22 Soviet divisions. West Germany was a forward military area as well as a nascent democracy.

Nato troops were kept on a war footing, and the American, British and French ambassadors retained some of their former proconsular authority. The American had a private train, not a private railway carriage but a complete train with priority of movement on the *Bundesbahn*. West Germans tended to defer to nationals of the three powers, and policemen were polite and forgiving if you spoke with an English or American accent. The consequences of defeat were very much in evidence. The economic miracle was only just beginning, and living standards were lower than in Britain. The rate of exchange was DM12.50 to the pound. The memory of Hitler still pervaded the country. Konrad Adenauer, the chancellor, rightly rejected the idea of national shame, but some West Germans were ashamed of their immediate past and many more knew that they were regarded abroad as moral lepers. In the west, they were disliked most in Britain, as we discovered when we drove home for vacations or visits.

Very few German cars were to be seen in Britain in those days, and our Mercedes with its Bonn registration plates provoked some deep prejudice. Drivers expressed their hatred or ire as soon as we got off the car ferry. They would cut in front of us as we drove up the London road from Dover, and occasionally shook their fists. *The Daily Express* rarely reported German news without sniping at Adenauer, and unreconstructed Nazis were reported to be training deep in the Black Forest for a war of revenge. This hangover from the war suprised both of us, although Pat's sister was killed in a London blitz. Perhaps we had been out of Europe too long, but despite my initial misgivings about working in Europe I liked West Germany from the beginning. Our unusual introduction no doubt helped.

When we landed at Cologne airport, a baggage handler carried Patrick from the aircraft and said, You will soon get well now that you are in Germany. The underlying arrogance escaped me. We were grateful for his genuine kindness, and he was the first of many. The physiotherapists at the university *Kinderklinik*, where I took Patrick for treatment, were wonderfully kind and attentive, especially Fräulein Marx, a handsome dark-haired woman in her late thirties. Her fiancé had been killed in Russia, she had no chance of marriage in a country which had lost so many men, and she enveloped her surrogate children with rich maternal love. Patrick loved her. Similarly at the hospital in Cologne where Patrick was an out-patient of Herr Professor Dr. Hackenbroch. He was world-famous in his field, perhaps because he had had so many broken and limbless bodies to mend and make workable with mechanical devices. Patrick's new leg braces were made by two of his former soldier patients, badly-crippled men whose physical losses had been compensated by gentleness and compassion.

It was an unusual introduction. Unlike other foreign correspondents or diplomats, we first met the cruel aftermath of defeat, the German victims of Hitlerism. It was infinitely sad. Even if I had been conditioned otherwise, I could not have behaved as a representative of an occupying power. The Marxes and Hackenbrochs made that impossible. They accepted their fate with fortitude and dignity. They were very fine people, much better than some of the Britons and Americans working in Germany. This proved nothing of course, except that not all Germans were fascist beasts.

We also lived among them, first in a little *Sachgasse* or dead-end street in the heart of Bonn, and not in one of the ghettos built by the occupying powers. Pat patronized the local shops, and the girls at the butcher's always sliced off a piece of one of the many sausages hanging behind the counter for Patrick. He soon became a *Wurst* expert. The baker, from whom we bought wonderful *Graubrot*, would always give him a sliver from the marzipan pig in the window. He played in the street with the local kids, and soon learned German, or rather Bonner plat. Indulgent mothers kept an eye on them, and the little street was pervaded with *Gemütlichkeit*. I should have disliked it, but German good manners and civility, cloying and too cozy as they could be, were pleasant and civilized.

We discovered that we liked Bonn, which then only attracted sneers from the foreign community. We used to say in self-defence that it was handy for trips to Brussels, Amsterdam and Copenhagen. At weekends, the Heren household echoed to the cry, To the frontier to eat, and we would drive into Belgium or Holland for a change from heavy German food. Maastricht, with its two very good restaurants, was a favourite. Nevertheless, Bonn was then a pleasant little town in which to bring up a young family. The toyshops, especially Puppenkönig's near the railway station, were delightful, as were the little cafés on the Rhine. Pat and I would share a bottle of wine, and Patrick and Katey would ask for cokes. Invariably the waiter would protest that apple juice was much better for them, but would fetch the cokes and then spoil them with attention while we watched the river traffic. I also walked regularly in the Siebengebirge, the range of hills on the other side of the river.

German formality was occasionally irksome or funny, depending upon my mood. I could be impatient with their earnest determination to state the obvious, and at great length. The self-pity of some was worse. We had a charlady who retold her experiences in the war. Pat commiserated, and also mentioned the London blitzes. I watched the char's face harden. She did not want to hear about what the Germans had done to us, and that was the last we saw of her. Memories of the war, although ten years old, were nearly always present. The men obviously felt compelled to explain that they fought in Russia but never on the western front. The one exception was Konrad Ahlers, the chief Bonn correspondent of *der Spiegel*, who later became the chief of the federal press office and then a member of the Bundestag. When asked by an American at a diplomatic party where he had served as a paratrooper, Ahlers said, Crete, Greece, Italy, France but never in Russia. I gave him a silent cheer, and we became good friends.

Some Germans were extraordinarily insensitive. We dined one night at a table where the inspector-general of the Bundeswehr was the guest of honour. He had been a member of Hitler's *Oberkommando der Wehrmacht*, and was in the bunker when the attempt on Hitler's life was made. He was perhaps understandably diffident, but his wife was complaining. She had been the wife of a senior staff officer for many years, but unlike British wives had never had the pleasure of being stationed in interesting places such as Cairo, Delhi, Rangoon or Singapore. I commiserated, and said it was a pity that Germany and Japan were defeated. She had been denied so many pleasures and experiences. I thought that she was about to agree, but a Prussian stare from the general silenced her.

On another occasion Dr. Etzel, the economics minister, was guest of honour at the dinner table of Nedville Nordness, an old friend who was a senior official at the American embassy. His wife Evy was a Norwegian, the widow of a resistance leader who was tortured and killed by the Nazis. Norway, exclaimed Etzel. *Ein schönes Land!* He had been stationed there during the occupation and had loved every minute of it. He established that Evy Nordness came from Oslo, and asked her if she had a lodge in the mountains. Yes, Herr Minister. Where? Evy said that it was way up in the mountains, outside a tiny village he could not have known, but he persisted. The general conversation ceased as he literally asked his way across the map of the Oslo fjords. The only other voice was Evy's as in a mesmerized monotone she answered his questions with, Yes, Herr Minister. Before he got half way up the mountain I knew, and I felt that the others knew, what was about to happen. He led Evy off the main road, through a village, and asked, Was it the lodge at the end with the blue shutters? Yes, Herr Minister. He had spent two summers there, and loved it. He was exuding bonhomie, warm and excited by a shared experience, and oblivious of the frozen silence of the other guests. The penny, or pfennig, only dropped when Evy asked, And how did you find Norway, Herr Minister? *Freundlich?*

The word got back to David Bruce, the American ambassador. Some discreet messages apparently passed between Washington and Bonn. Whatever happened, Etzel, who was then regarded as a possible successor to Adenauer, disappeared from view probably still dreaming of those two wonderful summers he spent in that mountain lodge requisitioned from a family whose father had been tortured and murdered by the SS. German life had many such oddities of fascinating interest. A truncated society was slowly coming to terms with its terrible past and doggedly learning to become a political democracy. The future, unsullied by that past, was for the younger generation. The interregnum, the period of painful adjustment, depended upon men such as Etzel. He was a shrewd economist. One could only assume that he too was coming to terms, and that he genuinely regretted the past, but he still remembered the good times and was clot enough not to realize that his reminiscences could cause extra pain for those who had suffered during the German occupation.

There were other interests. The wine, beer, *Wurst* and bread were excellent, and I fell in love with the baroque architecture which superseded my earlier interest in Middle East archaeology and the location of Somerset Maugham stories in the Far East. The work was essential for my future progress as a journalist, especially alliance politics and defence and the east-west confrontation. They tended to dominate the foreign news pages of *The Times*, and an understanding of them was part of the intellectual baggage which stood me in good stead when I was transferred to Washington in 1960. It enabled me to perform the diplomatic reporting role of the chief Washington correspondent as soon as I got off the plane. Only the faces were different. The work was of obvious importance, and newsworthy because Khrushchev seemed determined to pick a fight over Berlin. I had more than my fair share of space in the paper, but I was not overly enthusiastic about the work. I was by nature a reporter who preferred to report what I witnessed, not only action stories but the permutations of the human race with their occasional violent or destabilizing ruptures or adjustments. The east-west confrontation was largely a matter of attitudes and ideology, and I was persuaded that they had become too inflexible. Political and military leaders tended only to react to new situations. Very few people questioned the basic attitudes, and those who did were regarded by the suspicious as fellow travellers.

Among the senior members of the alliance, France was the

most awkward but Britain was regarded as the weakest. It protested its loyalty to Nato and the objectives of the alliance, but the Eden plans reflected flexibility and an impatience with those hardening attitudes. Whatever the merit of Eden's initiatives, they were doomed to failure; in part because of continuing Soviet sabre-rattling but mainly because the Americans loved concepts and doctrines. For all their individual resilience, they seemed compelled to work within a doctrinal framework. No doubt the difficulties of organizing public opinion and battling a programme through Congress required strict adherence to the finished product. They were also more passionately anti-communist than the British, but there was more to it than that.

Their political development had been shaped by doctrines and entrenched laws; from the Declaration of Independence, the Constitution, Washington's farewell address, and the Monroe and Truman doctrines to the North Atlantic treaty. Arguably Britain was way ahead of its allies in that it accepted the division of Europe which was recognized years later by Willy Brandt's *Ostpolitik* and the Helsinki agreement, but it was totally unacceptable by the United States in the mid-fifties. The change came very slowly, and was completed only in 1972 when President Nixon went to Moscow to announce the new era of detente. In effect he established a new doctrine, one more relevant to the times. History must give him the credit, despite Watergate, but confrontation in Berlin and the Cuban missile crisis had to be endured, the world had to be taken to the nuclear brink, before those old attitudes were changed.

The West Germans were similar. They loved order and discipline. They were unhappy without fixed sets of rules and political and philosophical concepts. Nato and alliance politics were also more important for them than for the British. The extra dimension was that they enabled West Germans to work themselves back into international society and become respectable again. All western European countries depended upon Nato and the American nuclear umbrella for their national security and survival, but the dependence was more obvious in West Germany. It was the designated battlefield. American support was essential if Germany was to be reunited again. Nobody understood this better than Adenauer.

Der Alte, as he was known, was by any standard a remarkable man. Ancient, he was 73 when he became chancellor, and the leader of a defeated and despised country, he nevertheless succeeded in pointing the alliance in the direction he wanted. He did not dominate the alliance, but for many years ensured that his objectives became the alliance's objectives. The Americans dominated the alliance of course, with the British hanging to their coattails, but Adenauer set the agenda. Neither Britain nor any other European member wanted the reunification of Germany; indeed, its continued division was their secret common aim, but Adenauer, whose earlier political experience was largely confined to being mayor of Cologne, made certain that *Wiedervereinigung* remained at the top of the agenda.

It was an extraordinary performance. In retrospect, he towered above the other leaders, Eisenhower, Macmillan and de Gaulle. He was careful to disguise his pre-eminence in the alliance pecking order. The Americans, British and French came first, and Adenauer always placed himself in the fourth position, just ahead of Italy but well behind the so-called Big Three. West Germany's increasing economic strength and the growing power of the *Bundeswehr* pushed him towards the front rank, but he always resisted. I admired him for it, especially when I compared him with Macmillan.

The British were shedding the last remnants of their imperial power, and their economy was failing to take advantage of the post-war transformation and expansion of world trade. They could not even afford to maintain the British Army of the Rhine, but by sucking up to the Americans they precariously retained some semblance of world power. It was shaming. Most of the British politicians and officials involved did not even like the Americans. Some felt infinitely superior, and saw themselves as the Greeks to the new Rome. The Americans suffered their pretensions silently. They were extremely well mannered on the whole, but they knew that British power was rapidly diminishing and that the special relationship, much vaunted in London, would soon be largely meaningless in terms of diplomacy and defence. Worse, the British appeared to be utterly unaware of the ridiculousness of the position they strove to maintain. Fantasy and not reality governed British official attitudes in the fifties.

Adenauer had no love for the British. They had dismissed

him from his post as mayor of Cologne soon after the war, and the memory still rankled. He resented British posturing, but these factors did not seem to figure largely in his calculations. He was the complete realist, and knew as well as the Americans did that Britain was in a state of decline. He did not welcome Britain's belated efforts to join the European Economic Community because he shared de Gaulle's view that the British were offshore islanders and not true Europeans. The twin pillars of his foreign policy were friendship with the United States and France. He did not seek a special relationship in the British sense of the term, but set out to be the American's most loyal European ally. He believed that friendship with France was essential if the old enmities were to be finally buried. He gladly suffered the posturings of de Gaulle, which were even more ridiculous than those of the British, because friendship with France promised a complete break with the past. He meekly bowed to French blackmail during the negotiations for the Rome treaty, and accepted the agricultural policy designed to help French farmers. What does it matter, he rhetorically asked during a conversation at the Palais Schaumberg. We have the steel plants.

Adenauer had the instinctive German understanding of the value of propaganda. Goebbels was not the first German propagandist. Bismarck employed the first known government press officer, von Busch as I recall. The federal press office, a large government department, was part of Adenauer's private office. During the occupation, Adenauer had skilfully used foreign correspondents to influence allied opinion. One of my predecessors in Bonn had been his most fervent admirer, and willingly allowed himself to be used. That was unnecessary as well as bad journalism. Adenauer regarded *The Times* as a world newspaper. He knew that it was carefully read in the State Department in Washington and other foreign ministries as well as in Whitehall. My less than high regard for his policies annoyed him. He accused me of being a *Drahtzieher*, or wire-puller. Anglo-German relations would be fine if it were not for me, he added. This was taken seriously by the British ambassador, who complained in his parochial way that the West Germans regarded *The Times* as the official mouthpiece of the British government. I said it was time they learned that we were an independent paper, and suggested that Adenauer was more concerned about *The Times* than relations with Britain.

This infuriated him, but it was true in a way. Adenauer wanted good relations with *The New York Times*, *Le Monde*, *The Times* and the *Neue Züricher Zeitung*, probably in that order. Although Switzerland was neutral, the NZZ was important because it was the only foreign newspaper of repute which he could read. We were invited, collectively and separately, to the Palais Schaumberg for a glass of wine or afternoon tea. Occasionally the correspondents of *The Guardian* and the old *New York Herald Tribune* were present. The tea was ruined by thick cream, but the conversation was useful and enlightening. Behind that immobile Red Indian face and iron will were many doubts that rose and fell with the headline news. He was not fully convinced that the Americans would support him until German reunification was achieved. He worried about the backstairs influence of the British. He was not afraid of the Russians, but of the possibility that the Americans would become impatient or lose interest in Europe.

Some of his doubts should have been allayed after Khrushchev began to apply pressure on West Berlin. The Americans immediately reinforced their garrison in the divided city. I did not doubt their resolution, but Khrushchev did more than threaten Berlin. He exuded the confidence and rough humour of a peasant. In getting rid of some of the more hateful aspects of Stalinism, Adenauer feared that he could be seen to represent a new kind of communism, no longer cruel and repressive and therefore more acceptable in the west. He was also apprehensive of Khrushchev's cunning.

This became evident at one of his tea parties after the Russian leader had proposed a confederation of East and West Germany. It did not appear to be particularly dangerous. Each country would retain its sovereignty and political and economic systems. West Germany was by far the more populous, prosperous and powerful, and could preserve its own identity if not dominate the proposed confederation. I did not see much merit in the idea but there was no reason to be afraid of it, and I said as much to Adenauer. Why was he so apprehensive?

Adenauer answered obliquely. You know I was in a concentration camp, he began. This was not quite true. He had been held by the police for short periods, but over the years these inconveniences or minor harassments had grown in his mind until he seemed to believe that he had spent the war in Dachau. I was sitting in my cell, he said, when the SS guards were changed and I recognized one of the new men. He was the son of a good Catholic *Beamte*, or civil servant. He was not very bright, but Adenauer had helped to get him into the police force. I said to him, Adenauer continued, Hans, why have you joined the SS? After a good Catholic upbringing, what can your poor mother think of you? You have disgraced your family and your church. Hans looked at me, and said, *Herr Oberbürgermeister*, I am also a good German. I am doing my duty. Adenauer paused for effect. We were all hanging on his words, and I was wondering what it had to do with the confederation proposal. He leaned forward from the little yellow love seat and sipped the tepid tea without a grimace. Then he flung back his arms dramatically and said,There, you can't trust the Germans.

I was astonished. Here was the West German Chancellor telling foreign correspondents that his own people could not be trusted. I tried to imagine Eisenhower, Macmillan or de Gaulle telling West German correspondents that they did not trust their people. It was monstrous. I could not believe that Adenauer had such a low opinion of his own countrymen. I assumed at first that he was prepared to do or say anything to further his political aims, even to malign his own people, but the more I pondered his statement the more convinced I became that he did indeed distrust Germans. He had seen too much; two military defeats, the Weimar republic as well as Hitler, the Rippentrop pact with the Soviet Union, the concentration camps and the degradation of defeat, inflation and semi-starvation. He despised his cabinet colleagues, especially von Brentano, the foreign minister, and Erhard, the architect of the economic miracle whom he derisively dismissed as a *gummi Löwe*, or rubber lion. Prick him, he once said, and he will burst. He had the Catholic's distrust of the Social Democrats, and contempt for the Free Democrats who were members of the governing coalition. He was feeling his age, and could not see a worthy successor. Not trusting anybody, he was determined to involve his country inextricably with the west, especially the United States and France. As an Englishman, I could only applaud his ultimate objective, but eventually his price was proved to be too high. When the crunch came, despite the bold talk about the liberation of eastern Europe, the United States was not prepared to risk war to reunify Germany.

*

The hope of early reunification had been kept alive until then by John Foster Dulles, the American secretary of state, who was probably closer to Adenauer than any other western leader. They made a strange pair. Dulles came from the upper crust of American society, not the billionaires but the old white Anglo-Saxon Protestant families who regarded themselves as a natural elite. It was a crust that was not supposed to exist, and its members were happy to promote that fiction. Dulles's father was a Presbyterian minister and his mother was the daughter of a former secretary of state. That was not all. When he joined the state department, the secretary was another relative, his uncle, Robert Lansing. This gave him a proprietorial approach to the department and American foreign policy. He really believed that he, and only he, was fit to conduct the foreign business of the United States.

My most persistent memory of him was in Berlin during one of the many crises of the fifties. It was before the big showdown, but the Russians were making belligerent noises and he flew in like an avenging angel. Extra drama was added by the United States Army which provided a guard of honour, not dressed in regimentals but in full battle kit as if they were about to storm East Berlin. A large placard suspended from the cantilevered roof of the Tempelhof airport terminal building proclaimed *Peace is our business—United States Air Force*. The arrival statement read by Dulles was like a thunderbolt flung at the enemy. I looked eastwards apprehensively expecting at least a little mushroom cloud.

Dulles was convinced that Russian communism was a ruthless system determined to destroy Christian beliefs and the principles of western civilization. Nobody could argue with that, but the intensity of his abhorrence too long prevented him from understanding the realities of the nuclear age. He seemed determined to vanquish the anti-Christ even if his crusade involved possible nuclear incineration. Possibly he was incapable of imagining the horrors of nuclear war. Many men then in high places could not, including Adenauer who once told me that nuclear weapons were only an extension of heavy artillery. Dulles might have been occasionally carried away by his own rhetoric, but his righteous language reflected his religious background and the assumption of limitless American power. He was an American Cromwell convinced that he held the sword of the Lord and of Gideon— until he finally realized the full consequences of the American failure to stop the Soviet invasion of Hungary in 1956.

It took time, and he was a very sick man when the first indications became apparent two years later. The admission that the United States was powerless to prevent aggression within the Soviet sphere of influence without exposing its own cities to nuclear attack must have embittered him, but more was involved than the final disillusionment of an old man dying of cancer. In 1956, after his threat to bury the west, Khrushchev launched his broad offensive to swing the balance of super power from the United States to the Soviet Union. He began with a declaration that the four-power status of Berlin was illegal, and therefore null and void, and the three western allies, the United States, Britain and France, were given six months to quit.

The gravity of this manufactured crisis could not be exaggerated. Apart from its moral obligation to the people of West Berlin, which was indisputable, the United States had to defend the city and its access routes through East Germany if its trucial guarantees in Europe and elsewhere were to remain credible. The Americans had, with British help, overcome the 1948 Berlin blockade, but ten years later nobody believed that West Berlin, reviving and bustling with industry, could again be supplied solely by air. Moreover, the latest threat was oblique. Khrushchev did not threaten a blockade, but only to hand over to East Germany the responsibility for controlling the road, rail, canal and air routes to West Berlin. Nato could hardly go to war over who would check the travel documents of traffic beyond its jurisdiction, but Dulles's problem was that he had fallen in with the fiction invented by Adenauer and Dr. Hallstein, the state secretary of the West German foreign ministry, that East Germany did not exist. They insisted that it was still the Soviet zone of occupation, and that Moscow was alone responsible for its administration until Germany was reunified under Adenauer. Recognition of the Pankow regime, the euphemism for the East

German government, was as much anathema for Dulles as for
Adenauer. That he could not concede without making a mockery
of his own policy. Khrushchev must have enjoyed setting that trap.

Dulles' dilemma was painful. He would not, and could not,
abandon the West Berliners to the communist regime in East
Germany, which would have been their fate although Khrushchev
had promised Berlin the status of a free city. Nor could he treat
East German control of traffic as a *causus belli*. That righteous
sword of his wavered, and suddenly he conceded the possibility
that those non-existent East Germans might perhaps be allowed
to inspect civilian lorries passing through their non-existent
country.

Alas, he did not notify Adenauer before allowing this possibility, and he could not have spoken at a worse time. Adenauer
and de Gaulle were in Bad Kreuznach for one of the periodic
meetings which had been arranged under the Franco-German
treaty of friendship. The first had been held in Paris, and protocol
required that the second should be held in West Germany. Bonn
was the obvious venue, but de Gaulle, despite the treaty to bury
the old enmity, was less than enthusiastic and they met at the
little watering place in what had been the French zone of
occupation. The choice was odd. Bad Kreuznach was the field
headquarters of the German high command during the final
retreat in 1918. From its pretty *Kurhaus* on an island in the River
Nahe, was issued that cryptic and famous communique, *Nichts am
Westen*, or all quiet on the western front.

Bad Kreuznach did not long remain quiet when news of Dulles's
intended concession was received. When it arrived I was in the
office of the West German delegation, which with typical
efficiency was equipped with news agency teleprinters as well as
official communications equipment. The various electronic
machines hummed, as did the West German officials. I could
understand their satisfaction. De Gaulle had refused to go to
Bonn, but Adenauer's policies were paying off: sovereignty,
the economic miracle, membership of Nato, the founding of the
European Economic Community, and now the application of the
treaty of friendship with France. De Gaulle still called the tune,
their presence in Bad Kreuznach proved that, but, to quote
Adenauer, they had the steel plants. They could afford to wait
because with German reunification and the close relationship

being forged with the United States, they would emerge as the undisputed leader of Europe.

At that very moment Adenauer was discussing with de Gaulle how to avoid the economic division of Europe when the Common Market began to raise its outside tariff wall in the new year. The economic health of Britain and other countries outside the EEC depended upon their deliberations. This was power, and the officials knew it. Fifteen years earlier most of them were in the *Wehrmacht*, under oath to Hitler, and probably fighting on the western front or in Russia. Ten years earlier those fortunate enough to have some possessions were selling them on the black market for food. Now, dressed in dark suits, white shirts and gray ties, they were trying to persuade the French to be decent to the British. The irony could not have escaped them, but they gave no sign. They were still cast in the modest role of confessed sinners working their way back into a state of grace, and I suspected most of them would cling to that modesty in order to discipline their national energies and ambitions.

Felix von Eckhardt, Adenauer's press chief, came into the room and made commiserating noises in my direction. Apparently de Gaulle was still opposed to the idea of a free trade area, but he was sure that they would work out something to help Britain. I made suitable obeisances. A former script writer of some talent, who had managed to avoid Goebbels during the war, von Eckhardt was a little man, very fastidious and looked like Charlie Chaplin in *Monsieur Verdoux*. Some foreigners did not take him seriously, but he was shrewd and very close to Adenauer. I suspected that he was more influential than any cabinet minister. He also said that Berlin was being discussed when he left the conference room, and the full support of de Gaulle as well as Dulles was assured. He was chipper enough to make a little joke about Britain, whose unswerving support—here his eyebrows were raised to the ceiling—was such a comfort for all Germans.

At that moment the warning bell on the DPA teleprinter rang, and in retrospect I thought that in his scriptwriting days von Eckhardt could not have written a more dramatic scenario. One of the younger diplomats went over to the machine, and I saw his face tighten. *Herr Sekretaer, Herr Sekretaer*, he called. We walked over, and as von Eckhardt read the news bulletin he began to look like Chaplin in *The Great Dictator*. There was no carpet to chew, but he tore off the copy paper in a fury. He did not shout *Gott in Himmel*, *Schweinhund* or any other ridiculous nonsense the stereotype German was once required to ejaculate in B movies, but the effect was the same. I almost giggled, until I managed to read over his head that Dulles had in fact admitted the limitation of American power. There would be no German reunification, in Adenauer's lifetime, or mine.

Von Eckhardt managed to pull himself together, but not Adenauer. His old, wizened face remained as immobile as ever when he met journalists later that night, but he was in a state of shock. I had no objective evidence to prove it, but he never really recovered. Khrushchev's six-month deadline passed almost unnoticed, but Adenauer was a changed man. Later he announced to an unbelieving world that he would quit the chancellorship and become president, which meant that he did not want to carry on as chancellor but could still not trust his fellow Germans. He assumed that as president he could keep a sharp eye and a tight rein on his successor at the Palais Schaumberg. This in fact was what he told von Eckhardt on the Rhine ferry the morning after his surprising announcement when driving to the chancellery, and for the little press chief the announcement was no less appalling than that night in Bad Kreuznach. Adenauer, the man who almost singlehanded created West Germany, had obviously not read its constitution. At least this was von Eckhardt's conclusion, and he had to remind Adenauer that the federal president was almost as powerless as the British monarch. At first Adenauer could not believe it. He was *der Alte*. They argued about it all that day, until Adenauer was finally convinced and then he reversed himself and announced that he would carry on as chancellor.

That was not the only consequence of Dulles's concession to Khrushchev. Others were not so comic. The Soviet leader's attempt to change the balance of super power subsequently persuaded Kennedy to call up the reserves to defend Berlin, and led to the resumption of nuclear testing. It also took the world to the brink of nuclear war when he stationed missiles in Cuba in 1962. That crisis was one of the great turning points in modern history. Frightened by their own criminal lunacy, the super powers backed off, negotiated the partial nuclear test ban treaty and agreed to strategic arms limitation talks. There were hopes for a saner world, but the Cuban missile crisis revealed that the Soviet Union, for all its nuclear might, was still a continental power contained by the United States navy. The Russians then embarked upon a massive naval expansion programme which was to make them a world power. Khrushchev also expressed support for so-called wars of national liberation, which frightened the Americans and led to their tragic involvement in Vietnam. It seemed that for all the promise of *détente*, a word which became increasingly fashionable, the super powers had only decided to seek their objectives by non-nuclear means. Nevertheless, when Willy Brandt came to power in Bonn his *Ostpolitik* succeeded in securing the future of West Berlin and negotiating a central European settlement. This included the recognition of East Germany. To that extent Khrushchev realized his 1958 objective, but by the time the last protocol was signed he had long been deposed.

*

I shared the conventional wisdom of most Britons and other lesser members of the western alliance that we were safer with a divided Germany, but I regretted the plight of Berlin. Although only in the first stage of post-war recovery and divided into allied and Soviet sectors, it remained a great city and immensely attractive despite the acres of ruins. I felt at home there, as I have always felt at home in great cities: from New York, Chicago, San Francisco and Rio de Janiero to Rome, Istanbul, Cairo, Damascus, Jerusalem, Delhi, Calcutta, Singapore, Hongkong and even Shanghai. I suppose it was the Cockney in me. I liked busy streets, avenues and *souks*; hotels, cafés, bars and restaurants; theatres, cinemas and cabarets; the sense of anticipation generated by crowds and the underlying suggestion of urgency.

I often felt alone, but that rarely bothered me. I could wander for hours in busy streets without being lonely. I never felt alien, despite the different tempo, climate, architecture, food and faces because I was a Cockney, an urban creature bred and conditioned for the adventure of living in great cities. One of my theories which has stood the test of time is that Cockneys are a universal race, scattered throughout the world like the Jews of the Diaspora. The London Cockney is only the British variety. The

theory is not so silly as it might sound. For all the differences of
language and skin pigmentation, the citizens of great cities have
shared similar experiences and developed qualities such as
quickness of mind, humour, low expectations and the ability to
survive.

West Berliners in the fifties probably had the world's lowest
expectations and the highest score for survival. They were
mercilessly bombed by the Americans and the British, terrorized
and raped by the Russians, occupied and divided, starved and
blockaded, and then largely ignored by the Bonn government
because of its provincial meanness and dislike of Cockneys. They
could not cherish the illusion that they were the masters and
mistresses of their fate. They knew that their future would be
decided by Washington and Moscow, and for reasons that had
little to do with their well-being. They knew that the communications to the west, the umbilical cord upon which their
measure of freedom depended, could be squeezed, blocked or cut.
They also knew that theirs was no mean city. No wonder West
Berliners were Cockneys, aware that they would not get an
even break but quick-witted and shrewd. They even spoke a
German Cockney, quick and abbreviated, sharp and mocking.

Berlin drew me like a magnet. On the long drive from Bonn,
my spirits would begin to rise after passing through the iron
curtain at Helmstedt. I would turn the Mercedes off the Berliner
Ring and drive fast, about 150 kph, down the last stretch of the
Autobahn until the *Funkturm* rose above the then low-roofed city.
Winter flying could not keep me away, although the Cologne-
Berlin trip could be one of the more disquietening scheduled
flights. The air corridors across East Germany were narrow and
occasionally buzzed by Soviet fighters, and during bad weather
planes were frequently stacked above the city. Landings could be
hair-raising. Tempelhof airport was only a short cab ride from
the heart of the city, and during the final approach planes let
down between apartment houses. They loomed up through the
swirling fog or snow on both sides of the plane, close enough for
passengers not rigid with fear to observe the domestic lives of the
tenants. Over the years I glimpsed all seven ages of man and more,
from copulation to a priest praying over a coffin.

Isolation gave Berlin a sharp identity and enhanced its inner
excitement. The claim that it was an island of freedom in a red

sea of communism was overly dramatic but nevertheless true. Doubters just had to cross into the Soviet sector to see, or read the party newspaper *Neues Deutschland* and the titles in the bookshop in Stalin Allee. Then there were the refugees. More than 3,600,000 fled to the west from 1949 until the Berlin Wall was erected in 1961. About 1,500,000 crossed over in Berlin, or rather crossed under because most of them travelled by the U-Bahn, or the underground railway which served all four sectors until the wall went up. The stations in East Berlin were closely watched by the police, but they still came across. The vast majority travelled without luggage to avoid search and interception, but not all. One East German brought across a library of 900 books.

I got to know him during a swan through East Germany. I was graciously allowed to drive my own car, but not to travel alone. I had to have a *Begleiter*, an accompanying officer who was a trusted member of the party. None of the regulars was available on this occasion, and I was given a youngish *Dozent* or lecturer from the Humboldt University. He proved to be an East German version of the good soldier Zweig. He had grown up under Hitler, had suffered the bombing and privation, and after the war found himself on the wrong side of the line. He had come to terms with the communist regime. He had no loyalty, he just wanted to survive. Presumably for that reason he was a little frightened of me at first. He distanced himself whenever we checked into a hotel or visited an office or factory, making it clear that he was with me, a representative of the capitalist press, only because he was under orders. He fabricated a kind of alibi in case I crossed the authorities. It was rather pathetic, but after two or three days he began to relax and enjoy himself.

One reason was that we stayed in hotels reserved for foreign visitors and delegations, and for the first time in his life he had all the butter and cream and as much meat as he could eat. Another was that his subject was English and American literature, and we discussed modern writers many of whom he had not been allowed to read. The drive from Rostock and Stralsund on the Baltic coast, through Magdeburg and Leipzig to Dresden near the Czech frontier, was for him a literary journey of discovery. Books obviously meant more to him than politics, and his inner reserve or protective mechanism finally gave way one day near

Karlmarxstadt when he asked about life in West Germany. I answered as truthfully as I could, and added that I would be glad to help should he decide to cross over. He shook his head; his old mother was still alive and he could not live without his library.

About six months later, he phoned me in Bonn to announce his arrival in the west. He was staying with a relative in Wuppertal, but was anxious to move to Bonn. Did I know of a room or flat, preferably a flat because of his books. All 900?, I asked. *Natürlich*. He had brought them across on the U-Bahn. Not in one go of course, but about 20 at a time. What about the police? He said that he had always boarded the U-Bahn at the mainline station for Mecklenburg, where he had an aunt. Whenever he was stopped and searched he said that he was paying her a visit. He made about 50 trips in about four months, each time leaving the books with a friend in West Berlin. He was a modern hero of sorts, or anti-hero, but in his own quiet way one of the indomitables. Certainly he was more impressive than the fictional spy who came in from the cold. He was apolitical, and as a university lecturer was comparitively well paid. Life was no doubt colourless, but he had security and status. He found it difficult to explain why he, a mousey little man, had taken so many chances. I supposed that he just wanted to read the books denied to him in East Germany.

Not many East German academics, writers and artists were willing to trade their favoured status in exchange for intellectual freedom, perhaps because they were also good soldiers Zweig and enjoyed so many privileges. During another visit I spent a weekend at a little resort on the Baltic coast reserved for intellectuals. Its unspoilt beauty and quiet affluence reminded me of Cape Cod. These privileged ones drove West German cars and their clothes had obviously come from the west. The drinks cabinets were also international. I could have been staying with Harvard friends on the Cape or Nantucket, except that the conversation was guarded. The intellectual freedom of America or Britain was entirely absent. They had paid a high price for their privileges.

At the other end of the social and intellectual scale, I met the manager of a farm collective near the Polish frontier who was an outrageous black marketeer. There was no question of passive resistance or calculated sabotage. His illegal trading was not a political act. He was a sly peasant who had done well during the war and continued to operate on the black market after the Russians came in and created their puppet state. I met him in a muddy farmyard as the spivish driver of a truck loaded with produce handed him a wad of marks and drove off. He had been drinking, and made no effort to explain away the transaction. Instead, he took me into the front parlour of the farmhouse, gave me a cigar and a large brandy from a well-stocked sideboard, and spoke mockingly of the glories of the East German democratic republic. I took a note of what he said, and it read like an editorial in *Neues Deutschland*, but the tone of his voice and his frequent winks signalled that he was enjoying an elaborate and secret joke.

He was a gross character, thoroughly unlikeable, but I did not blame him or those pampered intellectuals. Their experiences had been different from mine. I was rarely disposed to pass judgement on others, if only because I accepted that the flesh was weak. That said, it was always a pleasurable relief to meet men and women with principles and guts, and the lecturer was not the only one in East Germany. On one occasion I visited a factory outside Dresden which made television receivers. I was led into an office where the manager and the inevitable party spy sat behind a row of soft-drink bottles and plates of sweet biscuits. It was a familiar scene. I never saw anybody drink the lemonade or eat the biscuits but they were always there, apparently indispensable features of communist interior decoration. As usual the manager remained silent while the party man reeled off production figures, chided me for the sad state of British-East German relations and finally expressed complete confidence in the eventual victory of the proletarian revolution. I was accustomed to such claptrap, but it was particularly obnoxious that day perhaps because I had been in East Germany too long. Rather brusquely I asked the silent manager why his TV sets cost twice as much as in West Germany and were only half as good.

The party hack looked dumbfounded, but not the manager. Looking me straight in the eyes, he allowed that that was a fair description of his earlier product, but not now. He had been forced to produce a Soviet-designed set, and it was no damned good. He was now making a set designed in the factory, and with tubes imported from Britain. It was a much better set, perhaps not as good as western products, but it would be improved. He spoke evenly, ignoring the party man, and went on to tell me what his factory could do if he was only left alone. He spoke quietly but with great conviction. He was the archetypal German manager, confident of himself and his work force, and concerned only with making a good product at a reasonable price. This was the core of his integrity, his defence against the regime and system.

I saw enough of the East German economy to realize that it could become the most efficient in eastern Europe in spite of communism. The German work ethic, the love of order and talent for organization were blunted and misdirected by the system, but such national characteristics could not be wholly frustrated if only because the apparatchiks were also German. I was grateful that Russia and not Germany was the first communist state. If it had been otherwise communism could have been triumphant, but in the late fifties East Germany was a ramshackle state dependent for its survival not only upon Soviet arms but also upon the Soviet version of containment.

This was very different from the containment policy expounded by George Kennan in 1947. The American diplomat argued in an article published in *Foreign Affairs* quarterly, under the *nom de plume* 'X', that United States policy must be a long-term and patient but firm and vigilant containment of Russian expansive tendencies. The struggle would not be won by force of arms but by the dynamics of a free society. To avoid defeat the United States needed only to measure up to its own best traditions and prove itself worthy of preservation as a great nation. Kennan was right. Soviet society was not dynamic and could not compete in the same arena, and the very system demanded a police state. Its eastern European empire could only be maintained by excluding the outside world—in other words, containment. Hence, to quote Churchill, the iron curtain from Stettin in the Baltic to Trieste in the Adriatic—except Berlin. The city was a hole in the curtain, a wound through which haemorrhaged the life blood of East Germany. A tourniquet had to be tied, the Berlin wall had to be built, if that ramshackle state, and with it much of eastern Europe, was not to collapse.

In retrospect the building of the wall was inevitable, but not when Nikita Khrushchev, the Soviet leader, first visited East Berlin in 1956. I have forgotten the reason for the visit, but listening to him speaking at a public meeting in the Marx-Engels Platz the main object apparently was to express his hatred of Germany, East and West, communist and capitalist. The hatred welled out of him with terrifying virulence, and the vast silent crowd was cowed. Khrushchev recalled that Adenauer had gone to Moscow the year before to negotiate the return of prisoners of war. He had assumed that tens of thousands were still held in camps ten years after the war, and could not believe that the remnants of Hitler's once-conquering armies numbered only a few thousands. Khrushchev, his voice thickening with emotion, rhetorically asked what had happened to his own son during the war, and Mikoyan's. He did not know, Mikoyan did not know. They were buried in unmarked graves, the victims of Nazi aggression, of the fascists Adenauer wanted returned. Well, they were not coming back. They could not come back. They were under the ground. They were all dead.

Mikoyan, the Armenian who had survived so many purges of the Soviet leadership, stood silent on the platform while Khrushchev shouted and gesticulated. His hatred was now overwhelming. I was no less cowed than those miserable East Germans, many of whom must have still wondered if long-lost husbands, sons and brothers were still in Soviet camps. Until then I had thought that I understood Russian enmity of Germany, but the full horror of 20 million war dead was brought home to me by the Russian's snarling face. And for extra emphasis was the instant translation of the German interpreter, a tall man who towered behind Khrushchev and impassively boomed, *Alle tot, alle tot.*

That evening the mayor of East Berlin gave a reception in the *Stadthalle*, and the local communist party dignitaries stood about nervously sipping sweet champagne and awaiting some indication of what the night might bring. They received little help because unlike similar receptions in the west the hosts and guests of honour were at one end of the room segregated from the rest of the company by a long table cluttered with drinks and small eats. This was standard procedure in the allegedly classless societies of eastern Europe, but Krushchev was always approachable for western journalists. Only the timing was important, because the KGB bodyguards were inclined to toss out those who approached too early.

A few of us sidled towards one end of the table where a small group of correspondents had already taken up position. Seeing us, a Reuter man made a break for it and was stopped by the KGB men. He spoke politely in Russian, but two of them picked him up by the elbows and carried him from the room. He looked like Bugs Bunny as his legs moved uselessly in mid-air, and I laughed. I am told that I laugh loudly, even coarsely, and I attracted Khrushchev's attention. He waddled over, smiling broadly and his eyes, which had been red with hatred earlier in the day, were dancing with delighted anticipation. He obviously looked forward to a battle of wits. Then followed a knock-about comedy act with us first playing the straight men. He was alert, funny and enjoying himself. But even as he cracked jokes and invented peasant sayings we were sized up individually as he awaited the inevitable questions. The KGB men stood against the wall, and the room remained silent, apparently mesmerized by the extraordinary relationship he had established so quickly with western imperialists and jackals of the international yellow press.

This was one of Khrushchev's favourite phrases, and next morning I bought half a dozen yellow-and-black striped neckties in the Kurfürstendam and distributed them among my colleagues. We wore them that evening at another reception. A silly joke no doubt, but Khrushchev noticed them. We did not have to sidle up to the top table. He beckoned us forward, and roughly asked us why we were wearing the same tie. I said it was the old school tie of the international yellow press, and we wore them in deference to our socialist hosts. We did not want them to be unknowingly contaminated. An even sillier joke, I know, but he roared with laughter and seemed to remember it whenever he visited his eastern European empire. They were horrible ties, but they helped to break the ice and I felt that I could charge them to expenses.

Krushchev was a great historical figure. He was the first Soviet leader to come to power more or less bloodlessly. He denounced Stalin, and set out to improve Soviet agriculture and living conditions. He was the first Soviet leader to travel widely, and to show a keen interest in life beyond the Soviet empire. Those conversations he had with western journalists, ridiculous as they were in part, revealed a searching mind. He was too convinced of historical inevitability of communism to take us seriously, but he could not but be impressed by western achievements. He wanted to do good by his own people. He had fire in his belly, as did President Lyndon Johnson. I was always careful not to put too much trust in my own working class instincts, but at least they helped me to understand both men. I could recognize Khrushchev's potential for good when I subsequently edited his memoirs for publication in *The Times*. He had the right reflexes and yet he was gravely flawed. He wielded enormous power with ebullient confidence—and recklessness. His decision to complete what he described as the unfinished business of the second world war was fundamentally sound. There really was no alternative for the west, once Dulles recognized the limitations of American power. Willy Brandt was to prove that later, but Khrushchev preferred to bully his way to a settlement rather than negotiate. He could not understand the significance of West Berlin for the west. He might have been misled by his own hatred of Germans. He probably could not believe that the west, although not prepared to fight for German reunification, would stand firm in West Berlin.

Khrushchev also complained that West Berlin was a centre of espionage, and statistically it was probably the world's largest. At one time I counted 44 intelligence agencies. Many were in the business for money or were run by emigre groups and amateur American outfits fighting their personal cold war. The fabrication of intelligence became a minor industry. Much of it was sheer fiction, but the authors managed to generate a deliciously sinister atmosphere in many an obscure bar or restaurant. A zither player regularly strummed the Harry Lime theme in one of their hangouts, and I always expected to see Alan Ladd at the bar. Once again nature copied art, and exposed its own intrinsic nonsense. This aspect of West Berlin was successfully exploited by thriller writers as were the homosexual bars by Isherwood between the wars. Poor Berlin. It had its fair share of spies and homosexuals but it was grossly misrepresented by two generations of English writers.

Admittedly not all the spooks were phoney. British intelligence and the CIA were present in force. The British occupied the entire top floor of the Olympic stadium, which was the British headquarters in the city, and the Americans were more numerous. I often wondered what they were supposed to do. They could not compete with the Social Democrats' *Ostburo*, which kept in touch with former Social Democrats in East Germany. It was run by Stefan Thomas, who had battled with Nazi mobs in the streets of Berlin before the war. He had a lively Polish face—one attraction of Berliners was this Polish strain—and was touchingly pro-British. He was captured during the war in the desert when serving with the *Afrika Korps*, and when his British interrogators discovered his revolutionary past he agreed to be parachuted back into Germany as an agent. After training in Britain, he was taken to an airfield one night to be flown over, but at the last moment was told that he could not go because his wife had been sent to a concentration camp. It was feared that she would not survive in the event of his capture. The thought that the British were not prepared to risk the life of his wife made him an Anglophile for life.

Each of the four powers, including the Soviet Union, also had military missions attached to the headquarters of the others, and the American, British and French missions in East Germany were well informed on Soviet troop strengths and movements. With the help of aerial reconnaissance, it was most unlikely that the Soviet forces could have been reinforced or re-equipped without their knowledge. Russian troops were largely moved by train, and they still travelled 40 men to a cattle truck. I watched a division leaving Neubrandenberg for home, and it was reminiscent of the first world war. I occasionally spotted officers of the British military mission during my East German trips, which suggested that they were very active. They also attended Soviet army manouevres, and were well acquainted with the latest equipment.

Thus most of the intelligence agencies in West Berlin were unnecessary, and in any case the west could not hope to outdo the east in espionage. Many East German agents, who of course worked for the Soviet Union, entered West Germany as refugees, and there was no way of screening them. Some were painfully successful. The confidential secretary of the West German defence minister, Franz Josef Strauss, saw every top-secret document in his office and passed the contents back to East Berlin. The leak was discovered, but she disappeared before the security men arrived. She was eventually traced to the British embassy in Bonn, where she was working for the resident spooks. Their faces were red for weeks. Years later another East German agent was discovered working on the staff of Willy Brandt, who felt obliged to resign from the chancellorship.

Those West Berlin spies, even the non-spurious, could not compete, but Khrushchev's pressure on the city only relaxed because of American firmness. He had visited the United States, and, judging from his public statements, what he saw of the industrial power and vitality of that country made him more cautious. The cold war seemed to be thawing, and in 1960 a summit conference was arranged in Paris. Bonn would be of no news value until the conference finished, and we decided to see the passion play in Oberammergau in southern Bavaria. The play was a disappointment, but the beer was good and the area rich in rococo architecture. We indulged ourselves for a couple of days before heading north again. I was out of touch, the car radio was not working, but was not bothered until I saw a message chalked on a board outside a service area north of Limburg. It read, *Herr Heren. London ruft.* I wheeled in and called London, and was told that Khrushchev had quit the summit over the U2 incident and was heading for East Berlin. He was in a towering rage, and the worst was feared. Could I get into Berlin before he closed the road? I drove straight to Cologne airport, handed over the wheel to Pat, who only mildly protested and caught the last plane to Berlin.

The only other passengers were journalists. Here we go again, I thought. The vultures coming in at the death. And so it seemed when we landed. The people at Tempelhof were their usual stoical and efficient selves but the building was half empty and silent. The streets outside were also deserted although night had just fallen. One of my colleagues on the plane had arranged for his stringer, or local correspondent, to meet him, and we piled into his car and drove to East Berlin. The stringer said that Khrushchev was to speak that night at the *Seewindenhalle*, where Hitler had held mass meetings, and the allied garrisons were on full alert. The West Berlin police guard had been doubled at the Brandenberger Tor, where we crossed into East Berlin, and one of them said that a detachment of British troops was standing to in the Tiergarten. We drove slowly towards the East German

Vopos, and one of them sharply ordered us to dismount. Arc-lamps had been erected on their side, turning the Tor into a dramatic backcloth. Looking back, I could see the West Berlin policemen watching us intently, and the group stationed on the top of a nearby building who maintained surveillance of the crossing round the clock. Beyond the Russian guards at the Soviet war memorial stood impassively looking to their front. The road back to the centre of West Berlin was utterly deserted. We seemed to be isolated on a film set. No wonder English thriller writers were attracted to the city.

A young Vopo, with a burp gun slung across his belly, asked where we were going, and I said it was none of his business. We were British and Americans, citizens of occupying powers who could go where we pleased. He jerked the muzzle of the gun forward, and somebody behind said, Steady, Lou. I was not trying to be tough, but I was not going to kowtow to a commy cop at that early stage. He walked away stiffly, and as we waited I remembered the last time I had met Khrushchev. It was at the Leipzig fair, and on the last night there had been the inevitable reception in the Soviet pavilion. I had been in Leipzig for five days, sharing a room at the Bayerischer Hof, a crummy hotel at the end of a tramline. The trams turned round the hotel for the return journey, and had managed even to keep me awake as their steel wheels grounded protestingly on the sharp corners. That night in the Soviet pavilion I suddenly wanted the warm delights of West Berlin, and decided to drive back as soon as Khrushchev had gone. David Binder, a young American freelance who afterwards joined the *New York Times*, asked if he could come along.

The *Autobahn* was like the grave, and I drove well above 160 kph while Binder sipped vodka from a bottle he had taken from the Soviet pavilion. Somewhere south of Dessau a bridge across the road was being repaired, but I saw the red light and warning signs too late and zoomed past a 30 kph sign at four times that speed. Beyond the tunnel of scaffolding was a police motorcycle and sidecar. Binder urged me to keep going but we were more than 150 kilometres from Berlin and I stopped and reversed. Two policemen waddled towards us in heavy greatcoats, and I apologized. I had seen the warning sign too late. One of them inspected our papers while the other questioned me. I explained that we were western correspondents returning from the fair, but he was not impressed. He had a thick Saxon accent and only an approximate grasp of German grammar, and to my horror Binder began to correct him. 'Nein, nein, Herr Wachmeister, nicht. . . .' The copper was not unnaturally annoyed, and he wanted to know why we were travelling so late. I said that we had been delayed because of the Khrushchev reception, and assumed that the name would impress him. Not a bit of it. He wanted to know if I had been drinking, and guardedly I allowed that I had had a glass of wine, a mere *Viertel*. He clearly did not believe me, but triumphantly announced that I had broken the laws of the German Democratic Republic. It was forbidden to drive within twelve hours of having a drink. The fine was 25 marks. I gave him 25 East German marks, but he demanded West German currency. Clearly he was on the make. The East German mark could then be bought on the Berlin black market for one quarter of its official value, but I had bought mine at the official rate and we were in East Germany. To hell with it, I said. Let's go. Where? To your superior officer. Take me to your leader, I added theatrically, savouring the word *Führer*. We stared at each other, and then, using two words he had presumably heard uttered by some British or American soldier at the end of the war, he said in that terrible Saxon accent, Foock off.

We foocked off, at about 180 kph. In West Berlin, we drove straight to the Kempinski Bristol hotel, and although it was well after midnight, had a couple of double dry martinis at the bar and then oysters, steaks and a litre of black velvet. It was wonderful to be back in the decadent west.

Some of this passed through my mind as we waited. Not that it helped much. We were going in, not coming out of East Germany, and had no idea how the night would end. Also I had not eaten since noon, but that did not explain my mood. It was shared by the others. We did not scare easily, but there had been too many alarums and crises. Khrushchev had made too many threats. The theatricality of the scene; the silent city, the arclamps, the Vopos, the West Berlin police and the unseen British troops only heightened the mood. Finally the young Vopo returned with a sergeant, a polite almost fatherly man, who returned our passports with an apology. He asked if we were going to the Khrushchev meeting and gave us elaborate directions.

Although the tension was almost tangible, he was the archetypal German again doing his duty. We got back into the car, he saluted and said, *Aufwiedersehen*. I fervently hoped so. See yuh, said somebody in the back of the car, and we drove off into the ruins of East Berlin.

We parked the BMW near the entrance to the hall and a milling crowd, mainly men and obviously party activists, surrounded us. The big car, with its West German plates, our clothes, and perhaps even the soap, toothpaste and aftershave we used, separated us from the crowd. Generally East Berliners then treated visitors from the west with defensive indifference or envy, but that night they crowded us looking for trouble. We eventually pushed our way into the lobby where some functionaries made themselves difficult but we were rescued by the press attaché of the Soviet embassy. He spoke to another functionary, who led us into the hall and to a row of seats near the platform.

The hall was hot and crowded, and throbbed with the persistant beat of a brass band with a strengthened percussion section. The crowd was clapping in time to the beat, and it sounded like marching troops. They appeared to be mesmerized by the beat, and I was reminded of those old newsreel shots of Hitler haranguing the crowd in this very hall. Only the political insignia and slogans had changed. A couple of demagogic speeches were delivered to enthuse the crowd, and then to a great roll of drums Khrushchev appeared accompanied by Walter Ulbricht, the East German leader. His spectacles glinted in the footlights, but behind the Lenin-type beard his face was pale and drawn. He did not look like a man who knew that his time had come. It was the first intimation that Khrushchev had had second thoughts. The Russian, enormously impressive despite his waddle and ridiculously-wide trousers, acknowledged the cheers and forest of clenched fists but he was quiet, almost chastened. He looked like a patient man who had been wronged or misunderstood. Apart from a few salutations, he did not speak but stood, looking towards us from time to time, while his speech was read for him.

The usual harsh words were said about Adenauer and Willy Brandt, the governing mayor of West Berlin, but the speech made clear, to the point of repetition, that his intentions had suddenly become wholly peaceful. The summit conference had failed because the Pentagon did not want to resolve the world's problems peacefully. The U2 flight was an act of aggression, but in his view not a prelude to war. Rage made the attackers blind, and hot heads had to be allowed to cool off. He had postponed the summit to let the dust settle. There would be no separate peace treaty with East Germany before another attempt had been made to reach agreement with the west. Another summit conference could be held in six to eight months. Meanwhile, he would do nothing to increase tension or return to the cold war. He would follow the Marxist-Leninist policy of peaceful coexistence, and strive for international relaxation, disarmament and the peaceful solution of controversial questions.

I could hardly believe my own ears. I was both disappointed because the story was an anti-climax and relieved that the *Götterdammerung* had been postponed. The crowd reflected my reaction. The tense atmosphere dissipated itself before the end of the speech, and Ulbricht stared fixedly up at the ceiling. Belatedly I realized that the anti-climax was the story, and we made our way to the exit. The Soviet press attaché was suddenly jovial, he must have been as relieved as we were, and a path through the crowd was cleared for us. I pondered my lead as we raced back to West Berlin, and this time we were not delayed at the checkpoint. The Vopos waved us through, and a West Berlin policeman shouted, *Alles gut? Alles gut*, we chorussed as the driver gunned the car to the telephones. I dictated my story from the Reuter office, reporting the evening deadpan and quoting Khrushchev from notes I had scribbled in my notebook, below some thoughts I had recorded on the anti-Semitism of the Oberammergau passion play. Afterwards we had beers and Steinhagers somewhere on the Kür'dam, and I realized that I was famished. I ordered supper, not oysters and steak this time, but *Erbsensuppe mit Würstchen*. Later that night I called Pat, and said I would fly back on the morning plane. She asked about Khrushchev, and I said that we would probably survive for a few more months.

7   *Tieless to the Horizon*

The past may or may not be prologue, but on a number of occasions I was sent on special assignment because I had earlier worked in the area concerned or knew the people involved. There was probably another reason. The office knew that I liked hot-weather countries, that I disliked wearing a jacket and necktie and, I like to think, that I operated efficiently when away from established news sources. Whatever the reason or reasons, when I was the chief correspondent in Germany I was sent to some faraway places including the Horn of Africa. In those days, apart from Ethiopia, it was still largely a colonial area. The Somali littoral was divided into British and former Italian Somaliland, the French were still in Djibouti, and Eritrea had the status of an occupied enemy territory and was administered by Britain. Somalia was largely desert and very hot, but I had enjoyed my earlier visits. I liked Somalis—I was once a member of the Free Somali movement—and Ethiopia and Emperor Haile Selassie fascinated me.

I had had bouts of the giggles, mainly because the Ethiopian capital, Addis Ababa, so vividly reminded me of Evelyn Waugh's *Scoop*. It was then very much a shanty town, and it must have had the largest red-light district in the world. I had the impression that prostitutes occupied about half of Addis. This was no doubt a gross exaggeration, but whores were one of the country's largest exports presumably because Africans elsewhere admired their fine features. One night I was invited to dine at the British military mission, which was some miles out of town. Another guest was the resident English chaplain. It was the usual uproarious British military occasion. Even the chaplain had a drop too much to drink, and the commanding officer lent us a couple of horses. He thought that the ride home would clear our heads. We must have looked odd because both of us were wearing dinner jackets, but it was a beautiful night and our heads soon cleared. In fact, we felt so good that the chaplain pressed me to have a nightcap at his vicarage. To my amazement, the last half mile to the church was lined with brothels, or little bars with one or two prostitutes waiting for clients. They were very decorous, and I suggested that it must be the influence of the Church of England.

Before my first interview with Haile Selassie in 1952, the minister of the pen (a lovely title) instructed me to wear a morning coat and topper. I had never owned such an outfit, and as a compromise I appeared at the palace long before noon wearing my dinner jacket and black tie. I was also obliged to bow three times at frequent intervals as I approached the emperor sitting on a dais at the end of the long throne room. He watched me gravely as I made my slow progress apparently oblivious of the hissed instructions of the minister of the pen telling me when to halt and bow again. In comparison, Buckingham Palace was as informal as a disco, but clearly the emperor would have been affronted if strict protocol had not been observed. After all, he was the Lion of Judah, and claimed descent from King Solomon and the Queen of Sheba, but his enormous dignity did not rest upon such archaic nonsense.

The interview lasted about half an hour, and he then invited me to sit down and in turn questioned me closely on the state of the world. It was an eerie experience. Haile Selassie had been deposed by the Italians and put back on the throne by the British, but the outside world was still a threatening place. Western colonialism was dead or dying, but he must have known that the physical isolation of his highland kingdom was no defence against the disturbing ideas sweeping the Middle East and much of Africa. Ethiopia was much more backward than most of the old European African colonies, and in a determined effort to make some progress and avoid discontent he retained a number of foreign advisers. Presumably still suspicious of larger powers, he divided his advisers in order to rule without fear of foreign intervention. As I recall, the Swedes trained the royal bodyguard, which numbered 10,000, while the British took care of the army. An American was in charge of finance, and the education adviser was a Canadian. He seemed willing to try everything, except popular government. He was very much a medieval monarch. Power was his stock in trade, and he was determined not to relinquish or share it. There was to be his downfall eventually. I thought I saw it coming, and in my eyes his stature was enhanced by the inevitability of tragedy.

The Ethiopians had been colonialists in their time. They had descended from the highlands to seize the Ogaden, and only the arrival of the European powers prevented them from taking what was left of Somali territory. They had also laid claim to Eritrea in the north. The claim was renewed after the second world war, and in 1950 the United Nations sent a commission of five member nations to decide its future. I flew in to cover it. The commission was the usual UN farce. Britain, which had administered the territory since the war, wanted to hand it over to Ethiopia, and the commissioners divided not on the merits of the the case but whether they liked or disliked Britain. For instance, Britain was supported by a Scandinavian and no less automatically opposed by a Guatamalan because of his country's claim to the then British Honduras. Only the Burmese commissioner appeared to have an open mind, so open that it re-tained little of the testimony given. The British foreign office representative decided that whoever presented him with a case of scotch before the final decision was reached would win his vote. Whether or not the case was delivered, the Burmese voted for the British solution and Eritrea went to Ethiopia.

The locals who over the years had been misruled by Arabs, Turks and Italians, had already raised the flag of revolt. The British called them *shifta*, or bandits, but they saw themselves as freedom fighters. Whatever they were, they had the right to misrule themselves but the poor old British army was sent to chase them out of the bush. One night Dickie Williams of the BBC and I were told that intelligence had pinpointed the village where the headquarters was established, and we were asked if we wanted to be in at the kill. We had a wild drive across open country, then a long approach march to positions which we took up before dawn. We went in before first light, but the *shifta* had gone or had never been there in the first place. Nobody seemed to know for certain. We were offered the local beer, which looked like thin gruel and had to be sipped through handkerchiefs.

Rather sulkily Dickie and I said we were going back to Asmara, the capital, and the embarrassed company commander offered us two mules and an escort. We set out for the long trek home but soon lost the escort. They were two young national servicemen, and they were exhausted. Without a word being said, we dismounted and told them to hop on. Later that day, just as the sun was setting, we came in sight of the army camp and one of the soldiers said it was time for us to have a ride. Not on your bloody life, said Dickie, who was about 5 foot 3 and was wearing suede shoes, and I took the salute as we passed the guard.

In 1956, when Britain was preparing to invade Egypt and three weeks before Pat was expecting another baby, I was sent to the Horn on a final imperial mission. In those days the foreign pages of *The Times* were entitled Imperial and Foreign News, and although the paper had long advocated decolonization it still took its imperial responsibilities seriously. I was to decide whether the Haud should go to Ethiopia or to the then British Somaliland. The foreign office supported the Ethiopian claim for the contested area and the colonial office naturally defended the interests of its colonial charge. I was to be an unofficial adjudicator. The Haud was said to be vital for the Somali nomads because although grazing was thin, even non-existent by European standards, it kept their camel herds alive at certain times of the year.

My progress through the Horn of Africa was almost viceregal. For colonial governors and administrators *The Times* was still the house magazine of empire, and from Aden on I was gravely received at government houses and commissioners' bungalows. The conversations were extraordinarily frank. The original strategic reason for raising the Union Jack along those inhospitable shores had long ago lost its importance. The Indian empire had passed into history, and if admirals, generals and foreign office men in Whitehall still talked of keeping open its sea routes the men on the ground were concerned only with the welfare of the local people. They accepted that they would soon have to quit, and they had come to terms with the local politicians who expected to succeed them. Their main anxieties were for their pet projects, such as roads, water supplies, clinics and schools, which they had nursed along over the years. It was all very personal.

I was a long way from the rhetoric of empire and anti-colonialism, and the splendours of New Delhi. They lived very simply.

In Hargeisa, the capital of British Somaliland, I stayed with the colonial secretary and his wife in a bungalow not much bigger than an English suburban house. On my arrival I had a shower, and unwittingly used that day's ration of water. After supper we were joined by about a dozen Somalis. There was no colour bar. Everybody obviously knew each other well, and one Somali, who had learned his English in Cardiff's Tiger Bay, poured the whisky and gin. There was a lot of easy laughter until we settled down on the verandah, when I found myself conducting a kind of durbar.

Most of the tribes were in the Haud for winter grazing, and I joined the district officer who kept an eye on them. He moved with them, living in two large EPIP tents, one a sleeping tent with a screened bathing area, and the other served as a living room and office. I slept on a camp bed under a flysheet. His small encampment was comfortable by army campaigning standards, but still spartan. Most of the food came out of cans. In the evenings we had a couple of whiskies. It was like being back in the army, except for the loneliness and the local aperitif, gin and camel's milk. The spirit cut the heavy milk fat, and I suppose it was sustaining but I would have preferred a dry martini.

The Haud looked more inhospitable than the Jordanian and Saudi Arabian deserts, probably because of the rock-strewn ground. It looked completely barren, but the thin, almost-invisible pasture supported thousands of camels. The nomads were very different from the Beduin of the Middle East. They did not ride camels, but herded them as if they were cattle. The Somalis were also tall and more robust. The women were high-breasted, and in silhouette looked like drawings in *Vogue*. They were very handsome, except that they rarely washed because of the lack of water. They lived almost exclusively on camel's milk and blood. After trying the mixture, I decided that I preferred camel's milk with gin. Nevertheless, it must have been a sustaining if unbalanced diet because apart from their fine physique nomadic life was almost unbelievably hard. I saw more than one tribe on the move, and everybody walked, apart from a few old crones. They were perched on the camels carrying the hides and large hoops which were used for tents. In hard times, I was told, they were simply abandoned.

There could be no doubt that the Haud was essential for

nomadic survival, and after a few days the district officer drove me to Jigjiga, where I caught a plane for Addis. I thanked him for his hospitality, and invited him to lunch but he seemed to be anxious to get back. I think he enjoyed my company, but clearly he preferred the loneliness of the Haud to Jigjiga. In fact, the town had little to commend it, despite the jolly name. The airport was so much sun-baked ground and a small wooden building in which an Italian ran a restaurant. He was serving three Italian engineers with enormous helpings of pasta, which I refused because the restaurant was hot and fly-blown. They went on to eat steak and chips, and I settled for some ham, fruit and a bottle of chianti. The plane from Aden was late, and they ordered cheese and more wine. They were expansive and unbuttoned when the plane finally came in.

The Dakota belonged to the Royal Ethiopian airline, and I knew what to expect. They were like country buses, carrying freight as well as passengers. I had previously flown in them with a variety of freight, including bales of *kut* the narcotic chewed throughout the Horn and in the Aden territories. This one was carrying a spare radial engine, or it might have been a drugged bull. I had travelled with both cargoes, but have forgotten when. What I did remember was that in the rear of the plane were stacks of cases of coca cola. They were being flown to Addis to test the market.

The Italians followed me aboard, and they sat opposite on canvas bucket seats. They were smiling amiably, and I assumed that they would fall asleep after takeoff but I was in for a surprise. Jigjiga is at the foot of the Ethiopian escarpment, and a funicular railway would have been a more suitable form of transport. The plane seemed mainly to fly in wide circles to gain altitude because Addis, which was not so far distant, was 8,000 feet above sea level. The afternoon heat refracted off the escarpment, the plane bucked as if it was in a storm and the Italians began to vomit. The Dakota was of course not pressurized and as we reached our ceiling the caps of the coke bottles blew off. The contents filled the plane like a miasma in which floated pieces of pasta. Nothing could be done. I just crouched in my seat getting steadily wetter and trying to brush pasta out of my hair. The plane finally landed, and I was in for another surprise. For the first time in my career, the ambassadorial Rolls was waiting for me. The driver looked

appropriately aghast, but the young second secretary sent to meet
me roared with laughter and helped to brush the remaining
pasta from my clothes. Wrapped in a picnic tablecloth taken from
the boot of the car, I was finally allowed to step into the splendour
of that wonderful ambassadorial machine.

As mentioned earlier in this book, I was nearly interned in
Cairo when I flew back to Bonn for the birth of our third child,
but I was back again in the Middle East in 1958. David Holden,
then our correspondent there, was due for long leave and I
happily agreed to replace him for a couple of months. West
Germany was dull, Pat wanted the children to spend some time in
England because they hardly knew it, and trouble was again
brewing in my old stamping ground. This time it was Lebanon, a
once very pleasant little country.

Lebanon was a member of the Arab League and the language
was Arabic, but it was hardly an Arab country. A slight majority
of the population was Christian, but the Muslim minority was
further reduced by the large number of Druse who belonged to
an heretical sect and formed a distinct community. The country
had escaped the deadening hand of Muslim conformism and
puritanism, and was European, almost North American, in its
intellectual freedom and business acumen. They did well as
emigrants. Ralph Nader is an obvious example. They were also
great traders, and liked to see themselves as the Switzerland of
the Middle East. The French Jesuit and American Protestant
universities continued to be great liberating influences, and the
brief period of French colonialism had left behind a respect for
fine cooking and the best vegetable growers in the region. The
local wine was potable.

The religious differences created tensions, but they were kept
within bounds until President Camille Chamoun decided that he
wanted a second term in office. This was not possible under the
constitution, and talk of constitutional amendment appeared to
threaten the delicate balance between Christians and Muslims.
Occasional acts of violence developed into rebellion. The army
numbered only 9,000 and contained many Muslim units, and the
chief of staff, General Fuad Chahab, was unwilling to fight for
Chamoun's second term. This was the cause of the crisis, but
President Nasser of Egypt had recovered from his 1956 defeat
and was again supporting Muslim revolutionary movements

throughout the Middle East. Jordan was the main target, but the Muslim dissidents in Lebanon were supplied with arms by way of Syria.

The Lebanese crisis could have been quickly resolved if Chamoun had abided by the constitution and retired, but he chose to see himself as a defender of western civilization. The Americans accepted this fiction, and although they had opposed the Anglo-French landings in Egypt two years earlier a much larger force of American troops was eventually landed in Lebanon. They invented the Eisenhower Doctrine to make the intervention respectable and welcomed the landing of British troops in Jordan. The political ambition of Chamoun, whose name was previously unknown in the United States (How do you spell it, was the first question of an American reporter who came in with the troops) had created a very serious international crisis. It quickly spread with the help of Nasser. In Iraq the army overthrew the government and murdered King Faisal and the prime minister, Nuri as Said. The entire Middle East looked as if it might go up in flames.

My arrival was nicely timed. I arrived in Beirut less than three weeks before the American intervention, but already it was no longer the pleasant city I had long known. Not that all my memories of it were pleasant. I had covered the UN conference held there in 1949 to negotiate a general conciliation after the first Arab-Israel war, but the Arabs had made that impossible by refusing to resettle the Arab refugees. I could remember being appalled by their representatives sitting in the lobby of the St. George hotel, fuddling their beads and calmly stating that they would never agree to resettlement. Hundreds of thousands of men, women and children were condemned to a lifetime spent in the refugee camps. They were still there when I returned in 1958. I saw them driving in from the airfield, and by the seventies their terrorists were in action in many parts of the world. In the late seventies they were to destroy Beirut.

In 1958 only parts of it were being destroyed by gunfire and unexplained explosions, but life still went on. The CIA was there in force. Beirut was its main station for the Middle East, as it was for the Russian KGB. Kim Philby was also there, pretending to be the correspondent for *The Observer*. He spent most of his time in the bar of the Normandie hotel, conspicuous despite his retiring manner because of his seersucker suit and his drinking. He was always polite and stutteringly monosyllabic. Most nights he got helplessly drunk, which was why later I could hardly believe that he had been a double-agent. How could a man with so much on his mind remain discreet when he got drunk regularly? Of course, he might have been saved by the stutter.

I checked in at the St. George hotel, which I had always rated as one of the best pubs anywhere, and it was a pleasant place to return to after an arduous and occasionally dangerous day's work. Lucullus, the fish restaurant just beyond Digger's bar, was also as good as ever. I was enjoying myself, especially when some of my old friends and rivals flew in from different parts of the world to cover the best story going. Even Randolph Churchill arrived, but soon flew out when a friend at the British Embassy refused to put him up. It was too good to last of course. As the level of violence increased, the standard of the fresh salads at St. George became less than perfect, and it seemed wrong to go water skiing from the little jetty below the downstairs bar before leaving to cover the indiscriminate killing of innocent people. A curfew was imposed, except in a small area where most of the international hotels were then situated. This looked like gross class discrimination, but it did not help us much. The menu at the St. George became an empty boast. Much worse, the curfew at night turned much of the city into a free fire zone, and we had to file our messages at the central telegraph office which was directly in the line of fire.

The office stood on an avenue leading up to raised ground where the Muslim rebels were entrenched. Apart from machine guns, they were also armed with an anti-tank gun which they tended to fire whenever they saw a vehicle, even a taxi. Most of us accepted the inevitable, and became rather adept at dodging in and out of the telegraph office. A man sent out from London to cover the crisis, for, of all things, a gossip column expected the wife of his paper's resident correspondent to do his dirty and dangerous work for him, and a *Guardian* man became hysterical. It was difficult to understand. We were reporting a civil war, which because of its nature was very nasty. He was pro-Arab, which was unusual for a *Guardian* man. He was no doubt distressed because his beloved Arabs were being nasty to each other, but the only odd thing about that war was that foreign correspondents spent their nights in first-class hotels instead of slit trenches or press camps. It became even odder at the height of the war when a Swiss hotelier named Hoffmann made us an offer.

I had known him well when he managed a hotel in Cairo before he came to Beirut to take charge of the Palm Beach hotel. It was not quite in the same class as the St. George, but it had suites instead of bedrooms and they were all efficiently air-conditioned. The swimming pool was sheltered from shot and shell, and the martinis could have been mixed in the tea room of New York's Plaza hotel. Hoffmann had always preferred pro-fessional travellers such as foreign correspondents, but then we were the only travellers available. He offered us a ten per cent cut on everything if we moved across, and, even more enticing, round-the-clock service. We moved. Hoffmann was as good as his word, except that we were expected to dine in the night club with its strippers and French singers trying to sound like Piaf. My loyalty was sorely tried until Emile, a Greek who ran a bar and grill up the road, called to say that he was serving frogs' legs and lobster that night. He was trying desperately to salvage something from his Beirut investment to buy a taverne on some Greek island, and we were happy to help rescue him. I hope he made it. The frogs' legs were excellent.

Life was not all lobster and frogs' legs, or even arak and kebabs. It became increasingly dangerous—and frustrating. Censorship became unpredictable, in part because Levantine politics became incomprehensible even for the experts as Chamoun changed his political position. The British ambassador, George Middleton, whom I had known in Delhi, was helpful. He was also experienced and shrewd, but I suspected not fully informed. The American ambassador was too well-informed; he was actively organizing armed intervention and being too un-American to talk about it. The United Nations was as usual useless and insolent. The ob-server teams had taken over a splendid hotel on the corniche, and well away from the fighting. Their security guards, for the most part glass-eyed Swedes, treated us as if we were armed marauders. I was grateful, and not for the first time, that big-power politics had prevented that self-serving bureaucracy from assuming real power.

Dag Hammerskjold, the secretary-general, arrived and was just as bad. He was always accompanied by a bodyguard who looked as if he had been seconded from the Mafia. On one occasion he elbowed me away when I politely asked a question, and Hammerskjold smiled approvingly. That rough stuff was perhaps of no importance, but Hammerskjold believed his own propaganda. Men who worked closely with him were convinced that he thought he was God's gift to mankind, or whatever they acknowledge as God in Sweden. He knew he was always right, which was very dangerous. Fashionable liberals and the radical chic admired him, presumably because they hoped that the world could avoid its intractable problems by leaving them to the United Nations to resolve.

The Muslim rebels were even more frustrating because at first they appeared to have no approachable leadership. Ardent Baathists, for the most part attractive youngsters who unfortunately had exchanged the dead hand of traditional Islam for the equally arid local version of Marxism, were eager to explain what Nasser was trying to do for the Arabs. I enjoyed their company, Baathism had not yet destroyed their youthful enthusiasm, but they knew little about the local opposition to Chamoun. The only articulate spokesman was Saeb Salaam, a prominent politician who had sided with the rebels and lived in their stronghold above the city. I managed to make contact eventually, and was occasionally conducted through the lines for an interview.

I was blindfolded for my first visit, and when the bandana was removed I found myself in a courtyard surrounded by young men elaborately over-armed with every variety of automatic weapon. I was frisked for a final time, and taken into a darkened room where I saw the dim reflection of Saeb in the door mirror of a large Victorian almirah. The room might well have been darkened against the afternoon heat, but it was suitably sinister until I had a good look at Saeb Salaam. He was sitting at ease and in his braces, his plump hands folded over his tummy, and the jowly face was illumed by a pair of very shrewd and humorous eyes. I instantly warmed to him. Here was a real pro, a man in the same league as Mayor Richard Daley of Chicago. Neither was lovable, but they knew what they were doing. They made their calculations, and went ahead and did it. For that reason, Saeb was in his own queer way the only intelligent man in war-torn Beirut, and possibly its only saviour.

I did not believe his protestations that he would defend the

noble Lebanese constitution to the death, at least I was not prepared to believe that he was only moved to defend the established rule of law. I doubted that he approved of Nasser.
I knew that the western embassies in the city below regarded him
as a scallywag, but his own political ambitions coincided with
the best interests of Lebanon. Chamoun had to retire if those
fragile arrangements between Christians and Muslims were to be
revived, and without them peace was impossible. Saeb not only
knew this, but he had enough political sense and political allies
to revive those arrangements. He was conducting negotiations
while his wild men were firing that anti-tank gun at any moving
target below.

Despite his physical isolation, Saeb Salaam seemed to know
of everything going on in the city, including the presidential
palace and the American embassy. I knew that American intervention was inevitable. The US 6th Fleet was in the eastern
Mediterranean, and by all accounts just over the horizon, but I
learned of the exact day and hour from one of Saeb's henchmen.
Alex Valentine of Reuters and I laid our plans accordingly.

We had been in Korea together, and knowing that it would be
a long day we decided to have a good luncheon in the restaurant
on Pigeon Rock. It was an obvious choice; the Arab cuisine was
superb, the restaurant had a splendid view of the bay where the
troops were expected to land, and we would be beyond reach of
those of our colleagues who had not been forewarned of the
landing. We had eaten and were finishing the half bottle of
arak—the slightly-scented Lebanese variety is by far the best—
when the 6th Fleet came over the horizon. It was a splendid sight,
and we watched appreciatively until we established which beach
the landing craft were likely to use. Then we were off in a hire
car along the corniche, and to our delight realized that the
landing craft were heading for an exclusive swimming beach. At
that time of the day it was usually crowded with girls in bikinis
and we anticipated the contrasts. Being a news agency correspondent, Valentine had to file quickly, and he tried out a couple of
possible leads as we speeded to the beach. Both were too hilarious
for publication.

We arrived before the boats, and not one of our colleagues
was in sight. The beach was ornamented with good-looking girls
in bikinis. Katie Antonious, the only woman intellectual I had

met who combined brains with good looks was also there. The
girls did not scatter when the landing flaps went down and the
Marines charged ashore. It was wonderfully funny, and I exposed
a roll of film. The first wave of men, heavily ladened with the
accoutrements of war, dug in self-consciously, and the second
seized the club-house and changing rooms. They tried to look
warlike, at least while the officers were watching, but looked
like film extras who had charged onto the wrong set. Years later
I remembered them when I saw *Blazing Saddles,* and laughed twice
as much.

The situation was of course intensely serious, and we had
messages to file. Valentine found a telephone in an obscure
office, dictated a couple of snaps, and then thoughtfully removed
the microphone from the phone thus making it useless for the
opposition. Whenever we wanted to file we put the thing
together again, and dictated to our offices in London, Rome or
Paris—whatever overseas number the operator could raise for
us. This worked wonderfully well, we both scored scoops, until
one of the opposition caught us at it. He screamed so hysterically
that we made him a present of the mike. In any case, there was
nothing more to be done on the beach and we headed for the
airport just in case reinforcements were to be flown in. It must
have been our lucky day. The transports bringing in American
paratroopers from West Germany were beginning to arrive. The
airport was closed to normal traffic, but I also managed to hand
the film to a passenger aboard a KLM flight from Bombay which
had to be given permission to land because it was short of fuel. It
was faithfully delivered, and one picture splendidly filled a half
page.

We celebrated that night, but not too well. The Americans
had only seized the airport and its approaches. Their beachhead
was small, and there was no indication how the landing would be
received by the Lebanese, Nasser or the Russians. Chamoun
obviously welcomed their arrival, but General Chahab was an
unknown quantity and Saeb Salaam was incensed. We got up at
dawn next day, drove towards the airport, and found the
Lebanese army, all 9,000 of them, apparently prepared to fight.
Tanks with loaded guns were in position, and although the
Lebanese did not enjoy a reputation as fighting men, they were
much too sensible for that, they had chosen their battle positions

well. They would not have survived a prolonged attack by the
fighter bombers of the 6th Fleet, but the Americans were clearly
in a quandary. They could hardly engage the armed forces of the
government they had landed to protect. We reached the airport
without being stopped by the Lebanese or Americans, and
awaited events. Once again they refused to follow the expected
course. I was enjoying a good cup of French coffee in the sun when
Admiral Holloway, the American commanding officer, and the
ambassador, Robert McClintock, emerged from the terminal
building to meet General Chehab, the Lebanese chief of staff.
They talked surrounded by a circle of advisers and an outer circle
of correspondents. It was doubly ludicrous because we pro-
fessionals were outnumbered by a mob of American hometown
reporters who kept demanding to know what was being said and
what the hell did it mean anyway. I do not want to sound
snobbish, but they did prevent us from hearing what was said.

A deal was reached, the Lebanese army stood down, and the
American troops moved into the city where they were welcomed
by the bartenders and brothelkeepers if not by the Arab nationalists. The British landing in Jordan went well, and although the
Iraqi *coup* was bloody and unsettling the disciplined exercise of
American power chastened Nasser and deterred the Russians.
This was the difference between real power and the pretensions
of Britain. I did not regret it. We had had our day, and not done
all that well. Eisenhower, accused of being bumbling and naive by
American liberals who later blundered into Cuba and Vietnam,
demonstrated his understanding of power. Saeb Salaam was permitted to do his Levantine best and was rewarded with the
prime ministership, peace returned to Lebanon for a few more
years, and the American troops were pulled out before Thanksgiving.

*

West German politics were very tame after the Middle East.
Christian Democracy, still in the ascendancy, had served its
historic purpose throughout much of western Europe in helping
to stem Soviet imperialism. New political ideas were necessary
if further progress was to be made internally, but in West
Germany the Social Democrats did not then seem to be an
acceptable instrument for change. The party was dominated by

bureaucrats, decent men who would have done well in Transport House but lacked vision and popular appeal. The party was still Marxist, which offended many Catholics and scared the middle class. Ideologically the Social Democrats were in fact moving towards the centre, and some were actively disengaging themselves from the Marxist past. The most prominent was Willy Brandt, who had fled Nazi Germany and served with the Norwegians during the war. He was almost bilingual in English, and his politics were similar to those of Hugh Gaitskell in Britain and Adlai Stevenson in the United States.

Brandt had an engaging and modest personality. He had become the governing mayor of West Berlin, a position which was beginning to make him an international figure. Western leaders who visited West Berlin saw him as a man who genuinely personified all that was best in the city and West Germany. Inevitably he became a contender for the leadership of the SPD. Even outside the party some Germans regarded him as a possible future chancellor, despite Christian Democratic propaganda which in an un-Christian way recalled his illegitimate birth and his service with the Norwegians during the war. The Christian Democrats seemed to suggest that he was unsuitable for high office because he had fled Nazi Germany to fight Hitler. It was very odd, but they persuaded some British Tories and American Republicans.

In many ways Brandt was an unlikely candidate for high office. He looked good, and was an effective speaker, but there was something tentative about him. He was a thoroughly nice man, which suggested weakness or softness. We first met in the mid-fifties at the Social Democrats' annual conference in Munich. He was standing at the back of the hall waiting to be elected to the *Vorstand*, the party's executive committee. Because of his West Berlin power base and his assumed leadership of the new generation of non-Marxist party members, his election was expected to be inevitable but there was a revolt from the floor. The old guard were still fairly strong, and Wehner, a former communist, was elected instead. The party did break with its Marxist past two years later at its Bad Godesberg conference, but the revolt in Munich was a setback for the party and Brandt. He had prepared his acceptance speech, and unexpected defeat brought tears to his eyes. He was struggling to pull himself together when I suggested a beer and Steinhager, which he gratefully accepted. Thereafter I called on him regularly in West Berlin, where he steadily grew in stature without losing any of his niceness.

He still appeared to be indecisive, which some people confused with weakness. It was nothing of the sort. The job of governing mayor provided him with an international platform, but little power to influence alliance policy. He was well aware of this. More important, he was pondering the future of Germany with an honesty rare in politics. He knew that his own people had committed terrible crimes under Hitler. He was also beginning to realize that Germany could not be reunified in the foreseeable future, and that there could be no peace and stability in Europe until men and women of his generation recognized and accepted the disagreeable fact that they would probably not live to see reunification. Few Germans were prepared to accept it publicly, and for Brandt the possible consequences of pursuing such a policy were dangerous. There was no real future for Berlin while Germany remained divided, and he was its governing mayor. He could not accept the continued division without appearing to agree with Khrushchev. Their reasons were very different, but that would be difficult to prove in an election campaign although his anti-communism and dedication to representative government and human rights were beyond doubt. Nor could he hope to expiate German war crimes, especially in countries such as Poland, without offending some Germans and appearing to play into communist hands.

Brandt had another problem. American diplomats liked him, but they still preferred to see him as a dependable bastion in West Berlin and not as a future chancellor. They remained committed to Adenauer and his Christian Democratic successors, in part because Adenauer and the Christian Democrats were admired at home by Republicans and Democrats alike, but also because like most people they preferred the devil they knew. Brandt had but one advantage. The Americans would prefer him to be chancellor if the Social Democrats came to power, but that seemed unlikely at the time.

I was in the United States when Brandt came to power, when his years of indecisiveness were over and he courageously began to apply the policies he had so carefully thought through. He did penance for German war crimes in Warsaw, and then launched what became known as his *Ostpolitik*. The Americans were very uneasy at first, in part because Bonn and not Washington had taken the initiative. That was understandable. The habit of authority was very strong after 30 years of superpower, and West Germany was regarded as a loyal but submissive Teutonic tribe defending the eastern glacis of empire. They were expected to obey orders, not give them. And like so many Britons and Frenchmen, secretly they still did not trust Germans. I had frequent discussions in the White House and the State Department, and in my immodest way like to think that I at least was a character witness for Brandt. My testimony might have been of some help, if only because I was an Englishman who was assumed to be more suspicious than most Americans of the Germans.

Brandt achieved what he set out to do, and then resigned because of that spy found in his office. It was a sad way to go, but probably he had little more to contribute. Certainly he was exhausted. I had a long talk with him in his office just before the resignation. His voice was hoarse, he sat heavily, as exhausted people do, and he looked as if he had been drinking too much. He was then probably the most admired politician in all western Europe. He would have been the favourite for the presidency or prime ministership if the European Community had agreed to become the United States of Europe. He had well served his own country and Europe, as had Adenauer in his time. The old Rhinelander had integrated his people into the democratic west and Brandt had settled the eastern frontier. Between them they made Europe as safe as could be expected in a divided world for the foreseeable future. They were good Germans, as my old mother used to say; but the Germans who followed Hitler had also helped to create West Germany as a genuine democratic state, as beyond the Elbe East Germans had created history's first efficient communist state. The German enigma still held many of its secrets, and as some Britons remembered the blitz and Belsen I could never forget a passage in Ernst von Salomon's *The Answers*.*

Von Salomon was an unreconstructed German nationalist, and he wrote the book as an answer to the questionnaire the occupying powers required all Germans suspected of Nazi sympathies

* Putman, London 1954.

to answer. It is an arrogant book written by a proud but misguided man, but it succeeds in answering one or two questions
only too well. Towards the end of the book he describes the end
of Nazi Germany as seen from his hideaway in Bavaria. American
troops were everywhere, and one night a retreating German
infantry platoon arrived. They had been ordered to make for
Max-Hütte and defend it. Von Salomon said that the order was
crazy. The war was over, and the German government had
collapsed. A soldier asked the lieutenant if he should knock the
stinking bastard's teeth down his throat. The lieutenant got to
his feet and put on his cap. Without raising his voice, he said
let's get moving. Von Salomon took them to some high ground
and showed them the way.

   The lieutenant, who had come forward with me to view
the countryside from this vantage point while his men remained out of sight on the reverse slope, surveyed the whole
prospect for some time through his field-glasses. I said nothing.
What he saw must surely speak for itself.
   When at last he lowered his field-glasses I saw that he was
smiling. He said:
'Many thanks. You may go home now. You have spared us a
great deal of trouble. As for the "stinking bastard", please
don't take that to heart. We realize perfectly clearly that you
meant well, but . . . we're German infantrymen.'
   The lieutenant shook me by the hand and left. I remained
where I was and followed him with my eyes. He said a few
words to his men and then turned away, his rifle in his hand,
towards Bergen valley. The troops moved off after the
lieutenant. The infantrymen marched past me, without hesi-
tation or uncertainty, with that same rhythmical and measured
tread that had re-echoed down how many of the road's of
Europe. They marched in column of two, their rifles slung,
machine guns on their shoulders. Not one of them glanced at
me.

I still find that passage both frightening and moving. Of all
the armies which fought in the second world war, the *Wehrmacht*
was undoubtedly the best, perhaps the best in history. It took on
most of the world, and almost won. Its purpose was evil, but the
vast majority of German infantrymen who marched with that

same rhythmical and measured tread down the roads of Europe and beyond, to Paris, Oslo, Moscow, Stalingrad, Belgrade, Athens, El Alamein, Monte Casino and Neimagen were not evil. And they were not zombies. They were Germans doing supremely well what they had set out to do. Even the *Einsatzgruppen* of the SS terrorized and murdered more efficiently than any of history's death squads or Praetorian guards.

Whatever the German enigma is, part of it could surely be found in that terrible slogan Hitler so often screamed, *Ein Volk, ein Reich, ein Führer*. In 1960, my last year in Bonn, they had become a genuine and efficient democracy. The *Führer* was dead, and the one-thousand-year *Reich* long forgotten, but they were still *ein Volk*. Although divided by the iron curtain, the west Germans at least had regained their national pride as the British had lost theirs. We had lost more than an empire. Behind the posturing of the politicians, we had lost our national pride and, worse, our national self-confidence and identity. A. J. P. Taylor somewhere wrote, I think in his *Course of German History*, that the Germans had never tried democracy. Well, they were trying it in 1960, and making a go of it while we were steadily sliding down the drain.

I was in a very thoughtful mood when Sir William Haley, the then editor of *The Times*, offered me the job of chief correspondent in Washington. It was the top foreign job and I was 41 years old, only one year behind the schedule I had set for myself. Since 1950, when I passed through the United States on my way to Korea, I had fallen in love with the idea of America. I knew that it was only an idea, and that Americans had not lived up to the high standards they set themselves, but it still had an immense attraction. I discussed the offer with Pat before accepting, but there really was no question of refusal. She liked Americans as much as I did. In November the five of us boarded the Cunarder *Saxonia* for Canada, where Pat and the children stayed with her sister Monica until I found a house in Washington. We were very happy, and pacing the decks of the *Saxonia* I found myself humming snatches of the *New World Symphony*.

Those were the days when we still travelled first class, although my salary had only been raised to £2,000 a year. The first-class dining room was half empty, and I seemed to eat about half a kilo of caviare every day. We also tried all the American dishes on the menu, but occasionally I longed for some good German *Aufschnitt*. I am a dry martini man, and the Cunard bartenders knew how to mix them, but I had an almost overwhelming longing for a beer and Steinhager. Grouse was served one night. It had been properly hung and was very good, but it was terribly cold outside and I remembered the *Erbsensuppe mit Würstchen* I had eaten that night in Berlin after Khrushchev had drawn back from the nuclear brink.

The *Saxonia* had a good wine list. It was especially strong on clarets, but I searched in vain for a decent German wine, a good Moselle if not a Schloss Johannisberger Spätauslese or a Schloss Volrads. As the children tucked into their steaks and cokes, I remembered the many *Weinreisen* I had made. In those days foreign correspondents of *The Times* serving in wine-producing countries were expected to produce a vintage report every year. Germany was always difficult because the harvest came so late. There was no romantic nonsense of colourful natives treading the grapes. By the time they had ripened in the Rheingau, the Moselle and Rheinhesse it was already cold, and the pickers wore gloves and wellies. Only Germans could have fought the elements to produce such fine wines.

I took the vintage reports seriously, and always organized my trips with the *Deutsche Weinbau Verband*. I spent five or six days every year on a *Weinreise*. I remembered one year especially. We had wandered from the Rhine to the Nahe, and eventually reached the Moselle. We visited a number of vineyards, but the most famous was the *Berncasteler Doktor Weingut*, the owner of which, I think, was a Frau Dr. Taunus. She was a big rawboned woman dressed in good tweeds, and looked like the wife of a Scottish laird. The cellars were under the vineyard, and on the fifth day of our journey we happily moved in for the tastings. Sixteen wines were listed, and unlike in France and other effete countries in West Germany you did not take a dainty mouthful and then spit it out. You drank a full glass of wine. We moved slowly into the cellar, enjoying each glass of progressively good wine. We reached number seven, and the Frau Doktor asked for my opinion. *Sehr lustig*, I replied, but rather like number five. The Frau Doktor exchanged a quick startled glance with the *Kellermeister*, and we trooped back to the fifth barrel. Everybody thought it was a wonderful joke, and when we reached number eight somebody was reminded of number four and back we went to make sure. Instead of sixteen glasses, which ought to have been more than enough for any man or Frau Doktor, especially after five days of tasting, we must have had at least twenty.

We reeled out of the cellar, and made for the local inn where the guest of honour was Herr Luebke, the Land minister for wine who afterwards became the federal president. At the best of times he was a rather earnest little man, and he had not been tasting fine wine for five days. The dinner was good, the main course was venison, and the wines excellent. Herr Luebke got up to make a speech, filled with dreary statistics about wine production, and a Swiss journalist responded. He was as high as the rest of us, and his speech amounted to a proposal of marriage to the Frau Doktor. She blushed like a seventeen-year-old, as he spoke of their rosy future walking together, hand in hand, down those long cellars tasting all those splendid wines. I could not forget Germany despite the approaching new world and my new assignment.

The engines slowed down during the night and I could feel the vast bulk of the ship gradually lose way. She was no longer straining against the North Atlantic, but gliding slowly as if up a placid river. I remembered other ships, the *Glenorchie* coming up the London river twenty days out of Singapore, those Straits Steamship and KPM boats nosing their way up palm-girt tropical estuaries. There is no better way of arriving in a strange land than by boat, except perhaps by flying into Rio de Janeiro aboard an Air France plane eleven hours out of Paris. Before breakfast we all went up on deck, and there were the bleak, treeless hills of St. John's, Newfoundland. The children did not say anything. On the way over they had talked excitedly about the skyscrapers of Manhattan. Pat had sung *On the Sidewalks of New York*, and there we were approaching what appeared to be an empty continent. It could not have been much different from when Cabot and Captain John Smith first reached the new world. Patrick, Katey and Sarah looked decidedly unimpressed, and Pat leaned down to comfort them. It will be alright, she said, when we get to Auntie Monica and Uncle Jacques in Montreal.

8 *The Kennedy Promise*

I arrived in Washington from Montreal in a snowstorm, and checked into a hotel until I could find a house. As usual my predecessor had already left. Not once in my career as a foreign correspondent of *The Times* had I met the man I was taking over from. Fortunately, in Washington, as in New York, Bonn and Paris, there was an assistant correspondent, and I met him at the office next morning. *The Times* office was in the National Press Building, two small rooms on the inside looking into a gloomy ventilation shaft. They must have been among the cheapest in the building, and they reminded me of Claud Cockburn's story of when he joined Sir Wilmott Lewis, the chief Washington correspondent for many years. Lewis never went near the office, presumably because it was so mean and dreary, and when Cockburn entered it for the first time he found the door jammed by a cascade of cablegrams and letters pushed through the letter box. Some of the cables had been there for weeks, and most of them urgently demanded complete coverage of events long since forgotten. Lewis afterwards said that he had always found it best to maintain a certain distance from London. Better decide for oneself, he said, what to send and when to send it.

That was good advice. I had followed it long before I knew of Lewis, but Washington in his time was a provincial capital of no great importance until FDR was elected president. In 1960 Washington had become accustomed to being the centre of much of the world, and if I had tried to be so detached I would have been overwhelmed by events. Anyway, *The Times* seemed determined to stop me from being another Sir Wilmott. My contract included a car, and the manager insisted that I buy a second-hand one. Fortunately this was regarded in Washington as an English eccentricity. My predecessor, who had been married to a successful German actress, had owned a Rolls Royce. That I should run a used Chevy put me in the same class as the English characters made famous by the Ealing comedies. The house was another matter. I had asked the manager for a company loan to make a down payment in order that I could get a mortgage. This was necessary because after being a foreign correspondent of *The Times* for 14 years I had less money in the bank than when I was mustered out of the army. He agreed, but after I had arranged to buy the house he insisted that it should belong to the company. He then tried to charge me about twice the going rent for what amounted to a tied cottage. I moved out after I had moonlighted for a couple of years and had saved enough to get a mortgage for a house of our own.

This meanness seemed all the shabbier because of the warm generosity of Americans, which enveloped us when I took possession of the tied cottage. Our furniture had arrived in Baltimore, and I arranged to have it delivered before Pat and the children were due from Montreal. For some forgotten reason it was not delivered, and the family reunion took place in an empty house. All the hotels were full because of the Kennedy inauguration, and the immediate future looked bleak. It could have been bleaker, but fortunately Americans sell houses complete with carpets, light fixtures, refrigerator, stove, dishwasher—the lot. Also the doorbell rang, and standing in the snow was a large man looking slightly embarrassed. He introduced himself as Robert Fluker, a neighbour and a member of the American foreign service. His children had seen us arrive, but saw no moving van. Was there anything wrong, and could he help? Within the hour his sons came across the unfenced backyards loaded with camp-beds, blankets and pots and pans, and they were followed by their mother, Helen, bringing hot coffee, cokes and hamburgers. Afterwards she drove Pat to the local supermarket. They also bought a television set, and gin and vermouth. That evening we had a couple of celebratory dry martinis, and squatting on the carpeted floor ate steaks and watched television. We were in business.

Kennedy, who was sworn in the following day, dominated the news programmes, as he was to dominate my work for many months to come. Inauguration day was wonderful; cold with snow underfoot, but exhilarating and brilliant; so brilliant that Robert Frost could hardly read his poems to the assembly of the great, the powerful and the fashionable seated below the steps of Capitol. Certainly there was no sense of foreboding although the economy was still in the doldrums and unemployment had reached an unacceptable level. Black Americans were becoming restive, and abroad Khrushchev was again making bellicose noises over Berlin. Nato was seen to be in a state of disarray. The faraway country of Laos, half way round the world, was said to be disintegrating under the constant communist pressure, and Vietnam and much of southeast Asia was apparently threatened. A communist regime had been imposed in nearby Cuba, less than one hundred miles from Key West, and diplomatic relations had been severed.

These could have been seen as portents of the gathering storm, but a young and vigorous President had been elected to lead the country to a New Frontier. Beyond that frontier, so evocative of the American past, was a new and more beautiful America to be explored and won. The promise and the challenge came in the inaugural address. 'We dare not forget today that we are the heirs of that first revolution. Let the word go forth from this time and place, to friend and foe alike, that the torch has been passed to a new generation of Americans—born of this century, tempered by war, disciplined by a hard and bitter peace, proud of our ancient heritage—and unwilling to witness or permit the slow undoing of those human rights to which this nation has always been committed, and to which we are committed today at home and around the world. Let every nation know, whether it wishes us well or ill, that we shall pay any price, bear any burden, meet any hardship, support any friend, oppose any foe to assure the survival and success of liberty. This much we pledge—and more. . . . And so, my fellow Americans: ask not what your country can do for you—ask what you can do for your country.'

The rhetoric moved millions. I was no less stirred, and rejoiced that I had arrived in the United States at the beginning of a new era of greatness. Perhaps for the first time in my journalistic career I was caught up in a sustained wave of enthusiasm for one man. I had learned to respect and even like other politicians and leaders, but Kennedy was different. In the eyes of most of my American colleagues he could do no wrong. The invasion of

Cuba in 1961 was indefensible unless one accepted the right of powerful nations, including the Soviet Union, to crush smaller nations which displeased them. Kennedy also ensured the defeat of the CIA-organized invasion when at the last moment he cancelled the aerial support promised. He disarmed critics by taking full responsibility for the debacle. It mattered not that he could not have avoided responsibility. We sided with him, perhaps because he seemed to represent our generation, the young platoon and company commanders of the second world war. I also thought that he was eager for social reform, but despite his comparative youth and vigour, Kennedy was a cautious man when it came to domestic politics. He was certainly not impatient to improve the lot of the blacks. His main concern was national security and foreign policy perhaps because in that direction he could wield presidential power directly. He wielded that power almost immediately by ordering the clandestine invasion of Cuba. The attempt failed, and soon afterwards he sent General Maxwell Taylor and Walt Rostow, a member of his national security staff, to South Vietnam to assess the situation. They recommended that American military advisers be sent to help the Saigon government in its struggle against North Vietnam. The promise he made in the inaugural address to 'pay any price, bear any burden, meet any hardship, support any friend' was thus quickly given. The long descent into war and national turmoil was begun.

That was not all. Kennedy began the separation of the White House from most of the departments of the executive branch. In the last year of his life he called only eight full cabinet meetings. With the exception of the attorney general, his brother Robert Kennedy, and the defence secretary, Robert McNamara, members of the cabinet were regarded merely as departmental managers, political appointees of whom not much was expected. The elaborate national security apparatus which Dwight Eisenhower had devised was discarded. The secretary of state was reduced to overseeing the humdrum work of diplomacy and the joint chiefs more or less demoted to the rank of super-sergeants responsible for discipline and efficiency. Grand strategy, overall command and the running of various alliances were concentrated into the hands of the President and a few advisers, few of whom had heard a shot fired in anger. Kennedy was of course a war hero, but the command of a small boat hardly fitted him for the tasks he assumed without much benefit of experienced advisers.

Much of this was applauded at the time, and I joined in the applause. The President was after all the commander-in-chief, and generals and admirals were dismissed as holdovers from another age without experience or understanding of nuclear war. The argument was that if the President had to make the awful decision to use nuclear weapons he should have full control of the decision-making process and complete confidence in his advisers. The logic was plausible but one obvious consequence of this concentration of power was that it tended to shut off the President from alternative sources of advice. Ben Cohen, who had worked for Franklin Roosevelt, remarked after Kennedy's first year how isolated the White House had become. The dangers were not obvious at the time. Many more Americans than had voted for him, with myself on the fringe, were carried along by Kennedy's charisma and the unspoken assumption that Kennedy's kind of politics could transcend the limits of the commonplace world. The dangers became apparent, one by one, only after Kennedy's tragic death.

The main danger inherent in this tightly-controlled national security decision-making process was extended when a few of Kennedy's advisers agreed to serve his successor, Lyndon Johnson. This unusual holdover—Presidents not unnaturally want to surround themselves with their own men—was necessary because of Johnson's sudden elevation. Most of them did not stay long, but one man who stayed to the bitter end was Walt Whitman Rostow, who had first proposed the dispatch of military advisers to Vietnam and remained to become Johnson's special assistant for national security affairs. He was a likeable man, burly with physical fitness, who more often than not beamed at the world through large round spectacles in a colourless frame. He had immense energy, and regularly played a hard game of tennis before beginning his killing twelve-hour day in the White House. He was the son of Russian Jewish immigrants for whom the American Dream was no folk myth. The eldest son, Eugene Debs Rostow, became a Yale professor and served Johnson as under secretary of state. Walt was a professor of economics at MIT before serving as deputy to Kennedy's national security adviser. He then went to the state department as chairman of the policy planning council and returned to the White House as Johnson's national security adviser. He could relax easily after dinner, and was known to accompany himself on the piano while singing rather bawdy undergraduate songs. He was also a hawk, who could not be persuaded that the commitment to Vietnam was questionable or that victory was not necessarily inevitable. Even when the 1968 Jet offensive finally crushed Johnson, I can remember Rostow, in his White House basement office, showing me aerial photographs of the bombing of Khesanh as proof of North Vietnamese defeat.

Rostow's personality was a key factor in this extraordinary display of White House self-deception. He did not have a negative reflex in his entire nervous system. He was an ideologue totally committed to the ideology he had propounded in his book, *The United States in the World Arena*. But he and his like were brought to the centre of power to wield extraordinary influence without ever running for elective office, because Kennedy established the small elitist group in the White House. Without Kennedy's desire for total control of the decision-making process, unencumbered by traditional advice and restraint, Rostow might still be at MIT dreaming up even more economic takeoffs for developing countries.

Kennedy's desire for total control led the United States, like a sleep walker mesmerized by elitist double-talk, into Vietnam, which so bitterly divided the country. More than that, the Kennedy charisma made publicly acceptable the idea of a government within a government, a personal government all the more powerful because of the protection of executive privilege. A secretary of state or a defence secretary can be required to give an account of himself to the appropriate congressional committee, but not a presidential assistant. In an area of grave responsibility, with even graver consequences for the American people, Kennedy established a degree of unaccountability positively undemocratic. More than that. He made Vietnam and Watergate possible because he avoided or ignored constitutional safeguards designed to prevent such an aggrandizement of presidential power.

The defenders of Kennedy's memory are legion, and I must therefore try to avoid misunderstanding. I am not charging him with some sinister motive or suggesting that the Watergate scandals could have originated in his White House. His intention was entirely honourable. He changed the chain of command because he disliked committees and a bureaucratic structure of any kind. He preferred to work with small *ad hoc* groups. He sought flexibility. It was argued that this was his right. Every president has his own work habits and is obviously entitled to organize his office as he thinks fit. What I am suggesting is that he was not entitled to change the constitutional balance.

Eisenhower's chain of command was perhaps too large and complex. It suited him as a former general accustomed to the army command structure. In the second world war he was responsible for tens of millions of lives and the fate of many nations. He could not afford to make mistakes. The army command structure, on which his was more or less modelled, had been tested and retested. It was the sum of hard-won and bitterly-learned experience. It might have been slow, but it was reasonably sure. One cannot be certain of course, but I am willing to believe that the United States would not have been committed in Vietnam if he had been allowed to run for a third term. Certainly the United States was at peace during his eight years.

The Watergate conspiracy would have been more difficult to hatch in the White House of Eisenhower or Truman. Both were touched by some scandal, such as staffers accepting deep freezers and vicuna coats, but they did not threaten the health and well-being of the nation. Eisenhower also developed the concept of executive privilege, but only to defend the White House against the damaging depredations of Senator Joe McCarthy. Eisenhower and Truman remained accountable to Congress and the nation. Their special assistants for national security affairs were no more than staff directors ensuring the smooth flow of information and presidential decisions to and from the White House. They were not unofficial secretaries of state unaccountable because of their privileged status as presidential assistants. The secretaries of state, Eisenhower's John Foster Dulles and Truman's Dean Acheson, were powerful men wholly accountable to Congress. Under Kennedy, Dean Rusk was accountable but he had little to account for because he was not a member of the intimate groups which constantly advised the President.

Kennedy could not of course have foreseen that the tight little staff apparatus he established in the White House could make possible the commission of indictable offences. His own staffers were also honourable men. For that matter, he could not have foreseen that it would be perpetuated by his two successors. Johnson's decision was understandable. He was a secretive man, but during his first year of office he retained the services of some Kennedy men because he wanted to demonstrate the continuity of the Presidency despite Kennedy's assassination. Nevertheless, the decision was tragic. It is just possible, had he returned to the more traditional arrangements for staffing the White House that Nixon, for all his secrecy, would have found it more difficult to establish his own government within the government.

*

That was for the future. In 1961 events moved too quickly for anybody to question Kennedy's operating methods. The Cuban invasion, the massive increase of nuclear missiles and submarines to meet the non-existant missile gap, the decision to land a man on the moon whatever the cost, the meeting with Khrushchev in Vienna, the callup of army reservists to defend Berlin, the posting of military advisers to South Vietnam and the resumption of nuclear testing in the atmosphere were only the highlights of a hectic year. In many instances Kennedy over-reacted, but I cannot recall that this was reported or observed in the American press at the time. He had an extraordinary impact on correspondents covering the White House. Shrewd public relations helped. Pierre Salinger, the press secretary, looked like a Mississippi riverboat gambler and regularly played poker with the old timers. The new generation of correspondents who had studied politics at university valued and boasted about their ready access to McGeorge Bundy, the special assistant for national security affairs. Never before had correspondents been allowed to get so close to the White House staff, and they felt themselves to be members of the team.

It was both exciting and cozy, but the relationship between President and press was not all public relations or news management. Most of us were genuinely attracted to Kennedy. He looked good, and he was cool, amusing and courageous. Our responses to most situations and crises were very similar because we were of his generation. We applauded when he called some steel barons sons of bitches for raising prices and I for one was captivated by his decision to fly men to the moon. Few of us questioned the wisdom of the involvement in Vietnam, although I could not understand the excitement over Laos. To my knowledge I was the only correspondent in town who had spent any time in Laos. Strategically it was of little or no importance, but my colleagues dutifully reflected the intensity of Kennedy's preoccupation. They appeared to attach as much importance to that faraway land as to West Germany. Kennedy even appeared on television to persuade millions of Americans who had never heard of Laos before that their future depended upon the survival of that plucky little Asian democracy.

Kennedy was very rich. He spent his weekends in the family compound on Cape Cod or at the mansion in Palm Beach. His path to power had been made easy by his daddy's dollars, but this did not rankle my egalitarian American colleagues. Indeed, some were un-Jacksonian enough to argue that wealthy men made the best presidents. Their superior education prepared them for power and responsibility, and wealth protected them from corruption. The gossip writers regarded him as a Renaissance man, which was a slight exaggeration. He had neither the intellect nor the cultivated tastes. His favourite books were Cecil's *Melbourne* and the James Bond stories. He was shrewd, very much a politician, but curiously also a mid-Atlantic man. It might have been his Irishness, or those English habits he acquired when living in Britain. Whatever the reason, I found him easier to understand than his successors and could even anticipate most of his reactions.

The Kennedys were also very close, again perhaps because of their Irishness, and this might well have explained the Kennedy White House. He and his small circle of intimates tended to see themselves as adversaries of Congress, the bureaucracy and any person or group which got in their way. You were either for Kennedy or against him, as some of us soon discovered. The old *New York Herald Tribune* was banned from the White House because of something it had published. Offending correspondents were put in the doghouse, in other words sent to Coventry until they toed the line. I was exposed to the presidential wrath because of a story I wrote about the activities of the CIA in Laos. It was true, but no matter. An interview with Kennedy was indefinitely postponed. I was called into Salinger's office like a recalcitrant schoolboy and questioned about my sources while some spook took notes. I refused to divulge them of course, and a witchhunt was launched in the State Department. My main source, a very, very senior official, looked uncomfortable for weeks. Under any other president the press corps would have been very indignant, but not under Kennedy. A great President, and they were already classifying him as great, was entitled to his little foibles.

This atmosphere nurtured the assumption of presidential omnipotence. Kennedy, I think, was more sceptical of his power than his staffers, but his grand design assumed that Washington was the centre of the universe. Allies were expected to do as they were told. Little was expected to happen without White House approval, which was why Kennedy reacted so slowly to the black revolution. Arguably this was one of the most important developments in recent American history, but the blacks were not one of Kennedy's priorities. They did not fit into the grand design.

This was established at one of the early press conferences when he was asked if he intended to introduce legislation to help the blacks. He said, no. There was sufficient legislation already on the statute books. I was new to Washington, and did not at first recognize the significance of his answer, but I felt and saw the tension of the other journalists. His answer was one of those signals so important in Washington, and which make presidential press conferences vital for those in government as well as the press. Kennedy did not say that the blacks would have to wait, but everybody in the room, in Congress and the bureaucracy knew that they would get little immediate help from Kennedy. He had other priorities, he needed the votes of southern congressmen, and assumed that the blacks would await his pleasure.

He was terribly wrong. The blacks were not prepared to wait any longer. Nineteen-sixty-one was the centenary of the beginning of the Civil War, which was supposed to have made them free and equal, and in many states they were still denied their constitutional rights. Elsewhere they were widely regarded as second-class citizens. Seven years earlier the Supreme Court had declared that racial segregation in schools was unconstitutional, but most schools were still segregated. Five years earlier Dr.

Martin Luther King, Jr., had successfully led the bus boycott in Montgomery, Alabama, his first campaign of Gandhian non-violence. And since then young black seminarians, organized by the students' non-violent coordinating committee, had held sit-ins at lunch counters and wherever they were denied entry or service because of the colour of their skins. The black revolution was beginning to sweep through the south like a forest fire. Nothing could stop it, certainly not the violence of white policemen, sheriffs and the mobs, or the indifference of Kennedy.

Soon after that press conference a small group of blacks and white supporters, organized by the Congress for Racial Equality, began the freedom ride through the south. They travelled aboard inter-state buses, which meant they could claim the protection of federal law. Their intention was to desegregate lunch counters at inter-state bus stations, which were also subject to federal and not state law. Their departure from Washington was hardly noticed, and their journey won little publicity until the bus was burned in Birmingham, Alabama. Clearly this was Gandhi's salt march all over again, and once again non-violence begat violence. I flew down to join them.

The next bus, to Montgomery, the capital of Alabama, was half empty. Apart from the freedom riders, only a few correspondents were aboard. It was like riding through Indian territory without the US calvary. We were marked men, and knew it. I expected to be ambushed at any moment, but nothing happened until journey's end. We were met by mobs, all the uglier because not a policeman was in sight, and the day ended in bloody rioting. The governor refused to impose law and order, and Kennedy finally intervened under a law of 1871 empowering the President to use militia, the armed forces or any other means to suppress an insurrection or domestic violence. About 200 US marshals were flown in, armed with truncheons and wearing civilian clothes, distinguished only by yellow arm bands with the legend, *US Deputy Marshal*.

The climax came the second night when Dr. Martin Luther King addressed a large congregation of blacks and freedom riders in the black First Baptist Church. The heat was intense, and tension mounted when the white mob surrounded the church and threw stones through the windows. The congregation panicked when King went to the door to investigate, but another minister led the singing of the old gospel hymn *Leaning on the Everlasting Arm*. We sang mightily as the mob stormed the ring of marshals outside. King said that he was going to telephone Robert Kennedy, the Attorney General, from the office in the church basement, and I stood in the doorway to see what was going on outside.

Dusk was falling, but somebody had set fire to a car parked down the block and in the light of the flaring flame I could see hundreds of whites battling with the marshals. For all their pot-bellies and rimless spectacles, they were brave men. Teargas bombs were thrown to hold back the mob, but the wind was in the wrong direction and the gas drifted into the church. A few of the bombs were also thrown back by the mob. The congregation panicked again, and I was no less anxious as the marshals began to retreat towards the church. I was convinced that they would be overwhelmed, and that the church would be burned down, when the local police finally intervened. They must have been lurking in the background, waiting until the very last moment before taking action. They threw more teargas and charged with batons, while a loudspeaker truck ordered the mob to disperse.

Governor John Patterson belatedly proclaimed martial law, and called out the national guard. The guard was similar to the old territorial army, and some of its Saturday-night soldiers were said to have been in the mob. Nevertheless, their presence was reassuring, if somewhat incongruous. They wore the old Confederacy flag as shoulder patches. The interregnum which followed was confused. Byron White, who was then an assistant attorney general, arrived and set up his headquarters in the nearby Maxwell air force base, which was federal territory. Over it flew the only stars and stripes in the city, apart from the post offices. Further comparison with the old frontier days was impossible to avoid. The air base was like an old wild-west fort, and White, representing the big white father in faraway Washington, had interminable pow-wows with the local Indian chiefs. They were in no hurry. Governor John Patterson was more concerned about his relations with the local tribes than with the distant white father.

Each day I went along to his office in the Capitol, a sad building where Jefferson Davis had been elected president of the Confederacy a hundred years before. Patterson told me how he loved all niggers, and how they loved him. Why, Alabama would be a paradise on earth if only Washington and those northern liberals would mind their own business. It was more difficult to keep in touch with the freedom riders. They were staying in the black section of town, and white cab drivers would not take me there and black drivers would not pick up whites. I had their telephone number, and was promised that I would be kept informed. One morning, about six, I was awakened by the telephone, and a conspiratorial voice said that the dogs would be running at eight. I was half asleep, and asked him to repeat the message but he rang off. I sat on the edge of the bed turning the enigmatic words over in my mind until I finally concluded that he was referring to Greyhound buses. We would be leaving for the next confrontation at Jackson, Mississippi, at eight. I dressed and packed and headed for the bus depot.

It was deserted when I checked in my bag, but in the street outside nature was once again copying art. A large sheriff's posse wearing five-gallon hats and six-shooters were seated on impatient horses. They looked as if they had just trotted off a film set. The national guard had taken up positions on the roofs of buildings. Most of them held their rifles at the ready, and one carried a large Confederate flag. Then preceded by the sound of sirens, a convoy of highway patrol cars came round the corner travelling in front, abreast and behind two battered taxi cabs. King and the freedom riders got out, and a hush fell upon the troops, posse and highway patrol as we walked into the depot.

We went through a door marked *whites only* and into a sleazy lunchroom. It had not been aired, and still smelled of last night's hamburgers. An old white couple took shelter behind a stack of luggage lockers. They clearly could not believe their eyes. Then the old lady screamed when she finally realized that blacks were in the whites' lunchroom. The white girl behind the counter also screamed and disappeared into the kitchen, and there was a pause until a policeman fetched the manager. King, his face grayly impassive, politely asked for a cup of coffee. We also ordered. The manager set up a line of chipped cups, slopped coffee into them and then disappeared. It was filthy coffee, but for some unknown reason I said, cheers. King smiled, and we stood at the counter silently sipping. This was what the violence was all about, the constitutional right of blacks to drink bad coffee at dirty inter-state bus stations. Another small but significant victory had been won.

The ride to Jackson was uneventful, and there was no violence. Instead, the freedom riders were arrested under some municipal vagrancy law. Lawyers came down from the north to defend them, and their learned arguments were of little news interest. It had all happened before. The National Association for the Advancement of Coloured Peoples had chosen the legal route for the liberation of blacks. They had argued the school segregation issue from state courts, through state and federal appeals courts and right up to the Supreme Court of the United States. They had won, but it had not established a precedent outside schools. To drink coffee at inter-state bus stations, to order a hamburger at a Woolworth lunch counter, or to spend the night at some motel, they still had to fight each case through the lower courts to the Supreme Court. To argue, as Kennedy did, that there was enough legislation on the statute books was nonsense, and I could not but admire those lawyers patiently and politely beginning the process all over again. I was probably more depressed than they as they began their preliminary arguments.

Before leaving Jackson I attended a large rally in the black section of town. The purpose was to rally the faithful after the sudden letdown of the freedom riders' arrests. It was terribly hot, and we tried to keep cool with large hand fans advertising some funeral parlour as speaker after speaker said his piece. They spoke well, as do most blacks with a religious background, and the audience responded with phrases such as *Tell it the way it is, brother*, *Thanks be the Lord* and long *A-mens*. Between the speeches prayers were said by a number of clergymen and songs were sung by Pete Seager. I thought it was strange, a white singer singing black folk and work songs to a black audience but they were deeply moved. Many wept, or stood up and ejaculated *Praise the Lord*. I was also wet-eyed, and not only because I was always sentimental. The hall had become a chapel or church. The audience, or congregation, was unburdening itself as if in the privacy of the confessional box. Faced with yet another disappointment, they naturally sought relief, comfort and grace from God.

Seager went on singing. He was in complete harmony with his black audience. The colour of his skin was of no importance.

The songs had been consecrated with pain, and although it was long after midnight they demanded more songs. The intervals between them became longer, and I supposed that Seager was exhausting his repertoire as well as himself when he struck a couple of chords and sang a long-forgotten hymn. It had been brought to America by English Baptists, who afterwards dropped it from their hymnals when black Baptists took it up. That was more than a hundred years earlier, and the hymn might have been lost but for a WPA worker during the Depression. His job was to record folk songs on an old wire recorder for the Library of Congress. He recorded this hymn when he heard it sung by black women strikers in some southern tobacco town. It was *We Shall Overcome*.

I was not impressed when I first heard it that hot night. It was too much of a dirge. In any case I preferred plainchant to non-conformist hymns, the civilized responses of the old Tridentine mass to the emotional outbursts of tin-roofed chapels. Musically I was a snob, but fortunately my reporting instincts were not dulled by that unlovely blemish on my character. Seager sang the first couple of verses clearly and without much feeling. He must have been very tired, but the funereal fans stopped fluttering, and I could have heard the proverbial pin drop until the hall began to pulsate with deep humming. I looked about me surreptitiously, and every shining black face was transformed. The entire audience, except for myself, seemed to be undergoing a fundamental religious experience. Then everybody stood up and sang, first hesitantly because of the unfamiliar words and finally in full voice. It was extraordinary. The hymn had lifted them out of the slough of despair, and they and millions of other blacks were to sing that hymn, in Selma, Alabama, and other vicious southern towns, in the march on Washington, in Chicago and other northern cities until they did indeed overcome.

I should not have been surprised. American blacks were naturally religious people, especially in the south where most of their leaders were clergymen. King was the head of the southern Christian leadership conference, and the students' non-violent coordinating committee still found most of its members on the campuses of southern black seminaries. King was from a middle-class family and had been educated in the north. He would not have been accepted as a leader in the south if he had not worn a clerical collar. He was a genuinely religious person, as I discovered after two long interviews. He really believed that unearned suffering was redemptive. He was incapable of hatred. He once said that the Negro must love the white man because the white man needed his love to remove his tensions, insecurities and fears. He could sound priggish at times, but he was a natural orator and had a superb voice. His greatest triumph was the march on Washington, when hundreds of thousands of people marched to the Lincoln memorial to hear him speak.

I can still hear his voice booming across the years: 'I have a dream that one day this nation will rise up and live out the true meaning of its creed: we hold these truths to be self-evident, that all men are created equal.' The dream refrain uplifted his vast audience, then in full voice he cried, 'We will not be satisfied until justice rolls down like water, and righteousness like a mighty stream.' Not all the oratory and rhetoric that day was of such a high order, but it was a triumph for King and the civil rights movement. He must have moved tens of millions of Americans who watched the march on television, but alas not the White House. Kennedy still had other priorities.

Among them was the Bomb, and no wonder. Ordinary mortals could worry about nuclear incineration, in Britain the CND could march in protest, but in the west only the President of the United States had the power of nuclear life and death. It was the ultimate power and ultimate responsibility, and both separated him from other men. Kennedy was also the first President to have this ultimate power. Truman had bombed Hiroshima and Nagasaki, but when he stepped down in 1953 the nuclear armoury was still comparatively small. Eisenhower had only just begun to move into the missile age, but Kennedy came to command an unholy trinity of nuclear bombers, intercontinental missiles and Polaris submarines powerful enough literally to kill all life on earth many times over. It was his, and his alone. Neither Congress nor the national security council shared that power, and that distinction made him the apex of a communications system which connected him with every bomber squadron, missile silo and submarine. He never escaped it. A warrant officer always accompanied him carrying a case holding the codes which could release hundreds of megatons of destruction. Wherever he went, to Palm Beach to swim or to European capitals to confer with his allies, the signal corps moved the communications with him. There was no escape.

This unprecedented power and responsibility weighed heavily on Kennedy, although he knew how to relax. That was part of his attractiveness, but the cold war was hotting up. Nuclear theorists were evolving strategies to replace the massive retaliation and mutual annihilation of the Eisenhower years. Henry Kissinger, still teaching at Harvard, formulated the policy of graduated deterrence, but his thesis remained disturbing. It argued for the use of tactical nuclear weapons against conventional as well as nuclear enemy forces. Kissinger was no Adenauer. A limited nuclear response would limit annihilation, presumably to the European battlefield although that remained unsaid. Kissinger argued that limited nuclear war offered the United States a choice of responses to nuclear and conventional aggression. Perhaps he and the other theorists who were thinking about the unthinkable were too pessimistic, certainly most of them were of German origin, but he saw Stalin and Khrushchev as successors to Napoleon and Hitler. In the perspective of history, the Soviet Union was yet another revolutionary and expansionist power threatening civilization and the established order. It was the historical task of the United States to resist, and Kissinger argued that it must not be afraid to use nuclear weapons. He said, The enormity of modern weapons makes the thought of war repugnant, but the refusal to run any risks would amount to giving the Soviet rulers a blank cheque.

Many Americans were badly frightened by this active preparation for nuclear war, and for a time air raid shelters outsold backyard swimming pools. A Catholic magazine told the faithful that it was permissible to shoot anybody who tried to use the family shelter. Robert McNamara, the defence secretary, one night worked out with the aid of the inevitable slide rule how much protective material was needed to make my basement safe from a near miss. It was all very disturbing, but the responsibility was Kennedy's. It was he who had to play the war games designed to make him act rationally—if that is the correct word—at the moment of supreme crisis, and essentially he had two problems. The first was to maintain his credibility. For the benefit of Moscow he had to demonstrate that he had the strength of will to order a nuclear bombardment if necessary. He also had to persuade his allies that in the event of war he would be prepared to exchange—as the nuclear jargon went—New York for Leningrad, Detroit for Minsk. Cuba provided the opportunity.

After the Bay of Pigs fiasco, and the Vienna meeting with Khrushchev, Kennedy had reaffirmed the Monroe Doctrine as legitimate authority for United States domination over the Americas. It was an extraordinary assertion of imperial power, no less than the doctrine subsequently expounded by Brezhnev after the invasion of Czechoslovakia. Whether or not it provoked Krushchev, in 1962 the Russians decided to station nuclear missiles in Cuba, and brought about history's first nuclear confrontation. For six days the world teetered on the edge of the abyss.

The confrontation was announced by Kennedy on television one Monday evening, but there had been warning signals. Senator Kenneth Keating of New York had publicized Cuban refugee reports for weeks, but they were denied by the Administration. Apparently nobody in authority could believe that the Russians would be so adventurous. The mid-term elections were also approaching, and Kennedy was campaigning hard in the hope of increasing the Democratic majorities in Congress. The next signal, muffled by a political white lie, came when Kennedy suddenly returned from a campaign swing. The White House announced that he was unwell, and although he looked spry enough the White House statement went unquestioned presumably because the weekend was approaching. The weekend might have been a British invention, but as with so many others the Americans had taken it over with many improvements. Official Washington was a dead town from Friday afternoon to Monday morning, and the weekend papers were largely filled with agency stories and fillers written by staff men before they disappeared from town.

The first undeniable signal came that Saturday evening. Pat and I were invited to dinner in Chevy Chase DC, and we were the only non-official guests at the table. The other men worked at the White House, in the Vice-President's office, the State Department, the CIA and the Pentagon. This was not unusual. I met some of my best sources at dinner parties, but it was Saturday and everybody was relaxed. There was a lot of easy laughter over the martinis. Kennedy was supposedly in bed with flu, and our hostess kept a good table. I decided that I did not have to be Hawkeye Heren, the ace reporter, and had another martini.

We went into dinner more or less on time because the first course was a soufflé, but as we were moving into the candle-lit dining room the White House man was called to the phone. He was away for some minutes, and the phone rang again—it was one of those Washington houses with three outside lines—and the Pentagon man was called away; then the State Department man and finally the special assistant to the Vice-President. The soufflé was on the table, and the hostess was looking desperate. I suggested that we should begin—there would be all the more for us, I said, or something equally silly—and the soufflé was served just as it was about to collapse. I tried to make bright conversation, but it was not easy. The women were Washington wives, and were wondering what was going on. I sensed a major crisis. I could see McGeorge Bundy discussing it with the President, and then sounding the general alarm. Presumably all over town other men were being called from dinner or the television set to crank up the crisis operation.

They came back eventually and tried to make conversation, but their minds were elsewhere. The evening was not a success, and we broke up early. By this time I was almost feverish with curiosity. I knew not what had happened, but clearly it was important. I noted that it was too late for the Sunday papers, but was raring to go. Our disappointed hostess suggested that Pat and I should stay for a nightcap, but I made some excuse and followed the others out into the frontyard. The White House man had already got into his car and was turning out of the drive in the direction of Connecticut Avenue, but I managed to pin the State Department man against his station wagon before he could open the door. What's going on? He looked at me appealingly. Gee, I'm sorry, Lou, he said. I just can't tell you, honestly. Shit, I retorted. We've been friends for years. When did I ever let you down—and you owe me a favour anyway. His eyes acknowledged the half-forgotten debt, but he whimpered that he was sworn to secrecy. His wife, who was waiting for him to open the car door and was finding the October night chilly, said, For God's sake tell him. I flashed her a grateful smile; I had always known that she was a good sort. He looked over and round me, and whispered, Cuba. What's happening? I can't tell you, he answered, and bundled his wife into the wagon and drove off.

It was not much, but I had been pointed in the right direction. Others were not so fortunate. One of the best-informed columnists in town had seen Foy Kohler, who took care of Germany in the State Department, going into the White House, and was convinced that Berlin was about to explode again. By Sunday afternoon Washington was seething with rumour. I knew it was Cuba, and remembered Keating's warnings of missiles. Refugees' reports were notoriously unreliable, and often politically motivated. The Administration had dismissed the reported missiles as anti-ballistic missiles, defensive weapons that were no threat to the United States, but what if they were medium-range missiles capable of knocking out American cities? I spent the afternoon phoning around town, and with one Pentagon source tried the old reporter's dodge of pretending to be in the know. What's this about Russian missiles in Cuba?, I asked belligerently. I almost felt sorry for him when he ejaculated, Who told you? One should not do it to a dog, I told myself, but nevertheless pushed on. How are you going to take them out? With another invasion? Alas, he recovered, clammed up and soon rang off.

I rolled some copy paper into the typewriter, and typed the slugline: WASHINGTON SUNDAY MISSILES FIRST BEGINS. I still did not have the full story, but it always helped to get something down on the typewriter. I knew that Kennedy had returned to Washington because of a critical situation in Cuba. The alarm bells had sounded throughout the national security apparatus, and presumably Kennedy and his advisers were planning an operational or diplomatic response at that very moment. I knew, or thought I knew, that the Russians had moved missiles into Cuba and that Kennedy could not accept such a decisive shift in the balance of power. The hawks would not be content with diplomatic negotiation, and the mid-term elections would give them a platform. In any case, Kennedy was not the man to reject such a challenge, not after the Bay of Pigs. This could only mean confrontation. I did not use the word, it was little used then, but thought of war, nuclear war.

This was the story of the century, I told myself, and then the implications flooded my mind. I shied away from the thought of nuclear war; it was unthinkable, although the theorists had been thinking the unthinkable for years. But what if I was wrong; if the missiles were really only ABMs? The paper would look bloody silly, and I would look sillier when in the subsequent post-mortem I would be asked to produce the evidence. And if I was right; if Krushchev was a wild man, would he launch an attack before the Americans were ready? I pondered the possibilities, then ripped the paper out of the typewriter and went home without filing a word.

Monday was horribly frustrating until the evening, when Kennedy went on television to announce the confrontation. He said, We will not prematurely or unnecessarily risk the costs of world-wide nuclear war in which even the fruits of victory would be ashes in our mouth, but neither will we shrink from that risk at any time it must be faced. It was a chilling moment, but I thrust my own thoughts aside and reported the speech as objectively as I knew how. Afterwards I went to State for a briefing and Nick Herbert, my number two, went to the Pentagon. The department was ablaze with light despite the late hour, and the atmosphere almost crackled with nervous energy generated by the crisis. After the meeting I managed to have a few words with Dean Rusk. He was desperately tired, but he had the toughness of a man born poor, and his years in the army had given him a sustaining discipline. I asked him if it was as serious as it seemed, and he nodded. You mean, I persisted, that the President is prepared to trade New York for Leningrad, or Washington for Moscow? He stared down at me for a few moments. He did not look like the friendly neighbourhood liquor dealer, as he had once wryly described his round undistinguished face. Lou, he said. We are all in this together, but this time, we are calling the shots. If I were you I would get your wife and kids out of town.

I had a feeling that with other ordinary mortals in Washington I was being abandoned. I knew that Kennedy had an underground command centre deep in the West Virginian mountains. I accepted the fact that as commander-in-chief he of all people had to survive if he was to command, but I also knew that he would be accompanied by his family and many senior officials. A friend at the Supreme Court had told me that Robert Kennedy had called on Earl Warren, the chief justice, and said that there was a place for him in that safe command centre in the event of nuclear war. Warren had refused, but other people regarded as important would go. They would survive.

The Cuban missile crisis, or Cuba Two as we afterwards remembered it, was the strangest story I ever covered. Every nuclear missile unit was on full alert, and bombers of the strategic air command were already in the air awaiting the coded order to attack. The navy was steaming out into the Atlantic to blockade Cuba, and army units were moving down to Florida to invade the island. It was war, but unlike any other war. There was no distant battle front to fly to, no slit trench in which to take cover. It would have been useless to attach myself to the navy or army because the war was being fought in the minds of two men, Kennedy and Khrushchev. Every day I padded down those corridors of power, and thought that for once a cliché was appropriate. At night I went home to listen to my children tell of the air raid drills at school. They were told to crouch against a wall and close their eyes. I asked Pat if she wanted to stay with friends in Charlottesville, Virginia, but she refused.

On the Tuesday Soviet freighters carrying more missiles to Cuba turned back when confronted by the American blockade, and on the Wednesday the crisis was referred to the United Nations. I talked to Eric Britter, our UN correspondent, and he said that the crisis was over. I warned him not to be too optimistic, that Kennedy had no intention of listening to the UN, but he was not convinced. My doubts were re-enforced when I met Dean Rusk in his office late that afternoon. He had invited about half a dozen American and foreign correspondents for a briefing. The gist of it was that the United States would not be deterred from its resolve to force the Russians to remove the missiles from Cuba. In his quiet, blunt way, he made it clear that the Americans would not back down come what may.

We questioned him closely. Somebody raised the suggestion that the United States should offer to remove its medium-range missiles from Greece and Turkey in exchange for the removal of the Soviet missiles from Cuba. We knew that one member of the joint chiefs of staff had suggested this to the executive committee of the national security council, but it was quickly dismissed by Dean Rusk, the secretary of state. There would be no negotiation, no trade. The Russians had flagrantly challenged the United States, and the President was determined to expel them from the western hemisphere. It was both alarming and impressive. Washington liberals were fond of sneering at Rusk, but he was loyal and steady under pressure. Johnson was to say afterwards that he was a man one would willingly go with to the well—an expression of confidence recalling the old frontier days when settlers had to brave Red Indian attack when in search of water. I was not convinced that the world had to be taken to the nuclear brink, and perhaps beyond, to teach the Russians a lesson. The removal of missiles from Greece, Turkey and Cuba seemed sensible, but the United States was indeed calling the shots. Britain, no longer great or powerful, was on the sidelines with the banana republics although Kennedy had forewarned his old friend, David Ormsby Gore, the British ambassador.

I wrote about 900 sombre words, and went home for a morose martini with Pat. We were eating supper when London phoned. It was Iverach MacDonald, who was editing the paper that night, and to my astonishment he agreed with Britter. I told him that Kennedy did not give a damn about the UN, that if anybody knew if the crisis was over or not it was Dean Rusk. MacDonald was not convinced, and the next day I discovered that my story had been spiked. It was the first and only time the paper had questioned my judgement, and I felt badly about it. So did MacDonald later. Many years later he wrote, We were not yet used to taking seriously a crisis in which Britain was not directly involved; by definition it could not be so very serious. MacDonald had been the paper's diplomatic correspondent when Britain still saw itself as a great power. He had been part of the world of high diplomacy, and had shared many secrets and confidences. Eventually I managed to understand why he could not believe my story, but at the time I said to hell with it and went on a silent strike for a couple of days. What was the point of writing if I was to be spiked. Nick Herbert was pleasantly surprised when I let him cover the last day of the crisis. I did not tell him why, and he probably still believes that I was a kind and understanding boss willing to share the best stories with his number two.

Khrushchev was the first to waver in the macabre test of will with Kennedy. As Dean Rusk said, We're eyeball to eyeball and I think the other fellow just blinked, but tension was to increase again when the official communications network proved to be inadequate and the two superpowers had to use the news agencies to carry their messages. Kennedy won, and to some extent Cuba eased the nuclear burden for him. Nobody could now doubt the strength of his will. He emerged from that high noon as a new kind of hero. He had shown grace under great stress and danger. He had joined the pantheon of brave men he had extolled in his book *Profiles in Courage*, but his second nuclear problem remained unresolved. While still assuming that nuclear weapons would be used to defend the national interest, he had to reduce the chances of another confrontation. He announced that the United States, the Soviet Union and Britain would negotiate a nuclear test ban treaty, and the hot line between Washington and Moscow was installed. Disarmament was the declared long-term goal, the arms control and disarmament agency was established earlier, but meanwhile he had to avoid situation such as Cuba which could lead to nuclear war.

This was the second half of his nuclear problem, and arguably it was more urgent than the right of blacks to eat at white lunch counters. Kennedy's first solution was the maintenance of the *status quo*, but it had been rejected by Khrushchev at Vienna. The Soviet leader naturally believed in revolution, and supported so-called wars of national liberation. He said that they were revolutionary wars, not only admissable but inevitable, and the Soviet Union would always support them. In historical terms, Khrushchev had only given a new label to guerrilla wars, as fought in Greece, the Philippines and Malaya, but for Kennedy it was the declaration of a new phase in the east-west struggle. He decided that brushfire wars had to be stamped out before they involved the interests of the superpowers and led to nuclear confrontation. The United States had to intervene at an early stage. Hence the intervention in Vietnam.

The logic of the nuclear theorists' argument was persuasive, but the United States had no interests in Vietnam until the military advisers were sent. The joint chiefs of staff had no enthusiasm for the task that was to be thrust upon them. After the Korean experience, they did not want to station American troops on the Asian mainland. A study undertaken by General Gavin before the French withdrawal from Indo-China had also concluded that the war could be won only if 500,000 troops were committed. Kennedy was not prepared to listen. All military wisdom was seen to have been cornered by the theorists

biguous about the text of the resolution. The majorities were a fair measure of the political support for the war, and the containment policy still enjoyed a large and undiminished consensus in and out of Congress.

Looking back, those brief years were the peak of one of the most creative and fruitful periods since the ratification of the Constitution. Much was achieved at home and abroad. Unprecedented prosperity was created by building on the foundations of industrial power mobilized during the second world war. The arts and sciences flourished. Education was a boom industry. Only in the United States was sixteen years of education regarded as the birthright of every child, and post-graduate students were probably more numerous than British undergraduates. Everything seemed possible, including reaching for the stars and abolishing poverty.

The leadership of the western world was accepted, at first reluctantly, and then gravely, imaginatively and generously. There were crises abroad and at home, and McCarthyism, but good sense and pragmatism largely prevailed. American soldiers had fought in Korea and were now being sent to Vietnam, but a third world war had been avoided. The record was good, and there was no reason to believe that peace and plenty was an impossible dream. Americans were resilient and inventive, generous and natural democrats. They were quick to respond. The ambitious and the greedy bent the rules, but the law, as enshrined in the Constitution, prevailed.

The health of American society could be judged by the abundance of leaders in most walks of life. Men such as Harriman, Acheson and McCoy, the great pro-consuls and diplomats who had extended *Pax Americana* into a troubled world, were getting on in years, but they were being succeeded by a new generation. McGeorge Bundy was still the special assistant for national security affairs in the White House. Unlike Johnson, he was an Establishment man, a Bostonian who had been educated at Groton, Yale and Harvard, and was dean of Harvard before coming to Washington. His brother Bill was married to Dean Acheson's daughter, and had served in the CIA before going on to the Pentagon and the state department.

Bundy was what the British used to call a muscular Christian. The British prototypes were the men educated at Rugby under

Arnold when a constant supply of such men were required to rule, administer and police the empire. Bundy was probably brighter, but I recognized the type when we first dined together in Washington soon after Kennedy had appointed him. Daily tennis had kept him in tiptop physical condition, and the eyes behind the goldrimmed spectacles were alive. His self-confidence was undisguised. He served first Kennedy, then Johnson, by controlling and analysing the constant flood of paper across his desk, and whenever necessary presenting the options. He marshalled the facts and allowed them to speak for themselves. He would have made an outstanding cabinet secretary in Whitehall.

Dean Rusk, the new secretary of state, had come up the hard way. He was a southerner, a poor boy from Cherokee county, Georgia, who had actually gone shoeless to school. One of twelve children, the son of a preacher, he almost followed his father into the pulpit. Instead, the stern Calvinist discipline and the constant Bible reading led him to high academic honours. He won a Rhodes scholarship, that foreign passport for so many poor but bright southern boys to the world of success north of the Mason-Dixon line. The Rhodes scholarship was also a membership card to a powerful freemasonry in the army as well as government.

As with many southerners, Rusk was attracted by the military virtues and rose to the top in his high school and college ROTC. Just before the second world war, when teaching political science in California, he was called to the colours and then posted to the China-Burma-India theatre where he eventually became deputy chief of staff. He enjoyed himself in India. During his two years at Oxford he had learned to appreciate the gentle English sense of humour, the little asides and quiet giggles, and this, with his tennis playing and capacity to hold his liquor, well fitted him for the British society which then set the standards in the sub-continent. He was also a good staff officer, and other Rhodes scholars in the army eventually arranged a posting to Washington where he joined a political-military planning group preparing for the post-war period when the United States was to become the dominant super power. Rusk had come in on the ground floor.

Apparently he did not see it that way. He preferred to stay in the army. It suited him, but his hero, George Marshall, wanted him at the state department. Rusk did well, rising to deputy under secretary, the top job for career officers, and then taking demotion to be assistant secretary of state for far eastern affairs because it was then the toughest job in the department. Rusk could be very tough, and proved it when South Korea was invaded from the north. He knew instinctively what had to be done, and did it. There were stories of those early frantic hours, when information was scarce and conflicting, of how he communicated direct with MacArthur's headquarters in Tokyo operating the teletype himself. Whatever the judgement of history, he proved that he could coolly rise to one of the toughest situations that ever confronted a President and his advisers.

Rusk had the usual southern respect and liking for Britain, and no doubt it was enhanced by his years at Oxford. He knew better than most that Britain was becoming increasingly weak and ineffective, but he still saw me regularly. We lived only three blocks apart after I had moved to the Spring Valley section of Washington, and occasionally he would give me a lift downtown in his limousine. We also met regularly in his office on the seventh floor of the state department at the end of the working day, to discuss policies and events over whisky. His scout, as he called the black who served us, would bring in two highballs, and then about a quarter of an hour later bring in another for Rusk. I would be ignored, until the third time round when I was given my second glass. I never asked why, I was there for information and not free booze, but I supposed Rusk thought he had the larger capacity.

The leaders among the black community were no less numerous Apart from King, there was Roy Wilkins, the executive secretary of the National Association for the Advancement of Coloured People. He was a handsome man of mixed blood who would have graced any boardroom. Indeed, he spent a great deal of time in such a rarified atmosphere; in the White House and wherever he could win powerful allies for his cause. The NAACP had taken the legal road to liberation, and worked happily with whites. They saw themselves as Americans and wanted to join American society by peaceful means. Thurgood Marshall, who had argued the school desegregation case before the Supreme Court was to become its first black member.

They were happy years for us as well as for most Americans. I was concerned about Vietnam. I knew the country better than most of the officials planning the war. I was not convinced that the new tactics of firepower and mobility were the best, but asusmed as did everybody that the United States would win. There was much else to report, we had a growing number of friends and enjoyed what is usually known as the American way of life. We liked the pragmatism, the good sense, the friendly simplicity, the lack of arrogance of the rich and the independence of ordinary working people. We dined out frequently, at the White House and the embassies as well as with friends who happened to be high up in government, but we loved the evenings at home spent in the unfenced garden, or backyard as Americans insist upon describing their well-manicured lawns. Neighbours would walk across, glass in hand, for a chat, and the kids played happily on the street. We decided to have a little Benjamin for our old age, and were blessed instead with a Benjamina—Elizabeth Mary, known for some forgotten reason as Beany.

Yet unnoticed the United States was even then moving into a state of disequilibrium. Pragmatism and good sense were the first casualties. The 1964 Republican national convention marked the first success of organized extremism since the McCarthy days. Barry Goldwater, the Republican presidential candidate, was dismissed as a joke in Washington, but he represented a large minority of unreconstructed Republicans, decent people who nevertheless resented the changes in American society. They wanted to put back the clock, to Eisenhower and perhaps even Harding or Coolidge. They did not like trades unions, social security and the promise of Johnson's Great Society legislation. They were impatient with the outside world, afraid of communism, and seemed to assume that the perceived red threat could be made to disappear in a nuclear mushroom cloud.

Not all of the crowd in San Francisco's Cow Palace were middle-aged. Many youngsters sat in the back rows, and although I did not know it at the time they were the young men who, four years later, would rally to Richard Nixon and Haldeman and Erlichman to defend America from what they saw as the enemy within. Those I spoke to had been weaned on stories of the international communist conspiracy, of home grown agitators and communist sympathizers plotting ceaselessly to bring about the collapse of the Republic. With hindsight I could see why they would go to extreme lengths to defend Nixon. In their eyes, they would do no more than what the FBI and the CIA had done in their unceasing struggle with subversion at home and revolution abroad. David Ellsberg would be just as much an enemy of the Republic as any black-pyjamaed Vietcong cadre in the Mekong delta. They would see no difference between the burglary of the Democratic national committee in the Watergate complex and the bugging of Jimmy Hoffa by Robert Kennedy, when he was attorney general. Who was the more dangerous enemy, the old Teamsters' boss or Democratic extremists threatening their America?

Many of them at the Cow Palace were physically impressive, the products of well-to-do families, balanced diets and regular visits to the dentist. Their hair was clean and neat, their summer-weight suits and button-down shirts machine-washed and pressed. They were deferential to older women and called their elders 'Sir'. They sat attentively, the very picture of a prosperous and well-ordered democracy seriously minding its affairs, but they stood up and howled like wolves when Eisenhower attacked the press.

I sat in the raised press area, seeking protection behind my typewriter from the sound waves of hatred. The worst was to come, when Nelson Rockefeller, then Governor of New York, went to the podium to speak for one of the minority amendments to the platform. That picture of a prosperous and well-ordered democracy seriously minding its affairs exploded into an American version of a Nazi rally, except that the screams of hatred had not been orchestrated. They welled out from an innermost spring of the dark American soul. They were frightening because the hatred had been nurtured in a free society dedicated to life, liberty and the pursuit of happiness. The party managers were embarrassed. It did not look or sound good on television, but the young radicals were commended by Goldwater when he accepted the nomination. 'Extremism in the defence of liberty is no vice. . . Moderation in the pursuit of justice is no virtue'.

This pressure from the right made it difficult for Johnson not to extend the war in Vietnam. Not that he was unwilling. He accepted the new military theory that brushfire wars had to be stamped out before they brought about a superpower confrontation. It appeared to be an extension of the containment policy which had worked so well for nearly twenty years. He was a Texan who believed in the greater glory and invincible might of the Lone Star state and its appendage of the 49 other states. In any case, it was too late to withdraw. The last opportunity when the United States could have withdrawn in good order and without being accused by its own extreme right of selling out to the communists was missed by Kennedy a few days before his assassination. Since then American troops had been killed, and South Vietnam was on the edge of defeat. Even George Ball, the under secretary of state, who afterwards became the Administration's leading opponent to continuing the war, agreed that the Americans had to fight.

The pleasant affluent life continued, but university students, led by the New Left, began to try out their newly discovered political strength. They organized talk-ins, and made themselves disagreeable to official speakers who tried to defend the war on the better-known campuses. At first they were little more than undergraduate larks. At one I attended, the students appeared to be more upset by the apparent intellectual arrogance of McGeorge Bundy than by the war. This was to change, but their first major impact on events was in the field of civil rights. It was terribly sad.

Racial violence had continued to simmer in the south, largely because of the non-violence campaign of King and other black leaders, and in 1964 thousands of young white students went down to Mississippi to work for voter registration drives and generally help the civil rights movement. Some were beaten, a few killed, but the summer appeared to be a splendid promise of youthful idealism rising triumphant above racial animosity. This was long before the so-called counter revolution. They were not working against the system, but cooperating with the established order to make the system work better.

On their way south, some of them came to Washington to attend a youth convention held in the old Harrington hotel, where for the first time they met members of the student non-violent coordinating committee. Snick, as it was usually called, was still very much a genuine student movement with religious roots. They were the veterans of countless confrontations

in the south. Most of them were poor, and from rural backgrounds, and the rundown hotel on E Street must have struck
them as the height of luxury. They also met the white students
from Berkeley, Harvard and other northern campuses for the
first time, and it was not a happy meeting. While the young
whites argued about participatory democracy, which was then
becoming fashionable, or grumbled about Vietnam, the youngsters
from Snick in their farm coveralls held prayer meetings and
observed periods of silence. They were from another country, a
very harsh place where stoicism was one of the few defences against
white prejudice and violence.

I am not sure of what happened. Perhaps the young Snick
workers had been exposed too long to violence, and non-
violence did not seem to be making much progress. Poor and
relatively unsophisticated, they might have been overwhelmed
by the bright white volunteers from the affluent north. Perhaps
they did not like what they saw or heard. The easy sexual
relationships, still fairly new even in the north, might have
offended their black Baptist morality. They might have resented losing their identity in a larger movement. Snick had
struggled and suffered alone for years, and suddenly their
campaign was taken up by strangers, friendly, but nevertheless
white strangers who had no concept of life in the south but
wanted to take charge. Snick went separatist, and new leaders
preached violence and subsequently black power. Another
fragile link between the races snapped.

Separatism afterwards swept through the northern ghettos,
where the foundations had been laid by the Black Muslims. The
more extreme, known as the Fruit of Islam, had dropped their
surnames and used the letter X as a rejection of the past, when
blacks had taken the name of their slaveowner. For all the talk
about Islam, the organization at times looked more like a black
Mafia. I tried to cover one of their meetings in Chicago, and was
very roughly handled. They wanted nothing to do with the
white press, domestic or foreign. The many murders suggested
that internal discipline was severe. Malcolm X formed a splinter
movement, the organization of Afro-American unity, and was also
murdered although not before launching the black separatist
movement.

The black majority almost certainly held to the hope of being integrated into the mainstream of American life. Martin Luther King was still their chosen leader, but not everywhere in the north. The years of black migration from the south had done more than change the demographic maps. When Roy Wilkins of the NAACP was a young man New York's Harlem was a pleasant residential area, rundown and poor but safe and respectable. By the sixties Harlem and other black neighbourhoods had become lawless and hopeless jungles. Thousands of youngsters had become rootless, no longer members of American society and responding less and less to preachers such as King. The rejection of white standards by Malcolm X, a product of the ghetto, made violence respectable. It erupted suddenly in Watts, and after three days and nights of rioting more than thirty were killed and hundreds injured.

It was the first of what were euphemistically described as long hot summers. It was also the beginning of the end of that creative and fruitful period. The past was catching up with the present and at the worst possible time. Johnson, I think, sensed what was about to happen, and did not campaign much in the 1966 mid-term election and the Republicans won some congressional seats and state governorships. Travelling about the country covering the election campaign, it was evident that the mood of the country was changing. The war was beginning to worry some people, but most peace candidates were defeated at the polls. The growing white backlash against black demands, and the attention and money Johnson was devoting to them was stronger than any longing for peace. George Wallace, the former governor of Alabama, said that he was seriously thinking of running for the presidency in 1968, and southern Democrats in the House of Representatives launched their campaign to unseat Adam Clayton Powell, the Harlem representative. Johnson's consensus was beginning to come apart, and the slide into greater violence had begun.

*

Soon after my arrival in Washington I had a phone call from the Supreme Court. A thin but imperious voice said, Frankfurter here, Mr. Justice Felix Frankfurter. I have not received my latest issue of *The Times*. Do you have a copy to spare? I did, and dutifully took it to his chambers at the court. It was the beginning of one of my strangest love affairs, not with Frankfurter but the Supreme Court of the United States. Frankfurter was not my first associate justice. I had met Willion Douglas in Singapore, and he got me drunk. He was returning to Washington from one of his regular trips to the world's wild frontiers, and was spending a few days with a mutual friend before taking the long flight home. Douglas was interested in the Malayan conflict, the mutual friend thought that I could give a more impartial account than any British official, and I was invited over. I put on a tie and jacket, and a grave expression which I thought appropriate for a judge, and drove through the hot and clammy heat for what I expected to be a sober conversation.

Not a bit of it. Our mutual friend, his wife and Douglas were sitting on the verandah and, although it was well into the afternoon each of them had a large dry martini in front of them. Now I am a drinking man, and believe that the dry martini is one of the great American contributions to civilization—but not in the middle of a very hot and humid tropical afternoon. A martini was nevertheless mixed for me, the glasses of the others were sweetened up, and I tried to explain what was going on in those jungles beyond the Straits of Johore.

It was not a success. Apart from the drinks, I was almost mesmerized by Douglas' face. It was a wild face, undisciplined even by conventional politeness let alone the heavy responsibilities of the federal bench. I had seen its like often enough in the bars of Glasgow and the lesser clubs of British Asia where Scots engineers got drunk on a Saturday night. Also he obviously did not like me. Not that he knew me. It was enough that I was an Englishman in a British colony. I was an imperialist. I cannot recall how many martinis we drank or what I said. I know only that I got drunk and that Douglas, in spite of that wild face, remained—well, as sober as a judge. All that I can clearly remember was that I had met my first genuine American populist and libertarian.

The second time we met was in Delhi, when he was returning from a Himalayan trip, and he got me drunk again. The two drinking bouts were a sufficient introduction when I went to Washington, and we occasionally met at other people's parties. We got on well enough, but more often than not he was anti-British. He was provocative, and I could be provoked. He once boasted about the Supreme Court decision defending the rights of the accused, and I said it read remarkably like the judge's rules which Britain had had for decades. On another occasion he said that Britain knew nothing about individual rights because it did not have a Bill of Rights. We were a class-ridden society. I said that at least our racial prejudice was not institutionalized. We did not need a Supreme Court to desegregate schools because British schools were not segregated. I suppose he was trying me on, although he had the chauvinism of an American populist. He could be an imtemperate man in more ways than drinking. He was the opposite of what a judge was supposed to be, but he was a great judge. Douglas was a dissenter and he was suspicious of the conventional wisdom and the majority view, despite his populism. His dissenting opinions made the law human and added to the radicalism of the Court.

The Supreme Court had become increasingly radical since 1954 when its *Brown v. Board of Education* decision ordered the racial desegregation of schools. Earl Warren, the Chief Justice, who launched this benevolent revolution, had the informality of the native-born Californian, and looked more comfortable in a sports shirt than in judge's black robe. He could easily have been mistaken for a politician, and this is what he was before Eisenhower elevated him to the bench. The story behind the elevation had an ironic moral of sorts. Eisenhower wanted a moderately conservative Chief Justice, and knowing even less about judges than politicians, listened to the advice of the then Vice-President Nixon and Senator Knowland, the Senate majority leader. They were Californians, and Eisenhower must have thought that they knew their man. They did. Warren had served three terms as governor, and was regarded as a future presidential candidate. To that extent he was a political rival for the Republican leadership in the state and for the presidential nomination in 1960. The most effective way to remove him from the political scene was to kick him upstairs to the Supreme Court. Eisenhower obliged.

What Nixon and Knowland failed to tell the President was that Warren had served his three terms as governor when California was very much a Democratic state. He was on the left of the Republican party, and one year won the Democratic as well as Republican gubernatorial primary. He had also been a crusading district attorney, probably because of his background.

He had been born Varren. His father was a Norwegian immigrant who worked in the railroad yards until he was blacklisted for joining a strike. Warren never forgot his early years or the injustice done to his father, but as with most second-generation Americans, especially those of Scandinavian descent, he had a profound belief in American democracy.

Eisenhower was in for a surprise. The *Brown v. Board of Education* decision launched the social revolution which with Johnson's help was to give the blacks their full civil rights. The decision, written by Warren, reflected his passion for equality before the law, and it was only the beginning. Warren was determined to do whatever was necessary to achieve what Martin Luther King and other good men struggled for on the streets and the barricades. And the glory of the Constitution was that the Supreme Court, as a coequal branch of government, could achieve what the White House and Congress, for a thousand and one political reasons, could not or would not do.

Its protection of rights was not confined to the blacks. The Court hastened the return to sanity after McCarthyism by invalidating sedition acts in forty-two states, and held that the state department had no authority to withhold passports because of the beliefs and political associations of applicants, and in 1964 it struck down unfair deportation, search without warrant and loyalty oaths. In a variety of cases it extended the protection of the Bill of Rights into state courts, and then attacked the flagrant malapportionment of seats in state legislatures and Congress. Warren argued that legislators represented people, not trees or acres, and they were elected by voters, not by farms, cities or economic interests. Douglas said that there could be room for but one constitutional rule—one voter, one vote. The degree of inequality that had existed in the electoral system for so long was made evident in the dissenting opinion of Justice Harlan. Assuming that a disparity of more than 100,000 voters between a state's largest and smallest electoral district violated the Constitution, he said that 398 members of the House of Representatives from 37 states had been uncon-stitutionally elected. That left a constitutional House of only 37 members.

The work of the Court was on the whole more fundamental and important than Johnson's Great Society legislation, but both

were making the United States a better place to live in. Both
proved that the system worked, despite the increasingly fashionable doubts of liberal academics. Given men of goodwill, and
large Democratic majorities in Congress, the system was also
resilient and responsive. There was no need for resort to the
barricades, except for students who wanted to live out their
fantasies, except over Vietnam. The Administration was im-
placable in its determination to fight and win the war, despite the
increasing evidence that it could not be won without destroying
the society it was supposed to be defending, and the growing
anti-war movement on the campuses.

By early 1967 I was convinced that the United States could not
win. I was also aware of the strong feelings among students
because I frequently lectured to university audiences, in part to
make an honest buck but also to keep in touch with the rising
generation. I did not take sides. My job was to report as honestly
as I could what was really happening, and that was difficult
enough with manifestations of discontent appearing in many
guises.

About this time, in the late summer of 1967, rumours
floated over from London that the Astor family wanted to sell
their controlling interests in *The Times*. They came as no surprise,
but I was obviously interested in one rumour that said I was likely to
be appointed editor when Sir William Haley retired. I thought it
unlikely, Iverach McDonald appeared to be the obvious successor.
He had served the paper as foreign correspondent, diplomatic
correspondent and foreign editor, and was editing the paper while
Haley looked for a new proprietor. I was not certain that I
wanted the ultimate promotion, at least not yet. It was a splendid
job, the best in British journalism. I could see the headline,
former messenger boy appointed editor, but I did not want to
leave the United States while it appeared to be falling apart. I
had also been a scribbling chap all my adult life, and was only in
my late forties. I liked working at the coalface, as we used to say,
and without thinking much about it assumed that I would go on
covering the world, seeing new faces, new countries, and new
situations, until I dropped dead or was put out to grass. Pondering
the possibility, I could not really decide what I would do if the
editorship was offered. In the event, I was saved from that
dilemma. One afternoon the bell of the teleprinter rang, and the

machine clattered out the announcement that the paper had been sold to Lord Thomson. The new editor was to be William Rees-Mogg. I went back to my typewriter and finished the story I was writing.

Haley wrote me a letter saying that in selling to Thomson he had made the paper safe for me and my children. And so it seemed. More changes quickly followed, most of them beneficial. A third correspondent was posted to Washington to take care of the economic news, and we moved into a larger office and bought new furniture. We even discussed buying carpets, but I decided against it mainly because I was inclined to stamp out cigarettes underfoot when writing at top speed. Anyway, I preferred austere working conditions. Travel became much easier, and the scope of our coverage improved when we were given more space and the new feature page was introduced. My salary and allowances were increased, and for the first time in our lives Pat and I were free of money worries. I did not moonlight as much. We were also given bylines after 182 years of anonymity, and I was awarded a weekly column with my picture over the byline. God bless Lord Thomson, we said that night after a celebratory dinner of steaks and a half-gallon jug of California wine, and we meant it.

The byline was in its way as important as the extra money. I was no longer faceless. I had a public identity, which was very good for me. I had been accustomed to anonymity, regarded it as part of the price, along with the bad pay, for writing for *The Times*, but it was a bad policy. The argument that everybody who mattered knew who were the correspondents of *The Times* was only half true at best. The byline and the little picture made my work easier. They also made me accountable to the readers, which I gladly accepted. I believed in accountability and saw no reason why civil servants and correspondents of *The Times* should not be exposed to its discipline. (It is about time the civil servants were similarly disciplined).

Not every change was beneficial. The new man on the back bench, where the paper was put together at night, had the strangest idea of news. The selection became arbitrary. The old standards were ignored. For instance, when Nixon and Kissinger announced their new foreign policy principles, which were obviously of great importance, not a line got into the paper. For a time the paper ceased to be a true paper of record. The lack of experience of the back bench also manifested itself in late telephone calls demanding followups of rumours I knew to be baseless. I used to say, Nonsense, buzz off, or balls and occasionally something much stronger. A rumour floated across the Atlantic of discontent among the old editorial staff in London, but there was a gradual improvement until the paper became much better than it was in the old days. Rees-Mogg proved to be a courageous and lively editor, and apart from the residual lack of confidence in the back bench, I was happy enough with the changes and my modest affluence.

The new management under Denis Hamilton was generous. Patrick had stopped growing, and the time had come for the surgeons to repair, as much as was possible, the terrible damage polio had done to his legs. The bill ran into thousands of dollars, and Hamilton cheerfully paid. Years later I went to China with Lord Thomson and his son Kenneth, and in Canton we saw how effective acupuncture could be. Ken Thomson offered to pay for Patrick to be flown to Canton and to keep him there for six months for treatment. Enquiries were made, Patrick's medical records were sent, but the Chinese regretfully reported that nothing could be done.

Free of domestic worries, I could give all my attention to the job, which was just as well. The new American tragedy was fast approaching, and at its centre was Johnson. He had never been wholly accepted. He was a southerner, and had succeeded to power after the assassination of a popular and youthful President. His landslide victory in 1964 had given legitimacy to his presidency, but he was always compared unfavourably with his predecessor. His great achievements in furthering the causes of civil rights and education and helping the poor had at best won him only grudging respect, and now they were forgotten. The Kennedy faction within the Democratic party had always resented him. They had said that his Great Society legislation was only the realization of John Kennedy's programme, which was nonsense. Now they attacked his conduct of the war, where they were on surer ground although Kennedy and the defence intellectuals were responsible for the original involvement. They were more determined than the Republicans to drive him from office.

Robert Kennedy had never liked Johnson, and had tried to persuade his brother not to nominate him vice-presidential candidate in 1960. He was now the heir to the Kennedy legend, a political property beyond compare. His supporters dreamed of a Kennedy restoration and a return to Camelot, and he was convinced of his right to rule. The Johnson Administration was regarded only as an interregnum.

It must have been doubly unsettling for Johnson because by 1967 Robert Kennedy was also seen to represent the younger generation, if not all the undergraduates who were flexing their new political muscle on campuses across the country. The assumption was growing that the old guard had betrayed the country and that youth must take over, and Johnson was approaching 60 and looked it. Participatory democracy, which was never clearly defined, was supposed to be the wave of the future, and he was a shop-soiled old politico, a wheeler dealer, and past master of consensus politics. He had in fact done more for youth and the blacks than any other President, and their ingratitude pained him. He could not understand his failure to win the affection of those he had helped so much, and was convinced that he was a victim of a Kennedy conspiracy.

This was only partly true. Even those who still admired him for his achievements, as I did, were wary of him. He was larger than life, and could be physically overpowering. He assumed that every man had his price, whether it was federal funds for a dam in a senator's state or patronage for a political hack. He believed that if he pressed the flesh enough—a typically Johnsonian phrase which made some people feel uneasy, even unclean—they would do his bidding and love him for it. In the belief that he could store up political IOUs to be cashed later, he was always prepared to do favours for almost anybody, including people standing on the sidelines such as myself.

For instance, I saw him regularly, perhaps more often than most foreign correspondents, and when William Rees-Mogg, the new editor of *The Times*, visited Washington he readily agreed to see us. We were led into the Oval Office, and he greeted the editor with genuine southern courtesy. Obviously incapable of mastering English hyphenated names, he said, with almost breathless sincerity, Mr Mogg, it is a great pleasure and a real honour. He added that he wanted Mr. Mogg to know that he was fortunate in having the best and greatest correspondent in Washington. He then winked at me, indicating that he was putting in a good word for me with the new boss man. When we were leaving, he paused in the doorway, enveloped me in an enormous hug, and said, Louis, you know that you are always welcome. Come back any time, and give my respects to your dear little lady.

I suppose there was nothing wrong with the Johnson treatment. American psychologists had long recognized the social value of what was known as stroking people, and I had to admit secret gratification if only for a moment. It was pleasant to be treated by the President of the United States as an old chum before a new editor. He did me what he thought to be a good turn. He did it naturally, as a Beduin sheikh would offer you the sheep's eye or an Indian garland you with flowers, but ulterior motives were always expected even when they were absent.

Johnson aspired to greatness. His two great heroes were Roosevelt and Churchill, and naturally—most politicians are vain —he believed that he had been cast in the same mould. His domestic policies were Rooseveltian, and as far as Vietnam was concerned he compared himself with Churchill when Britain stood alone in 1940. The comparison was absurd, only his political survival was at stake and not the freedom of his country. He believed that if he hunkered down—the Texan rancher's expression was wonderfully graphic—the storm would pass, victory would be his, and his reputation as a great President would be secure for all time. As the clouds lowered, and he became almost a captive in the White House, he would spend garrulous hours brooding on this theme. He once kept me in the Oval Office for more than two hours, and the session came to an end only when he recalled the spirit of the Alamo. I was unkind enough—I can be very trying when it comes to facts—to recall that Davy Crockett and the entire garrison were killed, and he snapped back that it was the spirit that counted.

Apart from his own fatal determination not to admit defeat, he was caught in a trap. In Hanoi, victory was not the only objective of the North Vietnamese commander in chief. General Vo Nguyen Giap had said that South Vietnam was the model of the national liberation movement, and that if the special warfare the American imperialists were testing in the south was overcome then it could be defeated anywhere in the world. In other words, a negotiated withdrawal was out of the question. Giap was determined to defeat the Americans. This was too unbelievable to be accepted in Washington, and Johnson's determination not to admit defeat was nurtured until it was too late by Robert McNamara, the defence secretary.

The influence of McNamara and the defence intellectuals could not be over-estimated. He had been brought to Washington from the Ford motor company by Kennedy, and was widely regarded as representative of the new generation of modern American technological man. The management tools he had brought to the Pentagon were seen to be a new form of rationalism, an extension by computer of the best of the new age of enlightenment. McNamara was in fact more gravely flawed than Johnson. His speciality was statistical control, and perhaps because he had had no military or political experience he and his whizz kids tried to run the Vietnam war by slide rule and computer. The joint chiefs of staff were ignored, and abstract theories and computer calculations shaped decisions without the benefit of experience and the lessons of history.

Nothing could have been more disastrous. Conscripts with service in the field limited to one year could not be expected to fight seasoned Asian guerrillas on their own terrain and terms. The objectives and progress of guerilla war could not be computerized and usefully subjected to statistical analysis. McNamara tried with his body counts. The progress of the war was assessed by the number of bodies collected after a battle or ambush. The body counts were militarily meaningless, and only disgusted and further alienated decent Americans.

The situation within the United States became desperate. To many citizens it seemed that their government was beyond control, that it had become a dreadful juggernaut which would not be stopped until it had brought about complete disaster. They were not far wrong. The defence intellectuals still defended the continuation of the war even when victory was seen to be impossible. The attempt to stamp out a brushfire war had developed into a major conventional war without triggering a superpower confrontation, but no matter. One theory had been proved false, but another was quickly formulated. The credibility of the United States was now at stake. The war had to continue because defeat might persuade the western allies that American guarantees were worthless. It did not matter that every allied government wanted the war to stop. A theory had to be defended even if it badly frightened the allies and further divided the nation.

The demonstrations and marches on Washington increased, and with mounting violence. The New Left produced some ugly splinter groups, among them the Weathermen who, like the Baader-Meinhof gang, wanted to destroy society. Other nasty people emerged from the national woodwork as the established order appeared to disintegrate. During the march on the Pentagon, one alleged pacifist pissed on a soldier guarding the approaches. His girlfriend unzipped her jeans and flaunted her genitals. Whole neighbourhoods were looted by rampaging blacks, and put to the torch. I flew over one city in a police helicopter and it looked like the London blitz. The juggernaut thundered on now completely out of control. Thanksgiving turkeys tasted like ashes in many mouths, and few people celebrated the new year.

It was a presidential election year, and Senator Eugene McCarthy nearly beat Johnson in the New Hampshire primary to everybody's amazement including his own. His campaign was run by students, who were dubbed the McCarthy children's crusade, and on the Saturday night before the election I went round to their headquarters in Concord and asked about the candidate's chances. The student who was keeping a tally of the canvassing returns said he would get 42.5 per cent of the Democratic poll. This was much more than McCarthy was expected to get, and I went round to his hotel outside Manchester to discuss it. He was lying on his bed, and when I told him the good news he literally jumped off it. He could not believe the projected figure and asked me not to publish it. He had been hoping for about 20 per cent. This would have been regarded as a modest victory, enough to persuade the fat cats to support him in other primaries, but if I published the 42.5 projection and he won 30 per cent of the vote the press would proclaim it a defeat. He in fact won 42 per cent, and with the write-in votes came within 230 votes of defeating Johnson.

His victory, and it was a great victory for a relatively obscure Senator to nearly defeat the incumbent President, persuaded Kennedy to announce his candidature and Vice-President

Hubert Humphrey was raring to follow. Then came the Tet offensive, which finally persuaded Johnson that he could not win although McNamara advocated sending more reinforcements. Instead, Johnson took advice from wise old men such as Acheson, and announced that he would not seek re-election in November. This seemed to change everything. Americans could now hope that the democratic process would save them from disaster, and others saw a brighter future because of McCarthy's children's crusade.

I shared their enthusiasm because I had covered the New Hampshire primary on and off since Christmas. I liked McCarthy. He was a grayly handsome man, an intellectual and poet with a sardonic sense of humour. He was not a good candidate, he was disdainful of baby-kissing and handshaking, and he was too lazy, but he appealed to youngsters. Idealistic and eager, they responded to McCarthy's challenge, perhaps because it was romantic. He was taking on the President, the parties, the state and defence departments, the CIA, the joint chiefs of staff, the military-industrial complex—the lot. They appreciated his learning and quiet wit as well as his courage. They thrilled when he said that men who challenge the king must be prepared to die. You could feel their excitement when he spoke of personal commitment, of the need for a renaissance of profession and vocation in modern society.

For me, the young crusaders were more significant than the candidate. They seemed to prove that the violent antics of militant students did not appeal to the majority, that many were looking for a constructive cause. They shaved off their beards and clipped their hair, wore conventional clothes and were polite to the voters. They worked hard at canvassing and getting out the vote. It was possible to believe that American common sense and decency would be reasserted, that the system would work, and that with a new President the juggernaut could be brought under democratic control.

In response to Johnson's appeal Hanoi professed willingness to negotiate peace, and with growing optimism I decided to accompany the President to Honolulu for talks with his generals. I kissed the family goodbye, promised to bring back the requested presents, and took a press bus from the White House to Andrews air base. About one hundred of us climbed aboard the 707 with our typewriters and cameras, and the stewardesses served drinks while we waited for Johnson to arrive. Through a porthole I could see his Air Force One heavily guarded by the military police and the Secret Service. One of the crew announced that the President was delayed, and that dinner would be served while we waited. The steak was good and the wine drinkable, and I thought that this was the way to travel. As soon as we got off the ground I would fall asleep, and apart from a refuelling stop would sleep all the way to Hawaii. I was unlacing my shoes when the captain announced that Dr. Martin Luther King had been shot in Memphis and that Johnson had cancelled the trip.

When the White House travel office sent me the bill later I found that those drinks and the steak dinner had cost *The Times* $181.50—actually my share of the charter although we never got off the ground—but I had other things to worry about that night as a cab took me home through heavy rain. Listening to the cab's radio, it was clear that nobody knew who was responsible for the murder. One station assumed a white racist conspiracy and another reported fears of a black uprising. Events began to outpace the wildest rumour. Angry blacks were already roaming the streets of Washington's ghetto, looting stores and molesting white passers-by. When I tried to speak to the black driver, he said, Look, Mac. I'm hired to drive you home, not to write your story. Right!

The heavy rain prevented instant combustion that night, giving Johnson time to alert more than 350,000 troops and national guardsmen across the country. All that could be done to show proper respect for the dead man, to avoid disorders, and take prompt action should they occur was done quickly and efficiently. The larger danger was avoided. I wrote an early story before lunch, and after a hamburger and a beer at the national press club walked down F Street towards the black section of town to see if anything was happening. On the way I met an old friend from the state department, Bob Miller, a tall man who always wore a five-gallon hat, and we strolled on together. F Street, the main shopping street in downtown Washington, was normally crowded during the lunch hour, but was deserted that day. We walked from Fourteenth Street to Seventh, where a smartly-dressed young black woman, statuesque and handsome, smashed the window of a jewellry store and began to help herself. A white policeman appeared and tried to arrest her, but she kept him at armslength and calmly went on picking up gold wristwatches and bracelets.

A police car arrived and the driver went to the assistance of his buddy when I heard a rush of rubber-soled feet and round the corner came a crowd of young blacks. They were prancing like so many basketball players, and looked not so much happy as liberated or released. There was no suggestion of grief or anger. As if playing a game, they broke windows and scattered the contents on the sidewalk. One young lad casually tried on some bright clothes suitable for a Caribbean winter and another exchanged his jeans and sweatshirt for a white dinner jacket and plum-coloured trousers. I could not help noticing their flair for choosing the right colours for their young dark skins.

More looters arrived, and the mood changed. The two policemen got back into the car and drove off as Miller and I were surrounded by a small mob. I thought his five-gallon hat had attracted their attention, and damned him for it. We backed up against a wall as the blacks became more pushing and menacing. Then an older man lounging against a traffic light standard told them to cool it. They did. He looked us over, and said, Why don't you go home.

We walked westwards, and the surge of looters followed slowly as they shattered more plate-glass windows and overturned cars. At the corner of Fourteenth I met one of the old black waiters from the press club. He was a tall man with immense dignity, and he asked what was happening. I could hardly hear him for the sound of shattering glass. Smoke was rising, and the street was jammed with honking cars heading for the Fourteenth Street bridge, one of the main routes to the Virginia suburbs. The whites were fleeing Washington. The nation's capital, the city which controlled the most destructive power in military history, was being abandoned to the mob.

The intersection where we stood was only two blocks from the White House, and at first I could not see any policemen or troops. It seemed that they had also abandoned the city. By this time the looters had reached Fourteenth Street. Some ran through the stalled traffic towards Garfinckels, one of Washington's best departmental stores, and others spread northwards towards the liquor stores, bars and strip joints of the city's brothel area. There

was still no anger. I could have sworn that most of the young
looters had never heard of King. They radiated the supreme
happiness of the utterly irresponsible, glorying in their sudden
power and eager for the riches of upper-middle-class whites.
The few poor whites waiting at a bus stop looked very frightened
and alone. Their gaze was averted, but the young blacks did not
spare them a glance. The racial situation had suddenly been
reversed. The blacks were in charge and the whites looked like
so many Uncle Toms, anxious to avoid the displeasure of the
master race.

I went back to the office and phoned Pat. She had collected
the children from their schools, and told me not to worry. Our
block on Forty-eight Street was quiet, and the neighbours were
home. She assumed that I would be late, and said that she would
fix a casserole supper. I reminded her to put the martini glasses
in the freezer. I filed a few more paragraphs, and decided to
walk across to the White House. Outside the situation had
changed drastically. The white refugees had fled to their Virginia
and Maryland suburbs, and the streets were rapidly becoming a
battlefield. Northwards, smoke from burning houses was already
darkening the sky, the sidewalks were littered with shattered
glass and debris, and the police were at last trying to restore
order. Wearing white riot helmets with face visors, they made
sudden forays up the street.

It was much worse in the black neighbourhoods, and I got my
station wagon out of the deserted parking lot and drove northwards up Fourteenth Street, which at midtown was the western
limit of black Washington. Farther north Sixteenth Street became
the boundary, although this was where the wealthy blacks lived,
among them Stokeley Carmichael, the young West Indian who
had taken over the leadership of Snick when it became militant.
He was very goodlooking, which probably explained why he was
popular with the radical chic, those rich bastards who lived on
New York's fashionable East Side and assuaged their nasty little
consciences by supporting jerks such as Carmichael. His voice
suddenly came over the car radio. He was addressing a press
conference somewhere, perhaps from the fancy house on Sixteenth which he shared with a successful dancer, and he urged
the blacks to arm themselves with guns and take to the streets.
He blamed Johnson and Robert Kennedy, along with all the

other American whites, for the murder of King. Bobby Kennedy
pulled that trigger as much as anybody else, he hissed, and then
promised executions in the streets. I wondered what the wealthy
liberals safe in their penthouses thought of their hero as Carmichael threatened to turn the country upside down and inside
out.

I tried to turn into the black section, but was stopped by a
police cordon, and was advised to turn back. I showed my press
card, and stood on the sidewalk as the troops finally arrived.
They looked as scared as I felt. In Washington the blacks outnumbered the whites four to one. In this neighbourhood it was
wholly black but it would not be habitable much longer. Streets
of stores and houses were going up in flames. Drunk on looted
liquor the blacks were now burning down their own neighbourhoods; killing, raping and roughing up their own kind. I could
still hear the screams and drunken laughter as I finally drove home
through the deserted city.

The death toll that night in Washington and other cities was
39 and nearly 20,000 rioters and looters were arrested. Property
damage was estimated at more than $30 million, and it could
have been worse if Johnson had not acted so promptly. I watched
him emerging from the situation room in the White House
next day. He was red-eyed, taut with fatigue and on the point of
exhaustion. It had been a terrible week.

The election campaign continued, and I followed the McCarthy,
Kennedy and Nixon campaigns across the country. Nixon won
all the Republican primaries, and Kennedy was doing well. I
spent a week in Oregon, where McCarthy won, and then went
down to California, the last and decisive primary. Polling day
was on a Tuesday, but the campaigning stopped on the Saturday.
I had been on the road for weeks, and decided to fly back to
Washington at the weekend. Whoever won the California
primary, the main story would be there—or so I thought.

There is a three hour time difference between Washington
and Los Angeles. The results would come much too late to
catch the last edition in London, and on Tuesday night we went to
bed fairly early. I still had to catch up on a lot of sleep, but I had
a terrible nightmare. I was in a dark corridor, and somebody
was trying to kill Robert Kennedy. I swung at the assailant with
my portable typewriter, we fell and grappled on the ground. At

that moment I woke up, and found myself on the floor entwined in the bedcovers. I was sweating and breathing heavily, and afterwards Pat said I looked absolutely terrified. At the time she soothed me, and then went down to the kitchen to make tea. Waiting for the kettle to boil, she turned on the radio just in time to hear the first news flash. Kennedy had been assassinated in Los Angeles.

*

Life changed in Washington when Nixon became President. Correspondents were kept out of the White House proper, and had to meet Ron Ziegler, the press secretary, in a new press centre built on the site of Franklin Roosevelt's old swimming pool. We met very few other members of Nixon's staff, and Nixon only at occasional and formal press conferences. I saw Henry Kissinger fairly regularly, at lunch, but the press was generally treated as the enemy. Similarly with the so-called Establishment, the men who had faithfully served the country as cabinet officers, proconsuls, ambassadors and generals, and who in retirement were available to serve successive Presidents in many functions. They were a kind of grand council of the Republic who helped to provide a continuity which no White House staff could provide. They too were excluded. It seemed that anybody outside Nixon's immediate circle who had some power and influence was regarded as the enemy. There was only one impersonal ally, the people 'out there', those to whom Nixon adressed his televised statements, somewhere beyond the Appalachians and far away from the eastern Establishment. Otherwise Nixon isolated himself in a cocoon of self-deception and the blind devotion of Haldeman, Erlichman and the other staff men.

Nixon had taken the Kennedy example of a small activist staff and used it for one purpose, to accumulate power and deny it to others. Quickly the White House came to resemble the Yildiz Kiosk where the Ottoman emperor, Abdul the Damned, made a virtual prisoner of himself. Enveloped in the seclusion of the Yildiz, the Ottoman got rid of reformers, reduced his ministers, whom he rarely saw, to executive officers, transmitted orders to them through the Maybeyn, his intimate secretaries, and left the chief eunuch to deal with other matters. In Nixon's Yildiz,

Haldeman and Erlichman were the Maybeyn, and John Dean the Chief Eunuch. Like Abdul the Damned, Nixon lived in the midst of alarms which were largely due to his own temperament and isolation.

Life in Washington was no longer much fun. The war continued, as did the violent demonstrations. It was like seeing a bad movie for the second or third time round, which was one reason why in the summer of 1970 I did not immediately turn down an offer of promotion. The editor was reorganizing the editorial staff, and he asked me to return to London to be one of two deputy editors and to be responsible for foreign news. The idea of two deputy editors sounded like a recipe for instant disaster, but I was 51. The children were growing up, and Patrick was due to go to Sussex university that fall. Pat was not well. The doctor's diagnosis was inconclusive. He thought it could be the menopause, and said it might be better if Pat was closer to her family.

We decided to go away and think it over, and stayed with friends, Mickey and Sam Pendleton, who lived in a lovely *ante-bellum* house outside Charlottesville, Virginia. It probably survived the vengance of the Union army during the Civil War because it stood far back from a county road in the foothills of the Blue Ridge mountains. It also stood in about 1,900 acres. We had always enjoyed staying with the Pendletons. Apart from the house with its view of the Blue Ridge, they were nice civilized people, and with our other friends in the United States personified much of what we liked and admired about American life. Pat was not well enough to do much, but the kids and I swam, fished and canoed in the one-hundred-acre pond. We visited friends, and sat out on the screened porch drinking mint julips or bourbon-and-branch and admiring the view. At the end of the week Pat said that after all of our wanderings perhaps it was time to go home. The children needed to put down roots.

Despite her Irish blood, Pat was probably fonder of Britain than I was. I had the usual atavistic attachment to home, but I had no illusions about Britain. Not after growing up in London's East End. I also knew that the country was going down the drain. I had observed too long and with growing distaste the pretensions of its politicians abroad. Their assumption of superiority, the ease with which they deluded themselves and apparently their countrymen, was hard to take. After living abroad for so long, the class presumptions of the Tories and the class hatred of Labour left were incomprehensible. I preferred the natural democracy and sense of equality of Americans. But Pat was ill and wanted to go home, and after twenty-two years of love and loyalty she had more than earned the right to be heard. We sailed home on the QE2.

She was a good ship, with fourteen bars serving very drinkable martinis, but I watched New York disappearing over the horizon with regret. In other circumstances—if Pat had been well and if I was not so deeply attached to *The Times*—I would probably have become a United States citizen. I felt more at home there than in Britain; perhaps because, as Jacques Barzun once remarked, Americans were the prosperous poor who had inherited from the European poor a diffused amiability, a restraint in social inter-course, and an inbred recognition that they must live together and had best be pleasant to one another. I shared their optimism and admired their spirit. That spirit had waxed and waned, but had been inextinguishable in every crisis. Its popular symbol was Uncle Sam, but for me since one early dawn in Chicago it had been a young girl in a blue denim skirt and a smudge on her tired but gentle face.

The 1968 Democratic national convention had been violent and divisive, and the morning after I was driven out of my hotel room by tear gas seeping through the air-conditioning ducts. The early commuter traffic had not begun and I sauntered across North Michigan to get some fresh air in the park opposite, which had been the field of battle waged between the police and the demonstrators. A few of them were no doubt agitators. Many were perhaps misguided, but the majority were decent young Americans who felt shut out by the system and believed that they could only make known their detestation of the Vietnam war by peaceful demonstration.

Their remnant, about thirty young men and women, was still there, sprawled out on the grass where they had spent the night. Men of the Illinois National Guard still stood guard between them and the convention hotel. The chill morning air was refreshing, but the scene was depressing, even heartbreaking, until what first appeared to be an extraordinary apparition crossed the deserted road. It was a bishop of the episcopal church dressed in cope and mitre and carrying a chalice. He went among the sprawling figures speaking words of comfort. Gradually and wonderingly, they got up, stretched themselves and gathered about him. He prayed, and one by one his informal congregation joined in. They prayed for President Johnson, the American fighting men in Vietnam and the poor Vietnamese. They prayed for the other demonstrators, the National Guard and even Mayor Daley of Chicago. I could see their spirits rising as the bishop blessed them with the words, May the peace of God be upon you.

Then the girl with the smudged face, now palely alive, suggested that they should also bless the guardsmen standing behind them. The bishop gravely warned her to be careful. There had been too much misunderstanding and violence in Chicago that week. The girl nodded and walked slowly towards the guardsmen, followed at a distance by the bishop and the others. She went up to a black sergeant holding his rifle at the port, and said, May the peace of God be upon you. He was desperately tired, and his eyes were reddened by the lack of sleep. But they smiled in response, and he said, Thank you, Ma'am. The girl smiled in return and went to look for breakfast. The others drifted away, and the bishop returned to the hotel walking with immense dignity through the increasing traffic. The guardsmen stood guard. Nothing more was said, but nothing needed saying. For a brief moment the young demonstrators and guardsmen were not on opposing sides. They were one nation again. The American spirit had worked its miracle.

The self-evident truths of the Declaration of Independence, alas so casually ignored or forgotten even when obesiances were made to the spirit of Jefferson, were being asserted again. It would take time. Perhaps the pursuit of happiness was an impossible goal, but many Americans believed that happiness was their birthright. They would go on trying, ever optimistic and often generous. This was why I was happy in the United States, and reluctant to go back to Britain.

The old Cockney self-compensating mechanism came into play when we got home. If we were up the creek, we were only up to our ankles and not our knees. Actually life was not bad. It was good to be back in London. There were trips, to faraway places such as Brazil and China, and every year I went back to the United States. During the Watergate years I went more often, and was foolishly proud of how Americans emerged from their greatest crises and faced life anew with all the old resilience and confidence. I gradually learned the new skills of editing—as usual I was not told what to do—and they became more pleasurable when after another reorganization I became the only deputy editor. Life now was not bad at all. We had a slummy, expensive but nice house in the Vale of Health, the rates were high but the natives friendly. On balance, even if I was not editor, life was amusing enough as long as I contrived to regard the antics of the Tory and Labour governments as something to be reported but not taken seriously.

As I said at the beginning of this book, I was lucky except that Pat's condition did not improve. She had always been fey, in the nicest and most endearing way, but slowly, almost imperceptibly she began to lose contact with what is known as reality. Much of the time she was more loving and lovable, and then would drift away into a secret world of her own. She went into the Middlesex hospital for tests, where it was discovered she had multiple sclerosis. The consultant suggested a new treatment, still in the experimental stage. Pat went away for a month, but continued to float away from us. She also began to fade away physically, almost ounce by ounce. The family doctor said a new neurologist had arrived at the Royal Free hospital, an appointment was arranged and we waited on little plastic seats for more than an hour. Nobody bothered, and I took Pat home in a state of near collapse. I tried to arrange another appointment; a long correspondence followed but nothing happened. This was the old enemy authority, but in a different guise and none of my old weapons was of any use. One day I was called at the office. Pat had collapsed and had been taken to the Royal Free hospital. They had deigned to notice her at last, but when I got there she was already dead. The bastards had won in the end.

Index